Silicon Values

The Future of Free Speech Under Surveillance Capitalism

JILLIAN YORK

UNCORRECTED PAGE PROOFS

Please do not reprint without publisher's prior approval

VERSO

Contact: Julia Judge
julia@versobooks.com

(845) 853-6429

ISBN 9781788738804 • $26.95

288 pages • Hardback

On sale March 2, 2021

Silicon Values

The Future of Free Speech in the Age of Surveillance Capitalism

Jillian C. York

VERSO

London • New York

For my father, Terry C. York (1952–2011)
and for Lina Ben Mhenni (1983–2020)

First published by Verso 2021
© Jillian C. York 2020

1 3 5 7 9 10 8 6 4 2

Verso
UK: 6 Meard Street, London W1F 0EG
US: 20 Jay Street, Suite 1010, Brooklyn, NY 11201
versobooks.com

Verso is the imprint of New Left Books

ISBN-13: 978-1-78873-880-4
ISBN-13: 978-1-78873-883-5 (UK EBK)
ISBN-13: 978-1-78873-882-8 (US EBK)

British Library Cataloguing in Publication Data
A catalogue record for this book is available from the British Library

Library of Congress Cataloging-in-Publication Data
A catalog record for this book is available from the Library of Congress

Typeset in Fournier by MJ&N Gavan, Truro, Cornwall
Printed and bound by CPI Group (UK) Ltd, Croydon CR0 4YY

Contents

Prologue

Silicon Valley, as well as the broader Bay Area, offers a landscape of contradictions. It's a place where the uber-wealthy, dressed like university freshmen in jeans and hoodies, saunter past homeless encampments on their way to their enclosed campus offices. It's a place where twentysomething engineers shell out upward of three thousand dollars a month to rent tiny, dilapidated rooms in San Francisco's most desirable neighborhoods, only to be bused out of the city each day to go to work an hour away.

It is a place where, according to its critics, "disruption is an inevitable force and not one based on [individual] choices,"[1] where techies "bemoan that people don't understand technology, while making it obvious that they wouldn't pass a 7th grade civics class,"[2] and where people see technical progress as something distinct from, or not in need of, ethical considerations and consequence.

It is a place where traditional or unspoken rules and structures go unacknowledged, where individual freedom is prized over collective action, where the idea of "changing the world" is centered in a narrow frame of what makes up a society, and where an ethos of moving fast and breaking things—removing deliberation and nuance from the iterative process—reigns supreme. And it is a place where the conceptualization of "freedom" is a libertarian one, and as such, executives see no conflict between aiming to "disrupt" governmental functions abroad or support an opposition movement while unabashedly collaborating with illiberal governments.

I am certainly not the first person to have these thoughts, nor will I be the last. In 1995—in the midst of the first dot-com boom but well before the creation of social media, and more than a decade before this book's narrative begins—English media theorists Richard Barbrook and Andy Cameron published an essay entitled "The Californian Ideology." The pair observed that a "new faith" had emerged from "a bizarre fusion of the cultural bohemianism of San Francisco with the hi-tech industries of Silicon Valley." It "promiscuously combines the free-wheeling spirit of the hippies and the entrepreneurial zeal of the yuppies," and was achieved "through a profound faith in the emancipatory potential of the new information technologies."[3]

However, they warned, "by championing this seemingly admirable ideal, these techno-boosters are at the same time reproducing some of the most atavistic features of American society, especially those derived from the bitter legacy of slavery. Their utopian vision of California depends upon a wilful blindness towards the other—much less positive—features of life on the West Coast: racism, poverty and environmental degradation."[4]

Unlike Barbrook and Cameron, many outsiders have depicted Silicon Valley as a center of innovation and success, but the view from inside the Bay Area easily leads one to a different conclusion.

In 2011, in the midst of a period of uprising and upheaval both in the Middle East and the United States, I was hired to work at the Electronic Frontier Foundation—one of the oldest and most respected digital rights organizations in the world. In April of that year, my father (may he rest in power) and I rented a U-Haul and embarked on a cross-country road trip, arriving in San Francisco on May 1, International Workers' Day, an auspicious day to start a new job that comes with great purpose.

Upon arriving at my tiny apartment in the city's central Mission district, I was immediately struck by the contradictions. This was a city renowned for being the heart of innovation and success and yet, on my first Saturday morning there, as I strolled down Twenty-First Street to buy a coffee at the legendary coffeehouse Philz, I watched as a man squatted and defecated right on the sidewalk. Later, I would learn about the city's failure to provide meaningful help to its seemingly ever-growing homeless population, and watch Silicon Valley companies try to step in where the government had failed by creating public composting "pooplets" for San Francisco.[5] Unsurprisingly, they never materialized.

I moved to Berlin just three years later, a decision based largely on the fact that, by then, my job was taking me to Europe and the Middle East on too regular a basis for me to stomach the constant twelve-hour flights. On trips back to the Bay, I have dodged piles of used needles, watched helplessly as historic bars and hangouts (like the Mission's last lesbian bar, the Lex) closed down, and witnessed as an ever-increasing amount of anti-tech sentiment was spray-painted and chalked on sidewalks and streets.

But this book is not about how San Francisco has changed, nor is it about the broader problems with Silicon Valley per se. Those stories have been written, and will continue to be written as time marches on, by people with far more connection to—and stake in—the Bay Area and its future. So allow me to take a step back.

As the world burns

As I write this on a calm morning in late May, safely isolated in my Berlin apartment, I'm watching rapt as the Bay Area—as well as Minneapolis, Brooklyn, and much of the United States—goes up in flames. I regularly read the *Washington Post* and still subscribe to the print edition of the *New Yorker*, but most of my news comes from people, people I may or may not have ever met in real life but who have been part of my network for more than a decade. This news, sometimes in the form of links to published articles, and sometimes direct from the streets, is shared on Twitter, Facebook, Instagram, Reddit. At thirty-eight years old—and like much of the world's internet users today—I am entirely reliant on media that is shared on corporate platforms.

How did this happen? That, dear reader, is precisely the question I hope to answer with this volume. But first, I would like to acknowledge a few things, namely what this book is, what it isn't, and why I'm writing it.

This book seeks to encapsulate the history of how Silicon Valley's major communications platforms created a system apart—specifically, a system that governs how we can express ourselves online. As the title of this book alludes, this system of governance is encapsulated within a broader system, that of surveillance capitalism, a term popularized by scholar Shoshanna Zuboff with her book *The Age of Surveillance Capitalism*—essential reading for those seeking greater understanding of how we got here. This volume is not, however, *about* surveillance capitalism per se; rather, I see it as the system that has enabled a milieu in which companies, not governments, get to decide how we may express ourselves.

The stories in this volume are at times personal, at times observed from afar, but come together to tell a story of how, over the past decade, Silicon Valley's mega-corporations have come to align with governmental power while people in countries around the world, though increasingly divided politically, have come to distrust both corporations and government.

My experiences over the past decade have largely taken place outside of the United States, and so too do most of the stories contained within. Readers wishing to gain a deeper understanding of the impact social media has had on democracy in the United States are encouraged to read the work of scholars including Siva Vaidyanathan, Joan Donovan, Nathaniel Persily, and Ethan Zuckerman, among others.

Although the battles over copyright that have been fought over the past decades most certainly have played a role in the development of platform governance, copyright law is a complex and divisive topic, and one that is simply outside of my expertise. Nevertheless, understanding the basic history of intellectual property regulation and moderation online is important for any understanding of content moderation, and a pursuit I would encourage of any scholar on the subject.

A few other things this book is not: a deep dive into the inner workings of content moderation (for that, see Tarleton Gillespie's *Custodians of the Internet*); a legal history of how online speech is governed and regulated (see Kate Klonick's *Harvard Law Review* article "The New Governors," or Nic Suzor's book, *Lawless*); a manifesto about how social media should be governed (see Rebecca MacKinnon's

2012 tome *Consent of the Networked*); a book about how social media undermines democracy (see Siva Vaidyanathan's *Antisocial Media*); or an exploration of the impact of content moderation on workers (see Sarah T. Roberts's *Behind the Screen*). I have learned from and cited all these scholars as well as many others, and highly recommend reading their books, as well as many of the scholarly and popular works listed in the endnotes.

Like any writer, I have often worried that there are important stories that I have forgotten. For that, I apologize—a life lived large has too many stories to fit in one volume. Still, I would be remiss if I didn't note the role that activists, non-governmental organizations, and scholars—who are far too many to name—have played in shaping the developments of the last decade. Since those lonely, early days, the field of digital rights—and more specifically, the field of those studying platform policies and content moderation—has grown immensely. I count among my friends and allies a number of activists and experts in this field and know that, without them, my views would be much different than they are today. I have learned and grown as a result of their contributions.

Finally, a few brief words on the term "censorship." In the early days of my career, I often spoke on stage in my advocacy for a free and open internet about "corporate" or "platform" censorship, only to be confronted afterwards by constitutionalists who saw my use of the term as undermining or contradicting their legal perspective. Even today, I am sometimes chastised, usually by law professors, for distorting the (US) legal definition of the word.

On this point I stand strong: censorship is not a legal term, nor is it the sole domain of government actors or synonymous with the First Amendment. Throughout history, censorship has been enacted by royals, the Church, the postal service, the Inquisition, publishers, the state, and yes, corporations. Though the details differ, censorship exists in some form in every locale throughout the world. Throughout history, censorship has most often served those at the top, allowing them to consolidate power while silencing the voices of anyone who might engage in protest. But the struggle for freedom of expression is as old as the history of censorship, and it isn't over yet.

Furthermore, the legal framework inside today's social media platforms was not inevitable, nor is it necessarily the "right" one for every person in every place. The US Constitution—to which, it must be said, women and people and color were excluded from contributing —is not a perfect document, nor (as the first chapter of this book argues) is Section 230 of the Communications Decency Act—the 1996 statute that professor Jeff Kosseff has dubbed "the twenty-six words that created the internet"—a perfect law.

It is important, then, that we view today's debates around free speech, censorship, and regulation in the context of existing laws, in various jurisdictions, while also thinking outside the box for answers. Our future may just well depend on it.

Introduction

In the summer of 2005, when I was just twenty-three, I took a job teaching English in Morocco, where I had studied abroad the previous summer. Like many young people, I had no idea what I wanted to do with my life. I loved to write, and I knew that getting good at it required practice, so a few days after arriving I sat down in the local cybercafé and did what any reasonable person in 2005 would do: I started a blog.[1]

Blogging connected me to local communities, and it kept my friends back home informed of what was happening in my life. Eventually, writing about my own life became boring, and I began writing about Moroccan politics instead. I found someone to design a website for me as a repository for those writings. I would read the local magazines in my poor French and talk to friends, then write up summaries of current events, sometimes adding my own commentary.

Morocco and all its complexities (and yes, contradictions) have kept writers busy throughout history. On the one hand, and especially compared with some of its neighbors, the country's laws are liberal and modern: women more or less have the same legal rights as men, and labor and other laws are catching up fast. On the other hand, and despite decades of colonization that infiltrated everything from language to food, it remains incredibly traditional—something which, for me, stood out the most when it came to the nation's pillars: *Allah, al-Watan, al-Malik* (God, the Nation, the King).

Any Moroccan will tell you that there are three red lines you should never cross, verbally or in writing. First, you must avoid denying—or especially, cursing—God or Islam. You may ask questions, or debate whether the Qur'an actually prohibits alcohol (that one's quite popular), but crossing certain lines will land you in trouble. The second red line is country, or homeland. Morocco is rife with nationalism, certainly, but so are a lot of places. The specific line here is that you must never question Morocco's sovereignty over the Western Sahara, the land claimed in 1975 when 350,000 Moroccans marched into the then-Spanish territory, kicking off a war that lasted sixteen years and only strengthened the Moroccan government's resolve.

And finally—the king must not be disparaged. The Moroccan writers whose columns I used to read loved to criticize members of Parliament. They might even go after a member of the royal cabinet. But the king, as modern and fun-loving as he might appear in the ever-popular and ubiquitous photos of him on a Jet Ski, is beyond reproach.

Allow me to illustrate: In 2009, an independent poll conducted in Morocco found that 91 percent of the country's citizens approved of the king's leadership.[2] Now, anywhere else in the world, that would be an extraordinary number. Theresa May's approval rating never made it as high as 50 percent. President Obama's approval rating average was only 47 percent, not to even speak of his successor. But for the beloved king of Morocco, that 9 percent "deficit" was too much to bear, and when popular magazines *TelQuel* and *Nichane* published the poll's results, the copies were seized by the Ministry of Communications.

I immersed myself in stories and histories of censorship, first in Morocco and then across the Arab world. I began to write not just about my country of residence, but also Egypt, Tunisia, the United Arab Emirates (UAE), and Palestine. And I connected with others who were doing the same thing, first Moroccan natives and other expats for whom blogging was an outlet, and then, later, young people across the region.

In early 2007, confident in my writing abilities and yearning for a bigger outlet, I wrote to the regional editor of Global Voices, Amira Al Hussaini, asking if I might join the project. Much to my surprise, she replied immediately and enthusiastically, and on that day, my world was forever changed.

Global Voices was founded in 2004, just before the birth of modern social media. Its founders, Rebecca MacKinnon and Ethan Zuckerman, were fellows at the Berkman Klein Center for Internet & Society, a multidisciplinary institution with a mission to "explore and understand cyberspace" that was embedded at the time in Harvard Law School. MacKinnon had once served as CNN bureau chief in Beijing and later Tokyo, while Zuckerman's path to becoming a media scholar was more winding, taking him from Massachusetts to Ghana and back, where he then worked for early web host Tripod.com. Global Voices was born from a workshop attended by media scholars as well as a diverse and ambitious set of bloggers from all over the world. Within five years, it was a force to be reckoned with, providing an alternative view—and at times, a counter-narrative—to the often under-resourced and sometimes myopic mainstream press.

Global Voices' modus operandi, in those early days, was to report on what people were saying on blogs. Later, as blogging gave way to Facebook posts and tweets, and visual media gained ground, Global Voices authors were forced to innovate and find new ways to capture often-ephemeral content. But more on that in later chapters ...

I moved back to the United States in 2007 at the age of twenty-five, landing in Boston not far from my family and where I grew up. Although I had been on my own for a few years already, living in the US presented new challenges, and I hustled to make ends meet. Within a year, I was working full-time at a non-profit, volunteering for Global Voices, and snatching up every writing gig I could, from local restaurant reviews to narrative pieces for foundations.

And then I got my "big break": encouraged by members of Global Voices' core team, I applied for a fellowship to attend (with other members) a media conference in Miami. I arrived at a rented house in the middle of the night and joined my colleagues in person for the first time in the backyard the next morning for coffee.

I don't remember much of the actual conference, but a few memories from that week stand out: Everyone was talking about micro-blogging and couldn't shut up about a new platform called Twitter, which I joined that same week. My Global Voices colleagues were even kinder and more interesting in person than they were online; some had come all the way from Bahrain, Bolivia, Madagascar, Guatemala, Trinidad, and France for the event, and we spent the week joking and drinking and making up songs. They were all a little older than me, and they were all doing work that they loved—something that I still hadn't found for myself.

On my final morning in Miami, I sat in the garden with Solana Larsen, managing editor of the Global Voices' site at the time, and told her how unhappy and tired I was with the constant hassle of freelance writing gigs. She asked me what I wanted to do, and I rattled off a string of mildly incoherent thoughts: I wanted to write, and I enjoyed doing research, and I was fascinated by censorship and activism, and different cultures and maybe something to do with new media? "I might have some ideas," she said. "Send me your résumé and I'll see what I can do."

To make a long story short, I ended up at the Berkman Klein Center. I walked into my boss's office that afternoon and gave notice. And three weeks later, I walked across the Harvard campus and toward my new life.

The job wasn't easy, but I loved it. I was put in charge of coordinating the OpenNet Initiative, a multi-institution research project set up to study how governments conducted network-level filtering, or censorship. I had to coordinate technical testing of said filtering with the University of Toronto's Citizen Lab and dozens of volunteer and paid testers in as many countries, assist with research for a book being prepared on the subject, and write regular blog posts. I found the subject matter endlessly fascinating, and in my spare time would find myself reading up on the various countries we were studying. I was working with the world's foremost experts on internet censorship and absorbing everything I possibly could.

In the summer and autumn of 2007, there were numerous stories of governments blocking social media websites. Tunisia, Kuwait, Turkey, followed by Bahrain, the UAE, and Iran the following winter. China had never allowed access in the first place. No platform was spared—YouTube, Flickr, Facebook, Twitter were all targets. By the end of 2009, it had become hard to keep track (and we tried!), as different countries blocked and then unblocked (and sometimes blocked again) various social networks. The states were clearly enemies of free expression, and the platforms were the good guys … or so it seemed at the time, at least.

Around the same time, I was in touch with a young Moroccan activist, Kacem El Ghazzali, regarding a campaign to raise awareness for a blogger who had been arrested during a protest. After the campaign was launched, we stayed in touch, and he told me about his work fighting against religion in the public education system. It pushed right up against Morocco's red lines, and I worried about his safety because just a year before, the government had arrested a young man, Fouad Mourtada, for impersonating the king's brother, and while in custody, the police had allegedly beaten him.

Kacem was worried for his safety, too, but his convictions were strong. He ran a Facebook page called *Jeunes pour la séparation entre Religion et Enseignement* (Youth for the Separation of Religion and Education) but soon ran into a problem. On March 13, 2010, he sent me a message: "Facebook disabled my account."

A month later, I began researching "content policing," a subject that few had written about at the time. And thus began a decade-long personal obsession, taking my life and career in a new direction.

1

The New Gatekeepers

On a day to day basis, the rules that apply most directly to people on the internet are the rules set and enforced by intermediaries.

—Nic Suzor

Imagine a society where the laws are created behind closed doors, without public input or approval. This is a society where at any time the laws are subject to change, or be replaced with new ones altogether. There is no democratic participation, no transparency, and no due process—and the laws are enforced by minimally trained workers in faraway locales who often lack awareness of local conditions or, increasingly, by trained machines. Mistakes are, of course, inevitable and plenty, but when they're made, individuals rarely have the means to rectify them.

This society exists, inside the social media platforms created in Silicon Valley and exported throughout the rest of the world. These platforms—such as Google, Facebook, YouTube, Twitter, and Tumblr—now exert control over the speech and visual expression of billions of the world's citizens. As of 2020, Facebook alone has more than 1.7 billion daily active users—more than 3 billion greater than the population of China.

Although they lack the heavy weaponry of nation-states, the role of dominant platforms "in the international legal order increasingly resembles that of sovereign states," argues legal scholar Julie E. Cohen.[1] For the impact that their regulations on speech have on ordinary individuals the world over, this argument is absolutely true—and also runs counter to the ethos of both Silicon Valley and the early cyberlibertarian thinkers, whose optimistic philosophies still hold significant sway in the Valley today.

In his manifesto, "A Declaration of the Independence of Cyberspace," internet philosopher John Perry Barlow beautifully rails against the world's governments on behalf of fellow members of the online community, declaring "the global space [they] are building to be naturally independent of the tyrannies you seek to impose" on them. "Cyberspace does not lie within your borders," he claims, deeming it "an act of nature" that grows itself through "our collective actions."[2]

Barlow, who died in 2018 after a long illness, viewed the internet as a "a world where anyone, anywhere may express his or her beliefs, no matter how singular, without fear of being coerced into silence or conformity," a world where the legal concepts of "property, expression, identity, movement, and context do not apply …" for "they all based on matter, and there is no matter here."

The manifesto was written in 1996 during the World Economic Forum in Davos, on the same day that President Bill Clinton signed into law the Communications Decency Act, an attempt to ban "obscene" material on the internet. Barlow was well aware of the looming threat from governments to the freedom provided by the internet, having co-founded the Electronic Frontier Foundation six years prior.

Science fiction writer Bruce Sterling also stands among those who wrote of the early promise of freedom online; in his 1992 "A Short History of the Internet," he argues that the main reason people want to be on the internet is "simple freedom," adding that "the Internet is a rare example of a true, modern, functional anarchy. There is no 'Internet Inc.'"[3]

Growing up in the 1990s, I too believed anything was possible online. Although my first interactions with the World Wide Web were through Prodigy, an early provider not unlike the more popular AOL, I never encountered speech restrictions of any kind until well into the aughts. My early Web adventures were exciting—exhilarating even—and not without risk; I experienced harassment, hate speech. I witnessed images I cannot erase from my mind even today. All of the things, in other words, that today's platforms are attempting to banish. But I also made lasting friendships that took me on some of my first solo trips to other US states, and learned things about the world that were not taught in my small-town public school.

Barlow saw the internet as a place beyond the reach of states, an unregulatable space in which a new form of governance—based on the Golden Rule—might emerge. Sterling saw the internet as belonging to "everyone and no one."[4] Both of them foresaw the influence that states would inevitably exert over the Web, but neither quite imagined what the next generation, undoubtedly influenced by their ideas, might accomplish through unbridled neoliberal capitalism.

A brief history of censorship

Throughout history, various bodies have imposed rules on what ordinary citizens can see or say. Traditionally, this was the domain of the church or the monarchy, but with the emergence—from the 1648 Peace of Westphalia—of nation-state sovereignty as a basic ordering principle for societies, the nation-state and the lesser governance structures contained within it became the predominant arbiter of what people can do or say, and which information they can access.

Today, throughout the world, most societies have agreed that democratically elected governments have some right to control our expression and access to information, though the degree to which each society believes in such a right varies—as does, of course, the degree to which governments exert such control.

Until the advent of the internet, censorship was a localized endeavor. A government (whether democratic or not) might decide that a given book, film, work of art, or newspaper article violated its laws or its sensibilities and barred access to it. Methods of censorship throughout history and the world have varied considerably: Whereas in the Soviet Union, it was common for the government to withhold information from its citizens by erasing content from books and reprinting them anew, and jailing writers who crossed red lines known or unknown, in modern-day Saudi Arabia, the government prefers to black out or otherwise obscure offending words and images in imported magazines or films while simultaneously barring the creation of certain content locally. Both medieval Italy and pre-modern Britain utilized the fig leaf to desensationalize works of art, while present-day Turkey and Morocco—who share Islam in common but otherwise have considerably varied histories and systems of government—have imprisoned those who dare insult the country's rulers living or dead.

Often, the more democratic a state, the more transparent it is when it comes to censorship. Germany's Basic Law, adopted as the country's constitution when it reunified in 1990, guarantees freedom of speech, press, and opinion but allows for limits for the protection of young persons and the right to personal honor. Modern Germany's criminal code further restricts *Volksverhetzung*, or "incitement of popular hatred," Holocaust denial, certain forms of insult, and a handful of other things. Furthermore, provisions exist against "anti-constitutional politics," such as having membership in National Socialist and other neo-Nazi parties, but also the far-left Red Army faction. These laws, while often controversial, are fully communicated to the public and the text of them is found easily in libraries or on the internet. Though citizens of Germany and other states that apply such measures may disagree with them, those who violate the law do so knowingly and with the awareness that there will be consequences.

Defined by Wikipedia's global contributor base as "the suppression of speech, public communication, or other information, on the basis that such material is considered objectionable, harmful, sensitive, or 'inconvenient,'" censorship is essentially the act of an authority asserting its dominance—and its values—over the public by imposing regulations, punishments, or other measures on expression to which it objects.

"Censorship" is in itself an inherently value-neutral term. There is censorship of which one approves (a majority of Germans, for instance, support the prohibition on Holocaust denial) and which one finds unconscionable—and what constitutes each of these categories differs from one society, or even one person, to the next. Most of the world's governments see value in censoring hate speech to some degree, but relatively few impose restrictions on insulting the country's rulers.

Although censorship as a concept is value-neutral, it is all too often used only to describe the restrictions of which we disapprove. The United States, which has arguably the world's most permissible laws around speech, still enacts certain limits, one of which is on child sexual exploitation imagery (more commonly, and unfortunately, referred to as "child porn"). This is a restriction put in place to protect children that all but the most depraved individual might agree with; it is also—despite that consensus—censorship. It is, simply put, censorship of which we approve.

Furthermore, freedom of speech (or freedom of expression) is not a synonym for the US Constitution's First Amendment or equivalent legal rights.[5] Freedom of expression is, rather, a concept that dates back to, at least, ancient Greece. In Athens, all male citizens,[6] rich or poor, were encouraged to address the democratic assembly, thus participating in the governance of the city-state. This concept, *isegoria*, formed the fundamental basis for Athenian society, while another—*parrhesia*—gave license to society's philosophers to speak truth to power. Freedom of expression in Athens, as readers well know, was not without limits: the vote to convict Socrates may have been democratic, but it nonetheless resulted in the ultimate silencing of his speech.

Knowing the history of censorship—and resistance to the term—might help readers to understand our current dilemma. Today's gatekeepers of speech, as I will demonstrate in this book, are not only nation-states, but giant global internet corporations that have become, in the words of Australian scholar Nic Suzor, a "key actor in governing our lives."[7] They are simultaneously bound to no one and to many, resulting in a complex tangle of rules that has become unnavigable even to experts, let alone their users. And, as a result, they are having a massive and under-documented impact on our speech, our individual and collective agency, our culture, and our memory.

The new gatekeepers

While John Perry Barlow was brushing shoulders with the Davos elite, a young Mark Zuckerberg was at home in Westchester County,

New York, coding his first social network, ZuckNet, which linked together the computers between his home and his father's dental practice. Meanwhile, across the country, Larry Page and Sergey Brin were at Stanford, forming an unshakeable bond that, in a few short years, led to the incorporation of Google. And a young, restless Jack Dorsey was away at college in Missouri, ready to graduate so he could get to work.

These young would-be founders grew up with the same internet that I did, an internet where anything felt possible. They arrived around the turn of the century to a Silicon Valley whose predominant ideology was libertarianism, where laissez-faire capitalism was embraced and regulations pooh-poohed. They embraced the Californian Ideology and built their empires in its image.

The companies that Zuckerberg, Page and Brin, and Dorsey founded—Facebook, Google, and Twitter, respectively—launched during a period in which restrictions on online speech were minimal. The Digital Millennium Copyright Act, enacted in 1998, placed restrictions on the sharing and dissemination of copyrighted content, and extended responsibilities to platforms that might play host to such content. A handful of governments had found ways to restrict access to particular websites, while still others restricted access altogether, providing access only to certain citizens through licensing or other schemes. By and large, however, the electronic frontier remained a free-for-all.

Debates in the 1980s and 1990s over the widespread availability of pornography in the United States—dubbed the "porn wars"—led to the authorization of the Communications Decency Act in the United States, which was later deemed unconstitutional, though a piece of it—Section 230—survived that set the stage for social media platforms to flourish. Now known as Section 230 of the US Telecommunications Act and codified as 47 U.S.C. § 230, that original component of the Communications Decency Act was intended as a safe harbor for internet service providers and search engines,. It allowed for these providers to argue that they were not publishers, but only provided access to the internet or conveyed information, and therefore could not be held liable for their users' speech.

Section 230 has two components: The first prevents intermediaries from being held liable for the speech of their users, not unlike the protections afforded to telephone companies. This is an important provision, without which companies would be incentivized to proactively police their users' speech, thus inhibiting them from innovation and growth.

The second component gives intermediaries the ability to police their users' speech or actions without losing their safe harbor protections. Before the creation of Section 230, an internet intermediary risked liability for illegal or defamatory postings by its users if it moderated content on its services. Without this second component, it was more difficult for intermediaries to protect their customers from harassment or other abuse without facing legal risk for other content they might not be aware of.

Nic Suzor proposes that Section 230 "firmly establishes the ground rules for lawsuits over internet content: a victim can sue the person who is directly responsible for causing harm online but can almost never sue the service providers who host the content or facilitate communications. It is hard to overstate the significance of [Section] 230. The safe harbor that it provides is very generous: it gives platforms the right, but not the responsibility, to remove content as they see fit."[8]

The downside of how intermediaries are regulated, of course, is the fact that the rules of the road can be and are determined by unelected leaders with no particular qualifications, and can be changed at a whim. An intermediary can censor speech or permanently boot a user from using its services, for any or no reason at all. In other words, as scholar Rebecca Tushnet explains: "Current law often allows Internet intermediaries to have their free speech and everyone else's too."[9]

This matters less when a platform is small or niche, created for a specific purpose—few would argue that Jewish dating service Jdate should have to play host to Christians, or that a site for knitting enthusiasts should have to become a space for political debate. But over the years, a handful of large, all-purpose platforms have become the agora for billions of people worldwide. Although Facebook or Twitter are, legally speaking, akin to the shopping mall, to their early users they were more a virtual public sphere, in which ideas and information could be exchanged and all had an equal opportunity to contribute to public debate.

Though many would (and have, in criticisms of my work) argue that we should have no expectations of freedom within the corporate confines of these platforms, it is not without reason that many have that expectation. As the following chapters illustrate, these platforms' founders led us to believe early on that their sites were spaces for the free exchange of ideas. While none of them emerged without *any* rules, over time—as their popularity and user bases have grown—so too have the restrictions they place on what we can and can't do or say, as well as the pressure placed upon them by external entities. As such, we should view platforms as operating as the "New Governors" of online speech.

"These New Governors," writes legal scholar Kate Klonick, "are part of a new triadic model of speech that sits between the state and speakers-publishers. They are private, self-regulating entities that are economically and normatively motivated to reflect the democratic culture and free speech expectations of their users."[10]

The triadic model of which Klonick writes can be attributed to Jack Balkin, a US constitutional law scholar who has written extensively about civil liberties on the internet. Of the new governors, Balkin writes: "In the twentieth century model, the vast majority of people were members of an audience for mass media products, but very few actively used mass media as speakers or broadcasters. Twenty-first century governors of digital speech, by contrast, make their money by facilitating and encouraging the production of content by ordinary people and governing the communities of speakers that result."[11]

Balkin's triad model illustrates a pluralist concept of speech regulation that simultaneously contains significantly more complexity than those that preceded it, with a variety of actors playing a role in the governance of speech, and (perhaps as a result of the chaotic nature of this system) more opportunity for citizens to circumvent traditional state restrictions on speech.

But, as Balkin warned early on, the digital age has altered the importance of the First Amendment (and other legal provisions around the world) in securing freedom of speech, as the "responsibility for securing a democratic culture" has fallen to private actors.[12]

In the United States at least, the question of private governance in quasi-public spaces has been considered before, most notably in the 1946 Supreme Court case *Marsh v. Alabama*. In the early part of the twentieth century, it was not uncommon for a company to provide homes and other property to their employees. These spaces, known colloquially as "company towns," were owned and governed by a company but treated for most purposes as public space—that is, visitors were welcome to use the sidewalks and streets and to shop in the businesses located on company land.

But when Grace Marsh, a Jehovah's Witness, was found to be distributing religious literature on the streets of one company town in Alabama, she was told to leave. Marsh refused and was arrested, forming the basis for a constitutional challenge. The Supreme Court decided in Marsh's favor, with Justice Hugo L. Black writing for a 5–3 majority: "The more an owner, for his advantage, opens up his property for use by the public in general, the more do his rights become circumscribed by the statutory and constitutional rights of those who use it."[13]

This central holding of *Marsh* remained a guiding principle of constitutional law, forming a basis for subsequent cases, but has not as of this writing been applied to the quasi-public spaces of the internet. Nevertheless, one can quite easily imagine how its core principle could apply to virtual spaces.

In 2011, Facebook hosted a virtual "town hall" for then president Barack Obama.[14] In the United States, "town hall" meetings have historically been a way for politicians to engage with their constituents without regard to status—that is, ordinary voters and citizens are treated equally in this format. Although town halls are not inherently open and citizens could in theory be barred from attendance, many such meetings operate with an open-door policy.

A "town hall" hosted by Facebook, however, is in essence a closed-door meeting. Not only was a person required to have a Facebook account to participate, they were also required to abide by the company's rules—both using, and revealing to the public, their "real name." An individual who had been barred from the platform, either as a result of violating the rules or by mistake or misapplication of the rules, was also barred from participation in the town hall.

Similarly, an increasing number of businesses use Facebook for various forms of public engagement, from the restaurant that opts for a Facebook page instead of a website to the airline that uses Facebook to engage with customers. Not only are users who opt out—or are forced out—of participation unable to access these tools, the employee who does not use Facebook is at a disadvantage as well. In other words, if your job requires you to use Facebook, you must have a Facebook account—but if you are kicked off the platform, well, tough luck.

"The debate over how to balance the right of intermediaries to curate a platform while simultaneously protecting user speech under the First Amendment is ongoing for courts and scholars," writes Klonick, but for many users of these platforms—particularly those outside the United States—it's a debate that's moving far too slowly.[15]

The rules may differ from one platform to the next, but each has to put itself in the position of gatekeeper. And with each iteration of the rules, the platforms open themselves up to more pressure—from users, governments, and organizations—to censor different types of content.

We've now firmly reached an era where it can no longer be said, if it ever could, that the internet is a space where "anyone, anywhere" may express their beliefs, but one in which groups already marginalized by society are further victimized by unaccountable platforms, and the already powerful are free to spread misinformation or hate with impunity.

Welcome to dystopia.

Policing content in the quasi-public sphere

Mark Zuckerberg, the story goes, first conceived of Facebook in his Harvard dormitory as "FaceMash," a game that allowed Harvard students to compare two photos of female students—pulled from the university's "face book," a directory of students that contains their photographs—and vote on which one was more attractive. "I almost want to put some of these faces next to pictures of some farm animals," wrote the young Zuckerberg in his blog at the time, "and have people vote on which is more attractive."[16]

FaceMash got Zuckerberg in trouble with university authorities, who shut down the site, but the young student was not deterred. He created a new site, Thefacebook.com, which served as an online student directory. Launched in February 2004 for Harvard students, the site expanded the following month to Yale, Stanford, and Columbia, and later in the year to most universities across the United States.

Facebook was not the first social media platform of its kind—Friendster, MySpace, and the long-forgotten Orkut were already popular in various geographies—but it quickly grew to become the largest, reaching half a billion users by 2010, just four years after opening membership to anyone. A year later, it rolled out its first set of community standards.

That isn't to say that Facebook did not launch without rules: before the release of its standards, there were Terms of Service (ToS) that banned certain actions, such as "bullying, intimidating, or harassing any user"; posting content that is "hateful, threatening, pornographic, or that contains nudity or graphic or gratuitous violence"; and "using Facebook to do anything unlawful, misleading, malicious, or discriminatory." It further barred users from signing up for the service with anything but their "real name."[17]

While a company's ToS is a legal contract that outlines the terms between a company and a user of its services, the community standards or guidelines is a more human-readable document that explains a platform's rules and, sometimes, the consequences for violating those rules. Facebook's first community standards, launched in 2011, were clear but basic and prohibited violence and threats, self-harm, bullying and harassment, graphic content, and nudity. They further placed restrictions on copyright infringement, the promotion of regulated goods, the use of fake names or pseudonyms, and a handful of other actions.

A note at the bottom of the original community standards document explained that users should report anything they see on Facebook that they believe violates the platform's terms. Like most platforms, Facebook did not until recently take proactive measures to identify prohibited content, instead relying upon its users to police the site through a system known as community policing or "flagging." This system, argue Kate Crawford and Tarleton Gillespie, "act[s] as a mechanism to elicit and distribute user labor—users as a volunteer corps of regulators."[18]

Flagging works similarly across platforms: when a user stumbles upon something that they find offensive, they click a button (occasionally but rarely a literal flag) that presents them with a series of options. Facebook currently tells users that they can report the post "after selecting a problem" from a list that includes "nudity," "hate speech," and other forbidden content, while Twitter asks "What is going on with this Tweet?" with responses such as "I'm not interested in this Tweet" and "It's abusive or harmful." Depending on what the user selects, they'll be taken through a series of further questions or options that categorize the post in question before reporting it.

This practice of flagging has resulted in a culture of snitching, in which people are expected to monitor each other and report problematic activity to a central authority. This form of "community policing," like the "community standards," is hardly about community—rather, it would more accurately be compared to the US Department of Homeland Security program called "If You See Something, Say Something®." Designed in the wake of 9/11 to encourage ordinary citizens to report suspicious behavior to authorities, that program in numerous instances led to the reporting of innocent people of color to law enforcement for dubious reasons.[19]

On the modern social media platform, this translates to people reporting other users for violations both real and perceived, as well as simply out of annoyance or distaste. Once a post is reported, it then enters a queue to be reviewed by a human worker, who makes a determination about whether the content in question violates the rules.[20] If the content is found to be in violation, it is deleted; if it isn't, it remains online. Those who violate the rules repeatedly may be punished like kindergartners: they are put into "timeouts" lasting up to thirty days, hidden from search, or worse yet, permanently

booted from a platform, unable to access content—and networks—
that they've been incentivized for years to use as much as possible.

This process is what Sarah T. Roberts has dubbed "commercial
content moderation," a term commenting on the capitalist context and
scale at which these platforms now operate. Companies like Google and
Facebook utilize thousands of content moderators, dispersed around
the world and often employed through service firms like Accenture,
Cognizant, and Arvato. They labor, as Roberts writes, "under a number
of different regimes, employment statuses, and workplace conditions
around the world—often by design."[21]

Thanks to the work of scholars like Roberts and Klonick and journalists such as Adrian Chen and Casey Newton, we know considerably
more about the internal workings of Facebook's content moderation
than of other platforms. At Facebook, there are three tiers of content
moderation: Tier 3 moderators do the bulk of basic content moderation, Tier 2 moderators supervise them and review prioritized or
escalated content, and Tier 1 moderators are policymakers or lawyers
who deal with the most difficult content issues and are involved in
adjusting policy in response to them.

Commercial content moderation is a stressful and demanding job.
Moderators, particularly those at Tier 3–like levels, spend their day
viewing gruesome imagery and making rapid-fire decisions about
what to take down or leave in place. They're paid poorly: as little as
$28,800 a year in the United States, or $6 a day in India.[22] They receive
minimal training, little to no mental health support, and often work
in dismal conditions. And for what? So the platforms' users don't
have to see the same gruesome content that these moderators (often
themselves users of the platforms) have to see.

"It's humiliating," Amine Derkaoui, a former moderator for oDesk,
told *Gawker* reporter Adrian Chen in 2012. "They are just exploiting
the third world."[23] Derkaoui was among the first moderators to leak
a training manual to the media.

Today, Derkaoui works as a journalist, but when he was just twenty-
one, he took a short-term job with oDesk as a "pre-moderator" of
sorts for Facebook for $1 per hour. His job was to look at content in
a category of his choosing and determine whether or not it violated

the rules; the content was then passed to a full-time content reviewer in the company's Palo Alto office. "From the beginning, the whole project was only intended for people from the third world," Derkaoui told me. "It said that this project was intended for people from Africa and Asia, which meant that Europeans and Americans could not be candidates." When I asked him what the job was like, he told me in his Francophone lilt: "Being a Facebook moderator is a job where you have all the dirtiest, ugliest shit content on the internet." "We [are] bodies in seats," another moderator working in Tampa, Florida, for Cognizant told journalist Casey Newton.[24]

Moderation can be a harrowing job with lasting repercussions on workers' physical and mental health. For other moderators, it's not so bad—as Adrian Chen, who has interviewed dozens of content reviewers, tells me. For some, it's just a job. But, he says, "it's not a great job; it's pretty drudgerous no matter what you do. People feel like it's a necessity and they feel like they're more or less on the front lines against this tide of bad content they have to protect everyone else against … For me, the issue isn't primarily about whether these companies are controlling their platforms tightly enough, but it's about the power that they have. And giving them more power is bad, not just in terms of free speech but also in terms of necessitating giving these harmful, low-paying jobs to people in developing countries."

Alex,[25] a former YouTube staffer who began as a content reviewer and worked their way up to a policy job, told me they are proud of their time at the company and depict their overall experience as positive. Nevertheless, they feel the system of commercial content moderation is unethical. "You see that companies are hiring tens of thousands, but that's largely on the backs of undervalued labor—young people, immigrants, people of color."

One former Tier 2 moderator at Facebook described community operations, the department in which she served as manager, as one that "functions in permanent chaos." Anna* left her job after several years, having fallen into disillusion with the job. She describes part of the job as having to respond to the whims of governments without much regard for process. When, during the refugee crisis of 2015, the government of Germany wanted to see a policy that protected migrants from hate speech, Anna says that her team was expected to spring into action to create a policy in an unrealistically short time frame.

"The turnaround time for this policy was a few days and it didn't necessarily make any sense, but we had to operationalize it anyway," she says. "This became the most complicated policy possible, and we had to implement it within a week, whereas any other process would take months and would have gone through a long approval process, but we didn't do any of this because the German government said so."

But—says Anna, who is originally from a developing country, similar resources are rarely allocated when similar problems arise in the global South. Describing an example in which her team dealt with one group in a particular country who were at risk after other Facebook users labeled them as terrorists, she says: "This kind of policy would never get any face time with the policy team because they were always busy with ... whatever was prioritized by countries like Germany and the U.S. The policies would always be shaped by those countries."

Indeed, Germany—along with France and other powerful nations—has exercised a degree of influence through regulation that has had a lasting effect on policy not only in that country but globally. The Network Enforcement Act (referred to as "NetzDG", the short version of its German title) requires companies with a certain number of users to remove hate speech in accordance with German law in an impossibly short period of time. Furthermore, the law has effectively compelled Facebook and other companies to hire local workers to enforce it. It is difficult to imagine a country from the Global South being able to exert such influence.

"I sound like a jealous child, sorry," she joked—but in fact, this disparity has serious consequences for users in various locales. Take, for example, Facebook's failure to respond quickly to Myanmar government officials' use of the platform to spread hateful messages about the country's Rohingya minority, which has contributed to what many have described as an ongoing genocide. As activists repeatedly called on Facebook for more scrutiny of the situation, reports came out that the company's staff had only a handful of moderators who spoke Burmese.

Alex agrees that there's a disparity in the platforms' focus: "The press is focused on when it's white people or people from the global North dying ... That's going to be the content that gets the most attention."

"After [Myanmar] there is more concern for being reactive to things that aren't judged important," says Anna. But additionally, she adds, "content moderation has become a beat for journalists, and people care more," leading not only to greater scrutiny but also to more complex rules.

Moderators like Anna play a role in rule-making, but in most companies, the rules are ultimately decided by actors close to the very top of the hierarchy. And these are actors who, as many have observed, come from relatively homogeneous backgrounds, are not chosen by the people they supposedly serve, and are accountable to almost no one. Over time, they have accrued an unparalleled level of power over speech and access to information. Thus, by one road or another, the companies for which they work "create speech rules, enforce them, curate and censor content, and resolve user disputes, all in the course of moderating some of the most important channels of information in the world."[26]

Who watches the gatekeepers?

This therefore raises the question: If content moderators are the enforcement arm of the law, then who are the lawmakers, and from where do they derive their power?

Over the years, a number of observers and critics have attempted to answer this question. In a 2008 essay, legal scholars Jonathan Zittrain and John Palfrey called intermediary rule-makers "reluctant gatekeepers" who are forced to grapple with competing demands from states and the market.[27] Marvin Ammori refers to social media platforms as "the new speech vanguard," observing in a 2014 *Harvard Law Review* article that lawyers for these platforms are "shaping the future of free expression worldwide," their "paradigmatic decisions" having played significant roles in "some of the most important freedom of expression episodes in modern times."[28] Catherine Buni and Soraya Chemaly remarked in 2016 that early rule-makers "had yet to grasp that they were helping to develop new global standards for free speech."[29] And Jeffrey Rosen has referred to the companies' top brass as "The Deciders," in an homage to a nickname earned by Nicole Wong, former legal director of Twitter and current deputy counsel to Google, Nicole Wong.[30]

Wong is a revered figure in Silicon Valley. An attorney specializing in internet law with a master's degree in journalism, Wong is both thoughtful and pragmatic when she discusses the outsized role she and her peers played in shaping the rules of social media. Over breakfast in Oakland on a chilly December day, she told me how she and her peers at Google sought to work with civil society from the beginning: "There was a pretty fulsome group on content parameters that you could turn to" in the United States, she said, but "outside the US, that seemed to be missing." Although she admitted that was partly a result of her own American biases, she also correctly observed that "even if you could find someone who understood the content or media industry, it would be hard to find someone who also understood IP addresses."

Dave Willner has a similar perspective. At age twenty-six, he served as Facebook's first head of content policy and built the company's first set of community standards. We met on a rainy day near Airbnb's San Francisco headquarters, where he confessed to me that his team at the time was "a bunch of twenty-six-year-olds" who "didn't know what they were doing."

If, with Wong, Google's content moderation regime was the well-oiled machine, and Facebook's was the scrappy startup, MySpace's was the Wild West. At a 2007 conference at UCLA, my jaw dropped as I heard one of the platform's early content-moderation supervisors, Rasalyn Bowden, describe how MySpace's rules were created. "Going into it," she said, "it did seem like we were on this revolutionary thing, like nobody's ever done this before." She held up a three-ring notebook to the audience. "This is my bible from when we had our meetings ... when we would randomly come up with [rules] while we were watching porn."

"I went flipping through it yesterday," Bowden continued, "and there was a note in there trying to decide whether or not dental-floss-sized bikini straps really make you not nude, or is it okay if it's dental-floss-sized or spaghetti strap? What exactly made you not nude? ... These were the decisions we made in the middle of the night. It did feel like we were making it up as we were going along."[31]

For those users who feel as though the rules are arbitrary at times, these examples are cold comfort. They serve as reminders that some of the most important decisions about speech in our time have been made without regard to existing principles, sometimes on a whim, and have rarely been revisited or examined after the fact. "Once something is done, it's hard to convince the policy teams to roll it back," says Anna.

Make no mistake: the decisions that these policymakers must grapple with are, by any standard, tough. As Anna reminded me several times in our interview, "there's no textbook on how to be the moral compass of the world." Is an image of a nude girl fleeing from a napalm attack child-exploitation imagery, or is it a notable documentation of a war crime? Does the presence of a Hamas flag in a photograph of a legitimate protest constitute the promotion of terrorism, and should its presence warrant the removal of the image? Is the phrase "Men are scum" a popular sentiment in the #MeToo era, hate speech, or a permissible expression of frustration by a traditionally oppressed gender? Should rule-makers go against the grain and allow full-frontal adult nudity on their platform, despite much of the world prohibiting a nude adult from walking down the street? And how should the right to free expression be balanced with other, sometimes competing rights?

In her foundational 2012 book, *Consent of the Networked: The World-wide Struggle for Internet Freedom*, Rebecca MacKinnon observes that the unelected rule-makers at social media companies "play the roles of lawmakers, judge, jury, and police all at the same time," operating "a kind of private sovereignty in cyberspace."[32] She remarks that Facebook's core ideology is "the product of a corporate culture based on the life experiences of relatively sheltered and affluent Americans who may be well intentioned but have never experienced genuine, social, political, religious, or sexual vulnerability."[33]

These elites have, in recent years, reshaped some of their practices in response to critics. A little more than a decade after Wong and Willner were guessing at policymaking, the teams they helped create have expanded to include subject matter experts and input from mid-level operations managers with local expertise. Most major social media platforms regularly consult with external actors, including human rights and civil liberties NGOs as well as those focused on more specific subject areas, such as child protection or racism.

And yet, these teams are still operating with unchecked power. Over time, attempts to answer these policy questions—combined with growing pressure from a variety of external actors—have led to increasingly more complex rules on nearly every platform. Policymakers have demonstrated a predilection for giving the greatest amount of deference to state and other elite actors, rather than to their users. Increased complexity has led to a greater propensity for inconsistency and error, as the following chapters illustrate. This, combined with ever-increasing scale, has created a crisis of legitimacy and, for many individuals for whom these platforms constitute a vital tool, an untenable situation.

Offline Repression Is Replicated Online

Companies sometimes construct these quasi-public spaces in ways that seem like fun houses to their own employees but end up as houses of horror for other people who live and work in very different contexts.
—Rebecca MacKinnon

I n 2007, while still in its infancy, YouTube made a decision that would have an impact on its policies for years to come: after receiving multiple reports about an account containing graphic videos of police brutality, the company's operations team shut the account down.

That account belonged to Wael Abbas, an Egyptian human rights activist and a member of the early Arab digital vanguard, a loosely connected transnational group of bloggers and techies, many of whom had met through the network known as the "Arab Techies." Abbas was one of Egypt's first and most influential bloggers, known for being unafraid to tackle subjects like police brutality and corruption. His achievements had not gone unrecognized: just one year before, he had been the first blogger to receive the Knight International Journalism Award.

As cameras became smaller and less expensive, many bloggers began producing and sharing video content, to show what was not being seen on television. As such, when YouTube rose to popularity, it was a natural transition for Abbas to start posting videos there instead of on his own blog, which was a much more cumbersome process. He took advantage of the platform's centralized hosting and "discoverability" features to gain more attention for his videos of anti-government protests, voting irregularities, and human rights abuses.

By the time Abbas's account was suspended in November of 2007, he had posted hundreds of videos, dozens of which depicted police brutality. For many of his fellow activists, the videos confirmed long-held suspicions, but were nevertheless shocking to witness. One video in particular depicted a police offer sodomizing twenty-one-year-old microbus driver Emad el-Kabir with a stick. The video was recorded by another officer and sent to el-Kabir's colleagues in an effort to humiliate him. Egyptian newspapers only published still images from the video, but Abbas, after managing to get ahold of a copy of the video, published it to YouTube, where it quickly went viral in Egypt and ended up being used to prosecute two policemen who participated in the torture of el-Kabir. It was a rare moment of holding the powerful to account.

The suspension of Abbas's account made international headlines. Abbas contacted friends abroad and international human rights organizations and spoke to the media about the suspension. A Reuters newswire article from November 27, 2007, quotes him saying that YouTube had informed him that there had been numerous complaints about the content on his feed, particularly the videos that depicted torture.

Abbas also contacted the US Embassy, which in instructed the State Department to contact Google, as evidenced by a cable later released by WikiLeaks.[1] Abbas's account was restored shortly thereafter. Whether it was the government's intervention or that of human rights groups is a detail long forgotten by those I queried.

"The Wael Abbas case was really distinctive to me because it occurred around the time Google acquired YouTube," Google counsel Nicole Wong told me recently, "and I was trying to wrap my head around what it meant to apply content rules to a video platform. We were using a lot of the same rules from Blogger, because we wanted YouTube to be a robust, free-expression platform too. It hadn't really occurred to me how a visual medium would differ."

Unlike the detailed, serious community guidelines that exist for today's YouTube users, the platform's 2007 guidelines—like those of many of its peers at the time—were pithy and light. "Respect the YouTube community," they began. "We're not asking for the kind of respect reserved for nuns, the elderly, and brain surgeons. We mean don't abuse the site." Regarding graphic violence, however, the rules were fairly clear: "Graphic, gratuitous violence is not allowed. If your video shows someone getting hurt, attacked, or humiliated, don't post it."[2]

The company's process for moderating content in 2007 was fairly simple: if a user saw a piece of content they believed violated the guidelines, they could flag—that is, report—the video, which entered a queue. A human content-moderator then reviewed the video and made a determination as to whether it violated a particular rule. If it did, the user either received a warning or—depending on the severity of the violation—their entire account was suspended. And so, when one of Abbas's videos was reported by another user (or more likely, by numerous angry users) as containing graphic violence, his account was shut down.

The incident received so much attention in part because of Abbas's public profile, but also because, at the time, the restriction of speech by social media platforms was not yet a well-known phenomenon. People were giddily discussing platforms as enablers of participatory culture and activism, able to bridge geographical and cultural gaps and buck traditional censorship, including online censorship.

The online censorship of yesteryear looked different than that of today. Whereas today an offended government can request that a company remove or geolocationally block—that is, restrict access to content on the basis of a user's geographical location—a piece of content from their platform, in the era of a less-centralized, less-commercial Web, governments were forced to act as censors directly, blocking and filtering content for those within their borders. The techniques were limited, and the suppressed information varied greatly from one country to the next.

Before the advent of social media platforms, a government could choose from a handful of technical methods for censoring content that originated from abroad. It could filter by keywords; block a user's IP address or the address (URL) of a website; or engage in a technique known as domain name system (DNS) tampering, resulting in a given URL being redirected, usually to what's known as a "block page."

To engage in such censorship, a government needed access to certain tools. It might choose to commission custom-made equipment, as China famously did when it hired Cisco to create its "Great Firewall." A smaller country might purchase commercially available software off the shelf, as Yemen chose to do. Or, though rare, a government might follow the lead of the Palestinian Authority and install open-source software to get the job done.

In 2007, the OpenNet Initiative undertook the first large-scale research into how governments around the world filter content on the internet. By employing technical testing of hand-curated lists of URLs in cooperation with researchers in more than forty countries, the researchers were able to discern what types of content governments were most interested in pursuing.

What emerged was a broad portrait of what countries saw as harmful at the time. Cuba, Turkmenistan, and North Korea largely prevented ordinary citizens from accessing the global internet at all. Broadly speaking, countries across the Arab region targeted religious criticism, pornography, and political speech, but censorship in the region varied considerably, with the Gulf states among the worst offenders. Censorship across Asia was as diverse as the region itself. While Thailand went heavily after government criticism, for example, India's focus was on extremist content and reports about the country's human rights situation. Latin America's internet was by and large freer, with the bulk of censorship resulting from court orders. The internet across much of Africa remained free, owing perhaps in part to low internet adoption rates, with Ethiopia as a notable exception. And in Europe and North America, most restrictions were aimed at child sexual exploitation and copyright infringement.

In *Access Denied*, a book released by OpenNet Initiative in 2008, professors John Palfrey and Jonathan Zittrain wrote of "the emergence of an increasingly balkanized Internet." Criticizing the early idea of an "unregulatable" internet, they wrote: "Instead of a World Wide Web, as the data from our study of Internet filtering makes plain, it is more accurate to say we have a Saudi Wide Web, an Uzbek Wide Web, a Pakistani Wide Web, a Thai Wide Web, and so forth."[3]

From the beginning, many governments saw social media as a threat—it didn't just allow their countries' citizens to stay in touch with friends and family; it enabled them to mobilize, to find like-minded others and scheme with them, often behind the curtain of private groups. It emboldened people to do things—under the cover of relative anonymity—that they might not otherwise, like criticize the government. As such, a number of countries decided early on to block social media platforms. Thailand was among the first, blocking YouTube in 2006. Syria's government followed, blocking Facebook in 2007 ostensibly to prevent youth from having contact with Israelis (but more likely because it helped foster civil society). Over the next few years, these countries were joined by Turkey, Tunisia, Pakistan, and Iran in enacting wholesale or partial bans.

For executives at the companies, this spelled disaster. Countries like Turkey represented massive emerging markets, and the prevailing wisdom at the time was that once a site was blocked, it was rarely restored. At the time, governments could block individual YouTube videos or Facebook pages, but more often than not, they went for the whole platform instead. For both corporate executives and certain governments, it was time for a new strategy.

The internet may not be borderless, as early theorists suggested, but its borders have never matched up perfectly with those of nation-states. A website that tries to prevent, say, Germans from viewing its content will find that a few slip through the cracks. For example, two French groups had sued Yahoo! in 2000 to remove Nazi uniforms and memorabilia from its popular Auctions site on the grounds that users in France—where such sales are illegal—could access the platform. A French judge ruled that the company must comply with French law by blocking users in the country from accessing the materials or face a daily fine of around $13,000 in US dollars.

A panel of technical experts including Vint Cerf, one of the "fathers of the internet," argued that doing so would be impossible. Yahoo!, the experts argued, could block a large swath of French users by targeting their IP addresses, but that imperfect technique might cover perhaps 60 percent of users.[4] Yahoo! could require French users to validate their identity, but that could prove expensive. And in any case, those who really wanted to seek out the material could easily circumvent the ban. Yahoo! decided that selling Nazi items wasn't worth the trouble and changed the rules to disallow their sale, but the debate over geolocational blocking, or geo-blocking, didn't end there. Throughout the next few years, it would emerge again and again in discussions of how to regulate copyrighted content on the internet.

Before the internet, the application of copyright laws was a problem for individual states, but in a globalized world, enforcing copyright is a more complex process. When it comes to physical media, such as DVDs, technical restrictions can easily be applied, disabling say, a US-made DVD from being played on a European device. But in the early days of the internet, no such technology existed, and file-sharing sites like Napster—which allowed users to share their mp3s and other content with other users through a peer-to-peer interface—were able to thrive.

Enter geolocation technology, which enabled big players like music and film studios to place technical restrictions on digital content. The resultant effect is music files that disappear when one crosses a border, or Netflix content that differs from one country to the next.

Over time, improved location technologies and the emergence of content delivery networks, or CDNs, made geolocation much easier, allowing platforms to customize news sites and search and video hosting sites to comply with existing copyright and licensing requirements. Eventually, social media platforms began utilizing these technologies, first to geographically segment copyrighted material from foreign markets and later to narrow compliance with government orders.

Before, a company that received a court order from a government to remove something would be faced with the same difficult decision as Yahoo!—imperfectly block the offending content and risk a wholesale ban, or remove it entirely from the platform. The latter option was less than ideal; banning a foreigner from commenting on the Thai monarchy because Thailand forbids it creates a narrowing of the window for acceptable speech globally. The advent of geo-blocking enabled companies to tailor restrictions to only the country for which they were intended.

One early notable example of this tactic in use occurred in 2007, when a Turkish judge ordered the country's telcos to block access to YouTube following the posting of videos deemed insulting to Mustafa Kemal Ataturk, the founder of modern Turkey—a crime under the country's laws. As protesters took to the streets of Istanbul, it became the job of Nicole Wong to find a solution that would enable YouTube to remain online in the country while still complying with the law. The situation inside Google was tense, as executives debated the right approach. In the end, Wong told me, she made the decision to use IP blocking to make the videos inaccessible to Turkish users alone.

This was an important development, for by the middle of the decade, governments were inundating companies with requests to restrict content, or to turn over user data. Companies were wholly unprepared, as Yahoo! demonstrated in 2004, when again the company landed in the spotlight, this time for handing over information about one of its users to the government of China.

The email address belonged to Shi Tao, a journalist who had received a document from the Communist Party announcing there was a threat of foreign sabotage and instructing journalists not to report on the anniversary of the Tiananmen Square massacre. Shi used his Yahoo! email address to send the document to a Chinese-language website in New York. A few months later, he was arrested, charged with revealing state secrets, and sentenced to ten years in prison.

News later emerged that Yahoo! had provided to Chinese state security key technical information linking Shi to the email account, leading to his arrest. The US Congress formed a panel to investigate the events, and found Yahoo!'s general counsel's prior claim that he did not know the reason for the data request to be "inexcusably negligent behaviour at best, and deliberately deceptive behaviour at worst."[5] This incident led Rebecca MacKinnon to ask:

When change comes, will the new Chinese democrats thank companies like Google, Microsoft, Yahoo! and Cisco for bringing them the Internet as a catalyst for freedom? Or will they curse them for helping a corrupt and unaccountable regime hang on to power longer than it might have, thus ruining a lot of lives that might otherwise not have been ruined? Will the Chinese thank the American people for their support? Or will they mutter under their breath about hypocrites who talked a big game about freedom and democracy—but who weren't willing to forego a cent of profit to help non-Americans realize those ideals?[6]

This series of events led to the founding in 2008 of the Global Network Initiative (GNI), a organization with the goal of advancing its technology member companies' commitments to human rights. Yahoo!, along with Google and Microsoft, were the founding company members and were joined by half a dozen NGOs, academic institutions, and shareholder groups.

GNI was never designed to be an advocacy group. Rather, its principles—based on the standards put forth in the International Covenant on Civil and Political Rights and other charters—echo the Sullivan Principles, a set of guidelines companies were encouraged to adopt in order to "responsibly" operate in South Africa under apartheid. That is, the GNI's principles are designed to permit companies to do business in authoritarian countries, provided they follow the rules.

The launch of GNI was celebrated in elite circles, but while the organization may have prevented further tragedies in the vein of Yahoo!'s collusion with China, in my view, it has been largely ineffectual in furthering human rights online. The reason for this seems to lie in its reliance on the multi-stakeholder model, which follows the example of the Internet Governance Forum, a UN platform intended to further the discussion of policy issues relating to the internet. While such a model can indeed be useful for furthering debate, it has rarely led to meaningful changes in governance.

"Announcements of collaboration create a mirage of progress, without necessarily furthering the resolution of underlying issues," wrote scholar Evelyn Douek in a 2020 piece critiquing what she's dubbed "content cartels," or multi-stakeholder partnerships involving more than one company and, typically, state partners.[7] Indeed, GNI eventually lost one of its founding members, the Electronic Frontier

Foundation, as well as another group, NYU's Stern Center for Business and Human Rights, with the latter organization expressing concern that GNI's "current structure and funding model makes it unable to meet the pressing human rights challenges it was established to address."[8]

Giving in

Not long before GNI was formally launched, Nicole Wong noticed the press was reporting that the Turkish government had blocked access to YouTube by court order. The government was responding to videos found to be insulting the founder of modern Turkey, Mustafa Kemal Atatürk—a crime under Turkish law.

Users voluntarily removed the video, but the floodgate had been opened: Turkish prosecutors began objecting to dozens of videos which they claimed violated local law. According to reports from the time, these clips ranged from videos mocking Atatürk to those supporting Kurdish separatism. While Wong sought to determine which videos were actually in violation of Turkish law, a robust debate broke out within her team about whether it was preferable to protect speech as much as possible, or to compromise so that Turks could still access most YouTube content.[9]

The decision to balance these perspectives fell to Wong, who decided that the best course of action was to use IP blocking to prevent Turkish users from accessing videos that violated Turkish law. This decision was effective at first, and for a few months Turks were able to enjoy YouTube, but in the summer of 2007, a Turkish prosecutor demanded that Google remove the videos entirely, to protect the sensitivities of Turks abroad. YouTube has been blocked on and off by Turkish authorities ever since.

By the end of the decade, governments had grown savvy to the fact that companies readily responded to their takedown demands. In 2009, when Google issued its first transparency report documenting government requests for takedowns and user data, the company had received more than one thousand content removal requests in just a six-month period, a number that has only increased over time.[10]

At first, some companies were reluctant to respond to demands from countries in which they had no official business, and would ignore requests coming from places like China or Saudi Arabia. Facebook was likely the first major tech company to remove content at the behest of an authoritarian country.

Twitter was the last holdout to geo-blocking. In 2012, the company, whose own executives had once referred to as "the free speech wing of the free speech party," announced that it was launching a system that allowed the company to take down content on a per-country basis. Interestingly, Twitter based these takedowns not on user IP addresses, as its competitors did, but rather on the location selected by a given user—making it easy for users to circumvent the censorship by pretending to be located elsewhere.

At the time, a prevailing idea among civil libertarians was that companies should seek to limit censorship by responding only to court orders from countries where the companies had offices, employees, or other key assets—lest they become what my colleague Eva Galperin referred to at the time as "instrument[s] of government censorship."[11]

For a couple of years, Twitter kept to this ethos, but in 2014—just a year after Twitter's free speech–advocating general counsel Alexander Macgillivray departed for fresh waters—the company made the decision to comply with censorship demands from the governments of Russia and Pakistan. While the Russian requests were verifiably in line with local law, some Pakistani experts questioned the legitimacy of their government's requests. The Pakistani digital rights group Bolo Bhi wrote at the time: "Over the last few years, various authorities have arbitrarily blocked and censored the Internet, not over 'illegal' content, but to suppress political dissent. The process by which requests from governments are entertained by Twitter must also be made public knowledge. What is considered a valid complaint, through what process and policy?"[12]

Bolo Bhi's question remains an open one. Over time, it has become clear that in addition to the official requests received by companies for the removal or restriction of content, there are plenty of ways in which governments approach companies by going through the back door. And while transparency reports—now issued by all major social media platforms—show the number of items and accounts removed and, in some cases, the number of items *requested* to be removed, they do not include the secretive dealings that occur between governments and companies.

One early example of such an agreement is still shrouded in lies. In the summer of 2012, Nakoula Basseley Nakoula, an Egyptian-born Coptic Christian with a considerable rap sheet in the United States, posted two short trailers for the film *Innocence of Muslims* on YouTube using the pseudonym "Sam Bacile." The videos went largely unnoticed until September, when new versions with Arabic over-dubbing were uploaded, prompting Morris Sadek—a Coptic American blogger and notorious anti-Islam provocateur—to write about the film in Arabic, bringing it to the attention of the Arabic-speaking world. Then, just two days before the anniversary of the 9/11 attacks on the World Trade Center in New York, Egyptian television station Al-Nas showed a two-minute clip of the video, prompting calls for a protest to be held on September 11 in front of the US embassy.

More than three thousand individuals turned up to protest in Cairo, but in neighboring Libya—where protests had also been expected—things quickly took a turn for the worse. On the evening of September 11, the terrorist group Ansar al Sharia attacked the US Embassy, killing Ambassador J. Christopher Stevens and foreign service officer Sean Smith. The motive for the attack was at first wrongfully attributed by intelligence to the *Innocence of Muslims*.

That evening, I happened to be in Berlin at a cocktail hour of an internet and human rights conference and didn't hear the news until I went outside with a group of smokers that included a policy staffer from Google's Brussels office. We stepped away from the group, and the staffer informed me in a hushed and irritated tone that the White House had given his colleagues a call to request that the video be removed, a detail later confirmed by the *New York Times*.[13]

Google did not remove the video. It did, however, geo-block it in Egypt and Libya. In a statement issued to the press, the company explained: "This video—which is widely available on the Web—is clearly within our guidelines and so will stay on YouTube. However, given the very difficult situation in Libya and Egypt we have temporarily restricted access in both countries. Our hearts are with the families of the people murdered in Tuesday's attack in Libya."[14]

Nicole Wong recalled the incident to me on a phone call. "I remember having conversations around [*Innocence of Muslims*] knowing it would be really volatile ... There were a bunch of questions about sensitivity versus hate speech, and this notion of incitement," she told me. "That was really difficult for us and for all of the platforms to figure out where to draw the line—what is vigorous debate and what is incitement to violence? ... If it were incitement, we would go back to the test of time, place, and manner. That changed over the years, but we wanted to make sure there was a concrete call to action rather than things that would just rile people up."

Although Google's decision was widely reported as a voluntary measure, a source who worked for the company at the time informed me that pressure from the White House had continued, resulting in the compromise. Interestingly, Google refused to comply with court orders to remove the video that stemmed from other governments, including Pakistan's. Apparently, a phone call from the White House is worth more than a legal document from Islamabad.

Over the years, the methods that governments used have become even more casual. Some simply employ individuals to use companies' flagging mechanisms, while others pressure companies to remove content the governments dislike that happens to also fall afoul of the community standards. Whatever the method, one thing is clear: companies are far more adept at serving government demands than those of their own users.

Over the past dozen years or so, social media has provided a space for diffuse communities around the world to come together. Despite all my criticisms of social media—and there are many—in both my work and my personal life I have witnessed this power many times, and have even experienced it a few times myself. It is a matter of indisputable fact that my generation is more connected—in sheer network terms—than any before it.

It is not always merely the act of coming together, but what happens next, that makes social media so vital for some. As Jack Balkin has written, by arming themselves with digital technologies, "ordinary individuals [can] route around traditional media gatekeepers."[15] For historically marginalized or vulnerable communities whom the media has traditionally ignored or disparaged, social media can therefore be a powerful tool.

The civil rights movement of the 1960s, which had its origins in the Reconstruction era of the late ninetheenth century, marked the beginning of a new trajectory toward the goal of achieving equality for Black Americans. The movement utilized a multitude tactics, from legislative lobbying to direct action, and relied heavily upon the work of community leaders and physical gatherings, including the 1963 March on Washington for Jobs and Freedom. It was a pivotal movement, culminating in the formal desegregation of the South and the Civil Rights Act of 1964. Despite these historic achievements, Black communities across the United States have continued to face discrimination, inequality, and police brutality. Owing in large part to the historic indifference by politicians and the mainstream media and enduring racism, individual tragedies rarely make it to the national stage.

But in February 2012, one particular act of brutality found resonance: the shooting of seventeen-year-old Trayvon Martin in a gated Sanford, Florida community by neighborhood watch coordinator George Zimmerman.

As the story goes, the unarmed Martin was returning to his father's fiancée's home after a trip to a local convenience store when Zimmerman spotted him and called the police. Although the police told Zimmerman not to follow Martin, he did anyway, and after an altercation, shot Martin in close range with his registered semi-automatic pistol on the lawn of his relative's home.

Zimmerman was taken into custody, but claimed self-defense, which police did not dispute. In Florida, a controversial "Stand Your Ground" law, passed in 2005, permits the use of deadly force when an individual reasonably believes that they are at risk of great bodily harm. Because of this law, Zimmerman was acquitted at his 2013 trial.

The outpouring of grief and anger on social media was immediate. Local residents organized and spread the word on social media, which coalesced under a hashtag: #BlackLivesMatter. Social media amplified their organizing and resulted in solidarity actions in other cities, and ultimately major media attention—growing the local unrest into a major movement. So when, the following summer, another young unarmed Black man named Michael Brown was killed by a police officer in Ferguson, Missouri, local residents organized and took to the streets in protest. Social media amplified their actions, resulting in attention and solidarity actions in the region. The movement garnered attention from major media that allowed it to grow from local unrest into a national movement. In the days immediately after the shooting, the #BlackLivesMatter hashtag was used on Twitter nearly 150,000 times daily—before national media even began covering the protests.[16]

Numerous observers have remarked upon the myriad ways in which #BlackLivesMatter differs as a movement from its predecessors, but one is obvious: today's activists have the power of social media in their pockets. As Bijan Stephen put it concisely in a 2015 essay, "It took a lot of infrastructure to live-tweet what was going on in the streets of the Jim Crow South."[17]

All the modern activist needs to communicate is a smartphone loaded with a handful of apps. A video of police brutality can be rapidly uploaded to YouTube or emailed to a journalist. Protests can be organized using private apps like WhatsApp, Signal, or Telegram, and amplified on Facebook. Twitter is ideal for drawing attention beyond local boundaries, while Instagram is often used to share powerful protest imagery.

All of these apps have their downsides, and even the most tech-savvy activist is subject to platform policies and content moderation, as one powerful instance of police brutality in recent US history illustrates. Just as Wael Abbas's work on police brutality was erased by YouTube for its violent content, in the case of this particular incident, the evidence was almost lost to what Facebook called a "technical glitch."

On a summer night in 2016 in St. Paul, Minnesota, school cafeteria supervisor Philando Castile was stopped by police for driving with a broken taillight. What should have been a routine traffic stop quickly turned tragic as the police officer shot Castile as he reached for his wallet. Castile's girlfriend, Diamond Reynolds, whipped out her phone right after the shooting and streamed the aftermath on Facebook Live.

The video disappeared almost immediately, but was restored an hour later. In comments to the press, Facebook called the incident a "technical glitch," but refused to answer questions about whether the video had been flagged by a user or an automated technology.[18] The company's response was typical; in previous incidents where important content was erroneously removed, the company has nearly always cited "error" as the reason.

Despite this and other setbacks, the #BlackLivesMatter movement was incontrovertibly shaped and nurtured on social media, a fact which hasn't gone unnoticed by the companies. Their response has been positive in some ways—the hashtag's founders were verified on Twitter early on, and Facebook has made sure to verify many of the local chapters of the movement. Twitter added an image of three fists intended to represent three varying shades of Black skin to the hashtag to symbolize the movement, a tactic the company typically reserves for holidays or branded events like the Superbowl. Some activists within the movement have been grateful that they have direct contact with the companies, which allows them to more rapidly report harassment or content takedowns.

At the same time, some companies' top brass have been criticized once again for taking too much credit without acknowledging their platforms' flaws—most notably, Mark Zuckerberg, who took credit for the movement's virality in a 2019 speech on free expression, stating:

Movements like #BlackLivesMatter and #MeToo went viral on Facebook—the hashtag #BlackLivesMatter was actually first used on Facebook—and this just wouldn't have been possible in the same way before. One hundred years back, many of the stories people have shared would have been against the law to even write down. And without the internet giving people the power to share them directly, they certainly wouldn't have reached as many people. With Facebook, more than two billion people now have a greater opportunity to express themselves and help others.[19]

Alicia Garza, one of the hashtag's founders, was reportedly "enraged" by the speech, telling CNN that "what [Facebook] care[s] about more than civil rights is their bottom line."[20] Critics of Facebook pointed to the platform's propensity for spreading disinformation as well as maintaining policies that contradict Zuckerberg's claim of a strong belief in free expression.

One particular Facebook policy, which the company has dubbed the "newsworthiness exemption," has come under fire from activists, who believe it privileges politicians' speech above their own. The policy allows posts that otherwise violate community standards to remain on the platform if the company believes the public's interest in seeing it outweighs the risk of harm. In 2019, Nick Clegg—former deputy prime minister of the United Kingdom and vice president for global affairs and communications at Facebook—reiterated the policy, announcing that Facebook will treat all speech from politicians as newsworthy content that "should, as a general rule, be seen and heard."[21] Twitter has been accused of making a similar calculation in preserving hateful speech from US president Donald Trump that would otherwise violate its own rules.

In a blog post for Facebook, Clegg posed the question: "Would it be acceptable to society at large to have a private company in effect become a self-appointed referee for everything that politicians say? I don't believe it would be."[22] Indeed, the public has a vested interest in knowing what their elected officials, as well as those vying for office, have to say. But unlike activists and other members of the general public, politicians have numerous pulpits from which to speak; they're given airtime on television, can publish opinion pieces in major newspapers, and can fundraise to take out advertisements. If one social media company denies them a platform, their voice will still be heard.

The same cannot always be said for the activist. When Diamond Reynolds's video was removed from Facebook Live, it would have been gone forever had the company not restored it. When Wael Abbas uploaded his videos of police brutality and torture to YouTube, he did so because he had no alternatives. And when his fellow Egyptian activists later called upon their fellow citizens to take to the streets in 2011, they entrusted a single platform to galvanize supporters to hit the streets.

When the citizen's speech is deemed less valuable than that of the politician, when the activist is silenced by state or corporate powers (or both acting in concert), the same structures that enable offline repression are being replicated online. This is just as true in the United States as it has been in Egypt, Tunisia, and dozens of other locales around the world, and despite mainstream media's heavy focus over the past few years on the alleged censorship of right-wing populists, it is and has always been marginalized communities most affected by these new forms of censorship.

Backdoor collaborations

As we move into a new decade, a new threat emerges: backdoor collaborations between governments and platforms, or what scholar Evelyn Douek has dubbed "the rise of content cartels."[23] These alliances take a number of forms but their effect is often the same, and in essence, they constitute the powerful teaming up against the relatively powerless in opaque and unaccountable ways.

Some of these partnerships now seem inevitable in hindsight, foreshadowed by the actors' cooperation on key threats such as child sexual exploitation imagery. But in other ways, they represent a seismic shift from the days of roundtables at high-level multi-stakeholder events and visits by corporate heads to institutions like the Berkman Klein Center for Internet & Society at Harvard. In those days, companies seemed more likely to listen to academics and topical experts (still an elite bunch, no doubt) than to government officials.

But at some point, doubtless inundated with pressure and criticism, companies turned first inward, then to governments for guidance, resulting in opaque partnerships from which civil society is brought in late as window dressing, or excluded entirely. The degree to which citizens are shut out of these processes seems to correlate directly with how important the company, and the public, view the subject at hand.

The following chapters will explore some of the more formalized "content cartels" in further detail, but in seeking to illustrate how backdoor agreements further increase the existing repression, one example stands out: the close relationship between Facebook and the Israeli government.

For Palestinians, many of whom are physically cut off from the world by occupation and border controls, the internet is—in the words of author Miriyam Aouragh— "a mediating space through which the Palestinian nation is globally 'imagined' and shaped," bringing together a dispersed diaspora along with a geographically fragmented nation.[24] Social media has not only enabled long-lost relatives and friends to come together virtually, but has also provided space for organizing and the development of an alternate narrative to that provided by the mainstream media, which has long privileged the Israeli political position over that of the Palestinian one.

But just as Palestinian activist voices have been historically devalued and silenced by mainstream media, so too have they been censored by social media platforms—while Israeli hate speech on the same platforms often goes ignored.

In the summer of 2014, a few months after US-brokered peace talks faltered, three Israeli youth were kidnapped and murdered in the occupied West Bank. In retaliation, three Israeli men abducted and murdered a Palestinian teenager, leading to increased tensions, violent clashes, and an increase in rockets fired by Hamas into Israeli territory. Israel responded with airstrikes, raining rockets into Gaza and killing more than two thousand Palestinians and injuring more than ten thousand more—a majority of whom were civilians. As the violence played out on the ground, social media became a secondary battlefield for both sides, as well as their supporters and detractors.

As I arrived to work one day early that summer, I received a frantic call from a Palestinian friend in the United States. At that point, the kidnapped Israeli boys had not yet been killed, and my friend had discovered a Facebook page threatening the murder, every hour, of a "terrorist" until the boys were found. The page, in Hebrew, was quite clearly using "terrorist" as a stand-in for "Palestinian" and included comments such as "Kill them while they are still in their mother's [womb]," but when my friend reported it, she received a message that the page was not in violation of the community standards—despite existing prohibitions on both hate speech and credible threats.[25]

I emailed a contact on Facebook's policy team, who responded: "Seems like a violation of our terms. I'll run it by people here." As I awaited my contact's reply, the page began calling for the deaths of specific individuals. I wrote back to share that new information, and my contact replied to say that although they were still chasing down an answer, "if it's threatening people's lives, it seems to qualify, right?"

But later that day, my contact informed me over the phone that the page was not, in fact, in violation of the rules. The threat wasn't deemed to be credible, and on top of that, "terrorist" wasn't a protected category under the prohibition on hate speech. In a statement, Facebook's head of global policy management, Monika Bickert, explained: "We clearly list the characteristics that we consider to be hate speech, and if it doesn't come under one of those categories, we don't consider it hate speech under our policies."[26] The page remained up.

Two years later, the Israeli government announced that it had formalized a collaboration with Facebook's Tel Aviv office, which— according to Palestinian activists who have regular contact with the company—has jurisdiction over both Israel and the Palestinian territories. They were thus replicating, in virtual space, the occupation of Palestinian land. In a statement about the partnership, Facebook said that "online extremism can only be tackled with a strong partnership between policymakers, civil society, academia and companies, and this is true in Israel and around the world."[27]

Facebook's actions, however, speak louder than its words. When it comes to Palestinian speech, it is only Israelis who have a real say—no matter whether the Israelis involved even believe that Palestinians should have rights. Ayelet Shaked, who served as Israeli justice minister at the time the agreement was formed and was directly involved in dealings with Facebook, has herself engaged in hate speech on the platform. Of Palestinian mothers, she once wrote: "They have to die and their houses should be demolished so that they cannot bear any more terrorists."[28] A paper published by the Haifa-based Palestinian digital rights group 7amleh documented the disparities in how hate speech from Israelis and Palestinians is treated, noting that "Facebook is the main source of violence and incitement online" stemming from Israel.[29]

Meanwhile, Facebook censors Palestinian groups so often that they have created their own hashtag, #FBCensorsPalestine. That the groups have become prominent matters little: in 2016, Facebook blocked accounts belonging to editors at the Quds News Network and Shehab News Agency in the West Bank; it later apologized and restored the accounts.[30] The following year, it did the same to the official account of Fatah, the ruling party in the West Bank.[31]

A year after Facebook's relationship with the Israelis was formalized, the *Guardian* released a set of leaked documents exposing the ways the company's moderation policy discriminates against Palestinians and other groups. Published in a series called "The Facebook Files," the documents contained slides from manuals used to train content moderators. On the whole, the leaks paint a picture of a disjointed and disorganized company where the community standards are expanded piecemeal, and little attention is given to their consequences. Anna, the former Facebook operations specialist I spoke with, agrees: "There's no ownership of processes from beginning to end," she says.

One set of documents demonstrate with precision the imbalance on the platform between Palestinians and Israelis (and the supporters of both). In a slide deck entitled "Credible Violence: Abuse Standards," one slide lists global and local "vulnerable" groups; alongside "foreigners" and "homeless people" is "Zionists."[32] Interestingly, while Zionists are protected as a special category, "migrants," as ProPublica has reported, are only "quasi-protected" and "Black children" aren't protected at all.[33]

In trying to understand how such a decision came about, I reached out to numerous contacts, but only one spoke about it on the record. Maria, who worked in community operations until 2017, told me that she spoke up against the categorization when it was proposed. "We'd say, 'Being a Zionist isn't like being a Hindu or Muslim or white or Black—it's like being a revolutionary socialist, it's an ideology,'" she told me. "And now, almost everything related to Palestine is getting deleted."

Another former staffer told me under the condition of anonymity that it was a "constant discussion," and that the company was under pressure from the Israeli government.

As Maria tried to point out to her superiors, Zionism is an ideology or a political doctrine, akin to "communism" or "liberalism"—not an immutable characteristic. Treating it as such is not merely a mockery of actual characteristics that make a person or group vulnerable, but elevating it—and not Palestinians—to such a level also fails to take into account the power imbalance that exists between occupied and occupier. But, Maria told me, "Palestine and Israel has always been the toughest topic at Facebook. In the beginning, it was a bit discreet," with the Arabic-language team mainly in charge of tough calls, but after the 2014 conflict between Israel and Gaza, the company moved closer to the Israeli government. Somewhat notably, one of the first twenty members of Facebook's new External Oversight Board is Emi Palmor, under whose direction the Israeli Ministry of Justice petitioned Facebook to censor legitimate speech of human rights defenders, according to 7amleh.[34]

Israel was among the first governments to secure a backdoor deal with a social media company, but it's far from the last. A year later, Vietnam's single-party government announced an alliance with Facebook.[35] In 2018, the German government codified a law that required close collaboration from social media companies with more than two million users—a law that was later copied by several less democratic states, including Russia and Turkey. As states grapple with how to manage speech they find objectionable—but often not illegal—they simply circumvent traditional legislative processes, knowing that they can simply call on their friends at Facebook, Google, or Twitter to enforce their desires.

The result? An increasingly stratified online world in which the rules about what we can say are determined by a motley crew of elected officials and non-elected elites, some of whom have alarmingly close ties to government. Kate Klonick has expressed fears that Facebook is evolving into a place where world leaders and other important people "are disproportionately the people who have the power to update the rules."[36] Indeed, the very same repression that vulnerable communities have long experienced at the hands of state actors (and corporations) is playing out again, this time in the digital realm.

Abbas, revisited

A decade after Wael Abbas faced the Google Goliath, little had changed for the activist journalist and his Egyptian peers. In November 2017, Facebook erroneously issued him a thirty-day suspension for a post in which he accused another individual of threatening others. As a result of the suspension, I found it difficult to get hold of him, as his access to Facebook Messenger—our primary mode of communication—was blocked. As Facebook merges its various properties, the potential for such harm multiplies.

In 2018, I was able to help again: I contacted the company, and Abbas's access was restored, but not long after that, he was subject to a permanent suspension on Twitter, where he had long had a verified account. This time, despite a campaign that had support from prominent activists around the world and former Twitter staff, the company did not budge. Even David Kaye, the UN special rapporteur on the promotion and protection of the right to freedom of opinion and expression, called on Twitter to be transparent about the suspension, but to no avail.[37] In a Facebook post, Abbas called the erasure of his account, which contained ten years of activism and documentation, akin to "Hitler burning books."[38]

Not long after the suspension, Egyptian state security arrested Abbas and charged him with "involvement in a terrorist group," "spreading false news," and "misuse of social networks." He was held for several months without trial, his detention renewed every fifteen days, and eventually, to secure his release, forced to sign documents indicating his guilt. Egyptian media sources later claimed that his Twitter account was suspended for "incitement to violence" in an attempt to justify the government's extrajudicial actions. Twitter's silence on the matter is unjustifiable. As I wrote at the time, "These decisions are being used as evidence by media campaigns against activists, by real-world courts (some, like the "media committees" that judged Abbas, with little due process of their own)—and with real consequences."[39]

Abbas was released some time ago, but he remains silent. His Twitter account is gone forever, and he no longer posts on Facebook. His country's government—with the cooperation of two of the world's biggest social media platforms—finally got its way.

3

Social Media Revolutionaries

*I once said, if you want to liberate a society, all you need is the internet.
I was wrong.*

—Wael Ghonim

*There was a very famous quotation by, I think, Hosni Mubarak: "Let
them have fun," the kids on social media. And have fun we did.*

—Rasha Abdulla

On a hot Alexandrian day in early June 2010, an event occurred that changed the course of history. Khaled Saeed, a twenty-eight -year-old man, was sitting on the second floor of a cybercafé in the central area of Cleopatra Hamamat when two plain-clothes police officers entered the café and demanded to see everyone's identification, a fairly common under the emergency law that had been imposed in 1967 and in place more or less continuously since then.

Saeed refused, angering the police, who witnesses said began to beat him. They dragged him outside the café and continued to batter him, in full view of numerous witnesses who watched in shock. At one point, Saeed cried out, "I'm dying!" to which one of the officers responded: "I'm not leaving you until you are dead." The officers then loaded the dying Saeed into a van and drove off, returning ten minutes later to the same place to dump his body.

In the ensuing months and years, both Khaled Saeed and the circumstances surrounding his death were mythologized both in Egypt and around the world. He was held up as a martyr. Some early reports, quoting members of his family, suggested he was targeted because he was in possession of a video documenting police corruption, but the video—posted after Saeed's death to YouTube—is fuzzy and open to interpretation. One in-depth analysis depicts Saeed as an aimless stoner, deeply attached to his online connections, yearning to break free of Egypt's shackles and return to the United States where he had once briefly studied computer programming. Instead, this version continues, he found himself caught up with a group of drug users, one of whom would sell him out to the police.[1] But none of these details matter; the fact remains that he was brutally murdered by police.

Somewhat unusually for a young Egyptian, Saeed lived mostly alone, as his mother was often in Cairo helping his sister with her growing family—leaving much of his personal history up to the popular imagination. What we do know, however, is this: his tortured body was taken to the morgue, where his brother snapped a photograph of his distorted face with a mobile phone camera that the family later shared online. The photo was shared widely, and prompted the creation of a page, "We Are All Khaled Saeed." The page organized a series of protests against torture, and announced the details of Saeed's funeral, to which more than one thousand people showed up. The page quickly became one of the most followed in the Arab world, garnering hundreds of thousands of followers within a few short months. It later went on to call for the January 25 protests that would topple dictator Hosni Mubarak after thirty years of rule. But had circumstances been slightly different, it might not have happened at all.

In the years before the 2011 uprising, security forces had become more aware of the online activities of the country's young citizens. While some chose to boldly publish under their own names, others were rightly concerned for their safety and livelihoods. So the creators of "We Are All Khaled Saeed" made the prudent decision to manage their page anonymously, logging in with Facebook profiles that employed pseudonyms.

Although pseudonyms are common on Facebook, their use is against official policy. When Mark Zuckerberg first conceived of Facebook in his Harvard dorm room, he envisioned a platform where college students could identify and follow one another, necessitating the use of their real names. And so, from its early days, Facebook policy prohibited the use of pseudonyms or "fake names." Even as the social network grew and became open to the public—not just college students—the policy remained intact.

"There was a belief at the time—maybe it's not correct—that people were nicer to each other if they used their real names," said former Facebook head of content policy Dave Willner, who helped draft the rule. Additionally, he told me, "Facebook wanted to be accessible to mainstream people and get them to put their identities on the internet, which was not a mainstream behavior at the time."

By 2010, I was already angrily blogging about this policy. I'd been contacted by a Moroccan woman by the name of Najat Kessler. Her Muslim first name and Jewish last name were, I wrote at the time, apparently too improbable a combination for someone at the company, because when she submitted ID as requested, her account remained suspended.[2] The policy's enforcement reached peak absurdity the following year when world-famous author Salman Rushdie found himself booted off for not using his birth name of Ahmed.

But my concern went beyond the issue of unique names or famous pseudonyms. As I wrote in April of that year, Facebook's policy "gives would-be attackers a simple way to report a person's profile."[3] Reporting someone for using a fake name, both then and now, triggers a request for identification, and back then, the only way to submit a copy of one's ID was to submit it as an attachment in reply to a company email. Email has become more secure over the years, but back then email sent from most providers could easily be intercepted by a hacker or government actor, making it a risky option for an activist. Some users were rightly skeptical about Facebook's assurance that it would not share their information with governments. And as Najat Kessler's story shows, submitting ID was no guarantee that one's account would be restored.

Egypt's parliamentary elections were held in November 2010, and in their run-up, on the day before a planned Friday of protest, the "We Are All Khaled Saeed" page was abuzz with activity. Halfway around the world, a well-meaning staffer at an NGO sent a list of popular Egyptian pages to a contact at Facebook, with a note that they had come under attack and a request to keep an eye on them in case they were maliciously reported by state actors or sympathizers. That is what Facebook did, and perhaps even monitored things a bit too closely: upon discovering that the "We Are All Khaled Saeed" page's creators were using pseudonyms, the company removed their profiles, which resulted in the page being taken down as well.

Word of the page's removal reached Danny O'Brien, at the time the internet advocacy coordinator at the Committee to Protect Journalists.[4] Others had scrambled to reach out to Facebook—but it was Thanksgiving Day in the United States, and most employees of the company were at home with family. So O'Brien took a chance and emailed Elliot Schrage, the company's vice president of communications and public policy, who responded quickly from his iPhone that he was looking into it.

Schrage passed the message on to Richard Allan, then the director for policy in Europe and the Middle East, who offered up a creative fix: find a new administrator willing to use a real name. The page's anonymous admins mined their contacts and landed on Nadine Wahab, an Egyptian living in the United States, who stepped forward to volunteer. By the following day, the page had been restored. Wahab later told author Rebecca MacKinnon that she found Facebook's policies exasperating: "I don't think [the staff of Facebook] understand the implications that their rules and procedures have for activists in places like Egypt."[5]

I chatted online with one of the page's administrators in the days after the incident, who told me that it was his anonymous profile that had prompted the removal of the page. "I'd like to keep my anonymous identity," he said. "I have received numerous threats via [email] and wouldn't want to expose my life to danger."

In the weeks that followed, MacKinnon, O'Brien, and I debated among ourselves over email: Did the company mistake the NGO staffer's list as a guide for what to remove? Or was the page the target of malicious opposition? After much discussion, O'Brien compiled our thoughts and sent them to Schrage, copying MacKinnon, several additional Facebook staffers, and me. In his email, he thanked

Facebook for their responsiveness, addressed our concerns about the list sent by the staffer, and concluded with our concern about the timing of the removal of "We Are All Khaled Saeed"—as well as the page of Nobel Peace Prize–winner Mohamed ElBaradei the week prior. Two explanations could explain the page's removal—it either resulted from the sharing of the list, or it was an attack by malicious actors who were aware of the admins' anonymity and had sought to get the pages removed. "At the very least," wrote O'Brien, "[we] certainly need to spell out a better, more transparent, explanation for the timing of these and other takedowns—otherwise the most paranoid explanation will continue to trump all others in the public debate."

In his reply, Schrage evaded the questions:

> From our perspective, we disabled a page that violated our policies (unrelated to content)—one of millions we disable every day—and in this particular case we helped facilitate remediation by users to get the page back up within 6 hours following contact from human rights groups. The reason I am so impressed by the work and responsiveness is as follows: Under normal circumstances I believe we would NOT have facilitated the restoration of a page with the violations we discovered.[6]

It's true that Facebook went out on a limb to rescue a page based on our word that it was important to Egyptian human rights activists. It's also true that, in a series of emails spanning more than two thousand words, the company's reps never answered our questions about what happened with the page.

Maria,* a former Facebook community operations employee who joined the company's Dublin office in 2012, said she heard rumors about the person who had removed the page, himself an Egyptian on the same team, but chalked it up to human error. "Back then," Maria told me over Skype, "the Arabic team was just deleting fake profiles." Someone on that team, she recalled, had deleted the pseudonymous profiles, resulting in the removal of the page. "He was very stupid, he didn't calculate the results of his actions."

"You can't imagine how sometimes when you're so busy, you have this concept at Facebook that you have to move fast and break things, so it doesn't matter if you make a mistake," she told me, describing a similar incident in which she accidentally geo-blocked an important page organizing a major political protest in an authoritarian country. "It was horrible. Everyone was talking about it."

The admins of "We Are All Khaled Saeed" undoubtedly violated the rules, but the rules were not exactly clear in 2010. First of all, the "Community Standards," the guiding document for users of Facebook, didn't yet exist; rather, users were meant to rely on the Terms of Service (ToS), a lengthy document written in legalese. But that's if they could understand it—in 2010, the ToS was only available in a handful of languages, and Arabic was not one of them.

This was among the many issues we would raise to Facebook over the following months. At first it was a fruitful exchange, and company representatives were often surprisingly forthcoming with details. But that didn't last long.

First contact

The discussion that followed the deletion of "We Are All Khaled Saeed" wasn't my first contact with Facebook staff. A few months before the onset of the Tunisian revolution, I read a post on Palestinian Refugee ResearchNet's blog claiming that Facebook was blocking the term "Palestinian" from being used in page titles. The post included a screenshot of an attempt to create a page called "Palestinian Refugee ResearchNet," with a warning splashed across the top that read: "Our automated system will not allow the name 'Palestinian Refugee ResearchNet'. It may violate our Pages Guidelines or contain a word or phrase that is blocked to prevent the creation of unofficial or otherwise prohibited Pages. If you believe this is an error, please contact our Customer Support team."

The blogger, Rex Brynen, tested several similar titles, replacing "Palestinian" with "Israeli" and "Afghan." Both worked, so he wrote to the support team. At this point, I decided to write my own blog post about the problem, asking, "What is Facebook trying to accomplish

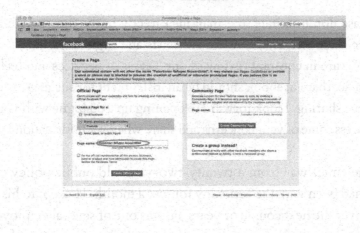

by eliminating page creation for a marginalized population?" and advising activists for the second time that week to stop using Facebook.[7] *Gawker* also covered the incident, noting Mark Zuckerberg's stated belief that Facebook could bridge gaps between the Middle East and the so-called West, and commenting that that would be hard to accomplish if Facebook were "arbitrarily—albeit innocuously— preventing words like 'Palestinian' from being used."[8]

Much to my surprise, I opened my inbox the next day to find a message from a facebook.com email address. "Ms. York—," the letter began, "I'm writing to offer you whatever help we can for either your blog or upcoming publications surrounding Facebook's content policies."

The email went on to say that the exclusion of the term "Palestinian" was the "result of an anomaly in an automated system" and that a "previously unseen bug" was the cause. It continued:

We realize that some of the automated systems we've built to protect the over 500 million people who use our service have caused confusion in the past. No system, let alone one that operates on our scale, is perfect, and we're constantly working on improving ours and making them more transparent. You can read more about these efforts in a recent blog post.

Additionally, we understand our product forms a valuable resource to many in the human rights and global advocacy community, and please don't hesitate to e-mail me directly in the future with any specific problems of bonafide activists and organizers.

We are in constant review of our Terms of Services and feel, as you do, that Facebook should be an instrument for social good and social sharing. I look forward to opening up a dialogue with you to address some of your concerns and share whatever information I can.

The email was from a twenty-two-year-old public policy staffer who had been with the company for just a month. He kept to his word and, over the next couple of years, he was one of several employees—almost all of whom were young, male Stanford graduates—with whom I would correspond when an issue arose.

In 2010, Facebook had been available to the public for less than four years and was a mere seed of the behemoth it is today. There was no global public policy team, no Middle East office. The teams in charge of creating and enforcing policy were, at the time, composed mainly of twentysomethings with bachelor's degrees and minimal policy experience outside of Facebook. Many of them had diverse portfolios and were quoted in the press on a range of subjects from Facebook's real-name policy to security vulnerabilities.

They were refreshingly honest at times, and other times bordering on rude. In one email exchange, during which I raised the deletion of a Tunisian activist page and questioned the policy that had resulted in the removal, a policy staffer admonished me:

As an aside, we've noticed a few public comments you've made recently about what you perceive to be a lack of transparency in our practices. We reached out to you precisely so that you could provide constructive feedback to us directly. We're still discussing internally the best way to assemble a small group of people in the activist community to help with these issues, and we hope to have a plan in place soon. Candidly, though, I'm not sure how enthusiastic folks here will be about including you in the group if they sense that you'd rather criticize us than engage.

I never did receive an invitation to that assemblage of activists.

In another incident, after I published an opinion piece for *Bloomberg* that suggested Facebook's real-name policy could put "pro-democracy activists [at] risk of being unmasked on social networks,"[9] a member of the public policy communications team called me to vent about my going public with my criticism—despite the fact that I'd been in touch with the company for more than a year about the policy in question.

I recently asked the former policy staffer who'd emailed me why he thought Facebook had reached out to me in the first place. "Facebook wanted to engage thought-leaders, bloggers and journalists to better understand the landscape, and become part of the conversation rather than merely a spectator," he wrote to me in an email. "This sort of outreach was increasingly common throughout the years I worked at Facebook."

At the same time, Google was putting in significant effort to be inclusive of civil society ... or at least certain segments of it. One month after Facebook first made contact, I received an email from Google inviting me to attend a conference in Budapest entitled "Internet at Liberty," featuring topics such as "the Internet's role as a democratizing force" and "the promotion of transparency and accountability." After conferring with my manager at the Berkman Klein Center for Internet & Society, I accepted the invitation.

A few months prior, I had the idea to write a paper about the account deactivations and content takedowns I'd witnessed. My manager, Rob Faris—who was at the time the Center's research director—liked the idea, and although I was just a project coordinator, he offered his assistance in writing it. Initially, the plan was to include it in a volume the Center was producing at the time, but when the Google conference was announced, we pushed the deadline up so we could publish the paper in time for the September event.

The paper was entitled "Policing Content in the Quasi-Public Sphere" and investigated the use of social media for political and human rights activism, as well as what I saw as a "pattern of deactivations" across four platforms: Facebook, Twitter, YouTube, and Blogger.[10] It cited work from scholars like Zeynep Tufekci and danah boyd, who had also just begun to write about content moderation practices. It was, as far as I'm aware, one of the first papers to interrogate the growing power of these companies.

At the Budapest conference, Faris gave the opening remarks and mentioned the paper. As a result, my blog received thousands of hits that day, and I was approached on the way to lunch by David Drummond, who served as senior vice president and chief legal officer of Google. Over the next few days, I spoke with a number of Tunisian and Egyptian activists and was privy to a number of conversations with Google staffers who, shortly after the conference ended, created a small private mailing list for human rights activists to interact with Google's policy teams.

Those early interactions between Facebook and Google staffers and activists, which took place over just a few short months in 2010, would prove to be vital in the months and years that followed, as first Tunisians and Egyptians, then Syrians, Bahrainis, Moroccans, and others took to the streets in an unprecedented series of uprisings across the Middle East and North Africa. Over the years, as these companies grew bigger, the interactions became impersonal, and the staffers less likely to offer workarounds in difficult situations. In retrospect, it's clear as day, but at the time I didn't realize just how much those vital interactions were so closely tied to the beliefs and values of whichever staffer one was speaking with.

A pioneer in censorship

A decade before Tunisians overthrew their government by taking to the streets in cities across the nation, the seeds of dissent were being planted online. In 1998, two students frustrated with the oppression and ennui of everyday life in the country set up a forum. Called "Takriz," after a Tunisian slang word that means "fury," the forum was hosted on foreign servers and provided its participants with a space to rage against the system that they felt was holding them back from opportunity.

Takriz was among the first online spaces to host open dialogue about the discontent that plagued Tunisians. The forum, initially conducted on a secretive mailing list, was "decentralized and intentionally disorganized," and discussion topics ranged from state media and internet censorship to gender relationships and virginity.[11] By 1999, Takriz had more than two hundred subscribers, and in 2000, it had launched a website and e-magazine.

It didn't take long for the public-facing iteration of Takriz to raise the ire of authorities, who blocked it within days, hardening the group's resolve. Members reached out to friends abroad who sought media attention for the ban, and pooled together resources on how to circumvent it using website proxies and anonymizing tools. But despite the valiant efforts of its members, the ban had a chilling effect on Takriz, and by 2002 the group's activity had ceased ... at least for a time.

From the ashes of Takriz emerged another platform, TUNeZINE, the title of which evoked the name of Tunisia's president at the time, the authoritarian Zine El Abidine Ben Ali. Created by Takriz member "Ettounsi," the site featured political cartoons and criticism of the regime's human rights abuses, and invited its Tunisian readers to participate. One poll asked visitors whether they considered Tunisia a democracy, a kingdom, a prison, or a zoo—"a prison" was the most popular response.[12]

TUNeZINE's readership increased, drawing the attention of authorities, who blocked the site and identified "Ettounsi" as Zouhair Yahyaoui, the nephew of outspoken judge Mokhtar Yahyaoui and the owner of an internet café. Yahyaoui was educated but had struggled to find employment. Bored and frustrated, he put his cleverness to good use by striking a deal with a local internet café—he would work without pay, in exchange for unlimited internet usage. It was there that he learned about internet censorship and circumvention and how to build websites, eventually leading him to launch TUNeZINE.

On June 4, 2002, Yahyaoui was arrested at the internet café where he worked. Authorities searched the premises, demanded the password for TUNeZINE, and subsequently destroyed the site. Yahyaoui was sentenced to twenty-eight months in prison for disseminating false information, undoubtedly in an effort by authorities to send a strong message to the burgeoning online activist community. While in prison, he was subjected to torture and went on several hunger strikes in protest. In response to increased international attention, he was released early, but died just a few months later of a heart attack at age thirty-seven.[13]

A pioneering state

Tunisia was the first Arab country—as well as the first on the African continent—to connect to the internet. In 1985, a grant to Tunisia from the US Agency for International Development (USAID) enabled the creation of the Institut Régional des Sciences Informatiques et des Télécommunications, or IRSIT, dedicated to the promotion of computer science and telecommunications in Tunisia. Early IRSIT engineers had studied abroad and brought back with them cutting-edge knowledge that put Tunisia's early networks on par with ones in Europe. By 1991, Tunisia was online.[14]

In 1996, the government mandated the creation of the Agence Tunisienne d'Internet (ATI), resulting in the consolidation of Tunisia's networks and the centralization of control under the government's executive branch. ATI became the sole operator of the country's internet backbone and took control over the registration of .tn domains. It issued contracts to five internet service providers, or ISPs, at least three of which were owned in full or in part by members of the Ben Ali family. It also served as the country's censorship bureau. By the turn of the century, nearly 3 percent of Tunisia's 9.6 million citizens were online, just in time to experience the self-publishing revolution. Brand new platforms like Blogger and LiveJournal offered spaces where individuals could share their uncensored thoughts with relative anonymity; in Tunisia, that meant criticism of the entrenched Ben Ali regime.

In 2005, Tunis was rather inexplicably chosen as host of United Nations–sponsored World Summit on the Information Society (WSIS), and Habib Ammar—a former minister and anti-torture advocate who as of 2020 is serving an eight-year prison sentence—was named as the head of its preparatory committee. Tunisians were justifiably outraged that Tunis was selected as host site, but used the opportunity to draw the attention of international attendees to Ben Ali's censorship regime.

The WSIS was marred by interference from government officials and attacks on local human rights activists but, emboldened by the success of their campaigns, Tunisia's bloggers continued their protests. Meanwhile, as more and more citizens gained access to the internet, the government's censorship apparatus grew increasingly vast and sophisticated. By 2008, nearly a third of Tunisia's population could access the internet ... or at least, what was left of it. To its website blocklist the ATI had added the video-sharing sites YouTube and Dailymotion, the pages of international human rights organizations, and proxy tools designed to circumvent blocks. Those attempting to access blocked websites reached a fake "error 404" page, an attempt by the government to pass off censorship as a technical problem. Clever activists anthropomorphized the 404 page, calling him Ammar 404 (or "3mmar 404," in the Arabic chat alphabet).[15]

But in late 2008, the government made a fateful error: it blocked Facebook. More than a decade later, the precise impetus for the ban remains unclear, though some have suggested the government was seeking to silence activists involved in protests against the Gafsa Phosphate Company that had begun earlier that year. Tunisians protested the decision, threatening to close their internet accounts and forcing the government to back down, with Ben Ali himself reportedly ordering the ban to be lifted on September 3.

Tunisia's blogging community was emboldened by their win, but their victory was short-lived. By 2010, the Ben Ali regime had ramped up its efforts to silence online discourse. At the same time, Tunisian activists who were using social media to document human rights issues began to run up against corporate content restrictions.

One such activist was Slim Amamou, who after the revolution briefly served as the minister for youth and sports. In October of that year, he wrote to ask for my help in getting a page restored. The page, Sayeb Sala7—short for "Sayeb Sala7, ya Ammar"—was an online representation of an ongoing campaign imploring the country's censors to ease up on censorship or, in the words of the campaign, to "let it go."

Another was Sami Ben Gharbia, who, along with two other Tunisian exiles in Europe, had co-founded the activist blog *Nawaat*. A longtime

activist on his own merit, in 2010 he spent his time between writing for
Nawaat and managing Global Voices' then-nascent Advocacy project
(now called "Advox").[16] Like Wael Abbas, he was well connected
with both media and international NGOs, and so when he learned
of YouTube's ban, he quickly emailed me and other members of a
mailing list to alert us to the situation.

The video that had prompted the account's closure depicted a
group of young children in Tunisia sniffing glue, an unfortunately
common habit among disadvantaged youth in North Africa. In a
short post for Advox, I shared the message that YouTube had sent
Ben Gharbia, which read: "It's not okay to post videos showing bad
stuff like animal abuse, drug abuse, underage drinking and smoking,
or bomb making. Any depictions like these should be educational or
documentary and shouldn't be designed to help or encourage others
to imitate them."[17]

As the depiction was intended to be educational, unblocking the
account was an easy ask; within twenty-four hours, Ben Gharbia
wrote that *Nawaat*'s access had been restored. That could have been
the end of the story, but around the same time, Rebecca MacKinnon
had been documenting a spate of account deactivations by Facebook in
Hong Kong. MacKinnon, the co-founder of Global Voices, had been
writing about social media platforms since the early 2000s and had
been instrumental in the founding of the Global Network Initiative
(GNI) just two years prior.

It has been a decade since these events, but what I can glean from
emails from that time is that her blogging, along with my own,
prompted colleagues within GNI to schedule a call on the subject
of account deactivations and content takedowns. On the invitation-
only call, policy executives from Yahoo!, YouTube, and SlideShare
detailed the inner workings of their content moderation practices,
while activists including Wael Abbas, Ben Gharbia, Hong Kong pro-
democracy lawmaker Charles Mok, and me shared stories of content
removal and stressed the importance of safeguarding human rights.

That call spawned a series of conversations—first private, then
public—between academic and digital rights organizations and Silicon
Valley companies about the human rights implications of content

moderation. It was still early days for social media, and the policy teams at most companies were open to listening and eager to get things right.

A month after that fateful call, I joined MacKinnon, Hong Kong–based activist Oiwan Lam, and Victoria Grand, YouTube's global head of policy, on stage at a Global Voices conference in Santiago, Chile, to discuss the issue. The videos from that panel discussion have long disappeared from the Web, but I remember Grand being surprisingly frank and thoughtful in her consideration of the issues we raised. MacKinnon's takeaways from the panel discussion, immortalized on her blog, are so prescient that I'll share them in full:

- Automated moderation and abuse-prevention processes will inevitably result in mistakes that hurt activists. Human judgment—informed by adequate knowledge of cultures, languages, and political events around the world—needs to be brought into the mix.

- Companies need to be as transparent and open as possible about how their takedown, moderation, and suspension procedures work. Otherwise they have nobody but themselves to blame if users cease to trust them.

- Companies should designate staff members to focus on human rights. Their job should be to develop channels for regular communication with the human rights community.

- It's almost impossible for globally popular social networking and content-sharing services to hire enough staff with enough knowledge of political movements and disputes in all obscure corners of the world in all kinds of languages. But communities like Global Voices and others with large networks of bloggers and online activists all over the world are ready and willing to help companies keep abreast of political hot-button issues and online movements around the world—and even provide help with obscure languages—so that extra care can be taken, and political activism won't be mistaken for spam or some other form of abusive behavior. We just need to figure out how to set up workable mechanisms through which this kind of feedback, advice, and communication can take place.

- Activists need to pay closer attention [to] the Terms of Service used by social networking platforms, and be more proactive in educating themselves about how moderation, takedown, and abuse-prevention mechanisms work. We probably need a "Guide to avoiding account suspension and takedown for human rights activists."
- It might also be good to have some kind of respected clearing house organization—or consortium of organizations—which can help mediate and resolve problems between activists and companies.
- People who rely on social networking and content-sharing platforms run by companies to do political and social activism should engage more actively with company administrators to improve policies and practices. Anticipate problems and help solve them not only for yourself but for everybody else in the community. Act like a citizen. Not a passive "user."[18]

Another prescient observation from that era came from Ethan Zuckerman, who wrote that the dominant strategy of activists at the time was to "hope service providers protect speech and attempt to pressure them when they don't." He also noted that this method "tends to reward the most shrill and the best connected—if you know someone [at a company] it's sometimes possible to get a decision about acceptable material reconsidered or reversed, but that's hardly a model for sustainable free speech over time."[19]

We were certainly aware at the time that our methods were unsustainable, but none of us could have imagined just how big these social media platforms—and how unscalable their practices—would eventually become.

A Facebooked revolution

By April 2010, Tunisia's ATI had blocked every video-sharing platform and most of the social media ones, and the government had begun ordering the blocking of individual activists' Twitter accounts. According to Amy Aisen Kallander, in April 2010 alone, the ATI blocked nearly two hundred websites. In an article published not long after the uprisings, Kallander wrote that "the arbitrary and unaccountable nature of censorship created a climate of intimidation that succeeded in dividing the blogosphere, and uniting activists."[20] That unity, coupled with the stifling online atmosphere, led the Tunisian blogging networks to plan a street protest. Slated for May 22, the protest was dubbed "The day Against Ammar," with activists using the slogan "Sayeb Sala7, ya Ammar" (Let it go, Ammar) to call for an easing of online censorship. The calls, posted on blogs and social media, reached new audiences both in and outside the country. They also reached the government, which quickly acted to shut down the protests, arresting several organizers the day before the protest and not releasing them until they published a video calling off the protests. In the end, only a few activists took to the streets, wearing white, the color of mourning.

The protests did not go as planned. "But things are about to change, since the new wave of online censorship is affecting everybody," wrote Ben Gharbia on May 27.[21] He was not wrong; the events of early 2010 were a catalyst in the uprising that began just a little more than six months later. While pundits and researchers, Tunisians and outside observers debated for years afterward the role that social media played in the Arab uprisings, it is beyond the shadow of a doubt that the offline repression that mirrored the online repression by Ben Ali's government was instrumental in creating the conditions for Tunisians to take to the streets later that year.

As revolutions go, Tunisia's was relatively quick, lasting just twenty-eight days. Following the self-immolation of street vendor Mohamed Bouazizi in Sidi Bouzid on December 17, which he carried out in protest of the police harassment he had suffered, protesters gathered to demonstrate, but authorities were heavy-handed in their response, and protests soon turned to riots. As the conflict between protesters and police escalated in Sidi Bouzid, videos of the violence reached Tunis, in part thanks to bloggers who shared them with international media. The demonstrations quickly spread to other cities.

Throughout this period, the government continued its online crackdown, arresting some of the country's prominent online figures, and instituting new measures to stifle the ability of activists to spread information about what was happening inside the country. One such measure was the institution of a malicious piece of code that captured the logins of individuals as they signed in to Facebook. The Electronic Frontier Foundation, which had contacts in Tunisia, issued a series of recommendations for users to remain safe, and urged Facebook to make user logins encrypted by default.[22]

Joe Sullivan, Facebook's chief security officer at the time, told the *Atlantic* that the company had "never seen anything like what was happening in Tunisia."[23] Sullivan's team responded with a technical solution, routing Tunisian requests to an HTTPS server and implementing a "roadblock" that required users who had previously logged in while the malicious code was running to answer questions to identify their account, then create a new password.[24] This special configuration for Tunisian users, though apolitical in nature, was unique and was replicated for the broader public for nearly two more years.

While Facebook was grappling with technical challenges, YouTube faced questions about the appropriateness of its policies amidst the violence in Tunisia. In early January, Ben Gharbia brought to my attention a video that had been removed from YouTube that claimed to show evidence of a civilian massacre in Kasserine, a town close to the Algerian border.[25] He shared a screenshot of a banner that stated the video had been removed as a result of the company's policies on "shocking and disgusting content."

The video was indeed shocking, but so were the circumstances: apart from Al Jazeera, international media was barely covering the violence against civilians, and the space for online activists to get the word out was rapidly shrinking. I contacted YouTube's policy team about the takedown and they deliberated: the video showed brain matter, which was typically a red line, but the team was sympathetic to the situation and asked me to send additional context in the form of news reports or other videos from the scene. In the end, they relented, restoring the video and advising activists to provide as much context as possible when uploading footage.

That conversation would have implications down the road, as demonstrations across the region were met with violence; but for now, at least, Tunisian activists had a solution for making sure that the outside world was seeing the brutality they were facing. Just a little more than a week later, their efforts paid off: Ben Ali stepped down after twenty-three years of rule and, in his final speech before fleeing to Saudi Arabia, promised his citizens a free and open internet.

The revolution will be tweeted

Less than two thousand miles to the east, Egyptians were watching the events unfold in Tunisia. Their own president, Hosni Mubarak, had been in power for six years longer than Ben Ali, and in the country of 85 million, poverty and repression were widespread. Police brutality —as Wael Abbas had long documented—was common, and many politically engaged Egyptians lived in fear of their government.

But unlike Tunisia, Egypt had never put much of an effort into censoring the internet, or into digital surveillance. Speech certainly was not free, but rather than block websites, the government was more likely to scapegoat prominent individuals in an effort to instill fear in others. In spite of these repressive measures, the county had a lively and relatively large blogosphere, as well as a growing community of social media users, who wrote in a combination of Arabic and English.

After witnessing Tunisians rise up against dictatorships, some Egyptians saw an opening.

"WE WILL FOLLOW!" tweeted revolutionary socialist activist Tarek Shalaby on January 14, 2011.[26] The next day, Manar Mohsen tweeted a link to a "Facebook event for a revolution in Egypt," adding, "Don't forget to RSVP!"

The Facebook event was connected to none other than the "We Are All Khaled Saeed" page, which had been gaining momentum—and followers—since its restoration in November. Now, it was being used to call for a "day of rage" on January 25, which coincided with National Police Day, a bank holiday in the country.

To many outside observers, the protests appeared spontaneous, or inspired entirely by Facebook, but they were in fact a long time in the making. Despite the emergency law that had been consistently in place since the assassination of Anwar Sadat in 1981, Egyptians had still found ways to register their disapproval of the government.

"If you're talking about history, [the revolution] was the climax of a process that started in the year 2000 with the outbreak of the second Palestinian intifada," explained Hossam el-Hamalawy over coffee in a Berlin café. The journalist, photographer, erstwhile blogger, and self-identified revolutionary socialist is a hair older than many of his activist peers, and as such, had studied Egypt's protests from a slightly different perspective. In an article for the *Guardian* published just after the revolution, he expressed a similar sentiment, calling it "a result of a process that has been brewing over the previous decade."

Rallies in support of the second Palestinian intifada in the early 2000s—"probably the first since 1977," says el-Hamalawy—emboldened Egyptians to take to the streets to protest the Iraq War, inspiring activists "to pull down the wall of fear brick by brick."[27] These early demonstrations led in 2004 to the creation of the Kefaya (Enough) movement, which took on the political corruption of the Mubarak family. Kefaya's use of early social media enabled Egyptians around the country to see what Cairo's brave activists were taking on.

But it was not until a worker strike in 2008 in the city of Mahalla that protests took on a life of their own. Mahalla's textile workers were able to claim victory, and news spread via traditional and social media throughout the country, inspiring further strikes. By 2010, recalled el-Hamalawy, small demonstrations had become commonplace. In a blog post that May, he recalled overhearing a phone conversation of a demonstrating worker, who said: "Listen to the chants ... Tell the people back home not to be afraid. We are demonstrating here in Cairo and no one touched us."[28]

At the same time that Egyptian workers were finding their voice on the streets, the country's literati were finding theirs through blogs. By the latter part of the decade, there were hundreds—if not thousands —of Egyptian bloggers from a variety of political persuasions, writing on a range of topics, including government repression. Blogs were a force that brought politically disparate individuals together: "Marxist bloggers such as Hossam al-Hamalawy and Alaa Abd El Fattah wrote and protested side by side with Islamists like Abdel Moneim Mahmoud."[29] By the time the day of rage arrived, many of Egypt's key bloggers had turned to social media and Twitter in particular, which enabled them to post updates from the streets. On January 25, 2011, many watched rapt as Egyptians tweeted their locations, and news from the demonstrations, in real time. The view of the streets through Twitter seemed determined, almost ecstatic.

But by late afternoon that day, Mubarak's government had taken the unprecedented move of blocking Twitter. Still, savvy protesters used proxies to circumvent the ban and continue sending updates. The following day, as the streets filled with demonstrators, the government blocked Facebook as well, but the protests continued to grow. "I blocked Twitter and Facebook so you could focus on your work, not run around the streets shouting #jan25," tweeted a parody account of Mubarak.

By January 28, the day of rage had become something much bigger, and the numbers continued to swell. Hundreds of thousands joined the demonstrations after Friday prayers, and the police responded with water cannons and tear gas. Terrified of the growing opposition, the government ordered ISPs and mobile phone operators to shut down. Only one ISP, Noor, remained online, ostensibly so that the country's stock exchange could remain live. Fortunately, a few key activists were customers of that ISP, and opened their homes to friends, who posted sporadic updates during their visits.

The internet remained unavailable to most Egyptians for five days in total, during which time only a handful of Twitter users kept the world up to date on the protests. The on-the-ground presence of the mainstream media was minimal, and, with the exception of the coverage by Al Jazeera's English bureau, many of the demonstrators took issue with the tech-centric reporting, much of which continued to resort to tropes like "Online Activism Fuels Egypt Protest" or "Movement Began with Outrage and a Facebook Page That Gave It an Outlet."[30] Amid the blackout, Hamalawy managed to access the internet for a few minutes to write: "All MSM reports about looting, violence [are] EXAGGERATED! Protests [are] still going on strong."

Just two days into the revolution, Wael Ghonim—a Dubai-based Google executive who had taken time off to join the protests—disappeared. He was one of many detained during the protests, but, owing to his stature and network, he became a symbol for those arrested, and an international campaign for his release quickly took root.

Ghonim was missing for twelve days, during which his case garnered support from Amnesty International and other human rights organizations. When he was finally released from police custody, on February 7, he took to a small stage in Tahrir Square and declared: "We will not abandon our demand, and that is the departure of the regime."[31]

That same evening, he sat for an interview with Dream TV journalist Mona el-Shazly and admitted to being one of the administrators of the "We Are All Khaled Saeed" Facebook page. He described the page as being democratically run, with decisions taken by vote among the administrators, and demurred that the page merely served as a megaphone for the hard work of political organizers who had come up with the idea for a day of rage.

In the lengthy interview, Ghonim was humble, giving all the credit for the uprising to those who remained on the streets while he was detained. The end of the conversation featured, over the sound of swelling violins, a series of screen images of the revolution's martyrs as Ghonim broke down sobbing, apologizing to the parents of those who died. "It's not our fault!" he cried. "It's the fault of everyone who held on to power and clung to it!"[32]

Ghonim's interview hit the right nerve in Egypt. "Everyone is crying, EVERYONE," tweeted Nevine Zaki. "MILLIONS WILL GO TO TAHRIR TOMORROW. MILLIONS!" proclaimed well-known blogger Mahmoud Salem on Twitter. "A revolution organized by [F]acebook, spread by [T]witter and organized by a guy working for Google," he later tweeted.[33] Hamalawy would later comment: "We need to spread images and videos of the revolt to inspire others into action. A camera, sometimes, is no less important than a Kalashnikov in a revolution."[34]

Four days later, Mubarak stepped down, and the global debate about whether Egypt's was a Facebook revolution began in earnest. "Can social networking overthrow a government?" asked a columnist for the *Sydney Morning Herald*, while the left-oriented publication the *Nation* proclaimed that "cyber-pragmatism brought down Mubarak."[35]

Dozens of articles took aim at pundit Malcolm Gladwell after he dismissively wrote in the *New Yorker*: "Please. People protested and brought down governments before Facebook was invented."[36]

Ghonim told CNN that "definitely, this was the internet revolution. I'll call it revolution 2.0." Not everyone agreed. Alaa Abd El Fattah, who had flown with his wife from South Africa back to Cairo to take part in the protests, may have been speaking for thousands of Egyptians when he asked a New York audience later that year what technology they thought he had used most in Tahrir. "SMS?" someone in the crowd queried. "Your phone!" "Twitter!"

"Nah. Rocks and clubs," said Abd El Fattah, laughing.

Abd El Fattah may sound cynical, but he's not alone. In the years immediately following the uprising, many of its key actors decried the Western media's perspective on their revolution as overly simplistic. Later, as the situation in Egypt worsened and the military took over in a coup that utilized social media in an attempt to give the appearance of having the masses' support, some would even call that narrative dangerous.

AbdelRahman Mansour recognizes the importance of the Facebook page that he, along with Wael Ghonim, created and administered—and yet, he too is wary of Silicon Valley. I first met Mansour online on November 26, 2010, when "We Are All Khaled Saeed" was removed by Facebook. We were introduced by a mutual friend in Cairo, a blogger who was publishing daily reports on the revolution. "Please I'd like to keep my anonymous identity, and wouldn't want to be known as the page's administrator," he wrote in an online chat at the time. "I have received numerous threats via Email and wouldn't want to expose my life to danger."

While Ghonim was thrust into the spotlight for his role, Mansour walked away from it, although by then his identity had become known. He's spent the past decade building a scholarly career, and for the past seven years has lived in the United States, participating in programs at some of the country's most prestigious universities and starting his own non-profit organization. Like his fellow Egyptians, Mansour experienced the disappointment that followed the revolution, but remains hopeful. In 2019, he wrote in a piece for *Foreign Policy*: "New waves of protests have gained traction every few months [in the Middle East and North Africa], showing that the popular movements that started eight years ago are alive and well and will not end anytime soon."[37]

In a phone call from New York, Mansour recounted his experience administering the famous Facebook page. "For me, Facebook was different before the revolution and after. Egyptian citizens discovered Facebook after the revolution," he explained, noting that before 2011, the platform was the domain of the country's educated middle class. "Then the revolution happened, and people read in the news that there's something called Facebook, and it's a website, and it happened to start the revolution." After millions of new users joined, he explained, "the type of communication on the platform changed."

The perception of Mansour and Ghonim changed as well. "Before the revolution, we were just the people who'd created the page ... but after, people were saying that we were the reason the revolution succeeded, and wanted our opinions," Mansour told me. He felt as if he'd been put into a box with which he could not identify.

Today, he says, things have not changed much on Facebook. "If you're hiding your identity, you are creating free thoughts and more flexible actions. If you are known, with name and address, you're part of the political game."

In our conversation, we revisited the story of how the page was removed and then restored. My recollection was that it was foreign NGO workers that had gotten the page back online. As Mansour tells it, Ghonim used his clout from Google to contact Facebook about the page. Both stories, it turns out, are accurate.

"Wael Ghonim reached out to Sheryl [Sandberg], who reached out to the policy team," says Maria, who worked in community operations at Facebook just after the revolution. "It was a big thing internally because [he had contacted] Sheryl." "At the time," Mansour recalls, "the communication with Facebook was based on Silicon Valley culture." That is, "if you know someone, or you work in a bigger company like Google, Facebook will respond to the request very quickly ... It brings questions about the authority of someone who knows someone at Facebook."

Indeed, had Ghonim not had connections, or had Mansour not known someone at that NGO, would the revolution have happened when and how it did? As my friend Mohamed El Dahshan—a participant in the revolution who is now a managing partner at a consulting firm—put it: "Would people have taken to the streets without the reassurance of 200,000 fellow Egyptians responding 'going' [on Facebook]?"

"I don't know," he concluded. "I want to say yes, but the truth is, everything was so precarious and there were so many moving parts and possible points of failure that, my guess is, if *any* of those moving parts had failed, we could have ended up with a very different outcome."

Rasha Abdulla, a professor at American University in Cairo who has written extensively about the role of social media in the uprisings, has a pragmatic outlook. Over a video chat, she told me: "Social media were a great accelerator ... a great facilitator, a great organizer. Would a revolution have broken out in Egypt anyway? Probably, but maybe it would have been delayed twenty years if we didn't have social media." She continued: "It made people feel like they had a voice, and that their voice counted. It was the first real space that afforded youth to have a voice in Egypt."

For Silicon Valley's executives, these details hardly seem to matter. From their vantage point thousands of miles away, they saw the tools they'd built serving a greater purpose. Although at first Mark Zuckerberg publicly stated that it would be "extremely arrogant" for any specific technology company to claim credit for the uprisings across the Middle East and North Africa, he changed his tune after Facebook went public, stating, "By giving people the power to share, we are starting to see people make their voices heard on a different scale from what has historically been possible."[38]

Zuckerberg's later take matches a memory of mine from those heady days. In March 2011, when I was working at the Berkman Klein Center, some of Facebook's top brass dropped by for a lunch meeting, among them Elliot Schrage, policy staffer Matt Perault, and Facebook chief operating officer Sheryl Sandberg. Near the beginning of the meeting, someone asked the inevitable question about Facebook's view of its role in the Arab Spring. I'll never forget the response:

Sandberg placed her hand over her heart and proclaimed her pride at what Facebook had started in Egypt.

Our meeting that day was otherwise fruitful, and set the tone for a working relationship over the next few years that—as things got worse across the region—proved to be vital in helping countless individuals regain access to their accounts, or get them shut down after an arrest in order to protect the members of an activist's network. And yet, it also laid bare for me just how much power was concentrated in the hands of a few Americans.

4

Profit over People

While Cairo's Tahrir Square was still being occupied by protesters in Spring 2011, calls to action began to resonate throughout the region. Jordanians began spreading calls for demonstrations in January using Facebook and live-streaming.[1] On Twitter, Bahrainis called for protests to take place on February 14. And Moroccans used blogs and social media to kick off what would later be called the "February 20 movement."[2]

But in Syria, things were a bit different. In 2011, only 22 percent of the country's 20 million residents had internet access, and unlike in the aforementioned countries, social media and blogging platforms had been kept on tight lockdown for years. There was nevertheless a small Syrian blogosphere and some Facebook traffic, but only those individuals able to use proxies could participate.

Despite such barriers, digitally savvy Syrians used Facebook and Twitter to call for a "day of rage" in Damascus with the goal of ending corruption, along with the state of emergency that had been in place since 1963. Around 250,000 people joined a Facebook group calling for a demonstration on February 4 and 5—more than the total number of Facebook users in Syria at the time, at least according to government sources[3]—only a handful of protesters turned up.[4] In an interview, Syrian president Bashar al-Assad stated that his country was "immune" to the kind of unrest seen elsewhere in the region.[5]

With the early calls for protest unsuccessful, it came as a surprise when, on February 9, Syrians could suddenly access Facebook,

Blogspot, and YouTube without a proxy. While some saw it as "a gesture to the people," and others were indifferent, I was skeptical.[6] Just two days after the sites were unblocked, I wrote: "Activists should remember that free access does not mean freedom of expression. Social media tools have been used for surveillance in a number of countries, and are easily exploited."[7]

It was not long until that prediction came true. In March, as demonstrations in the southern city of Daraa were met with state violence, rumors began to circulate of Syrian Facebook accounts being exploited by hackers using fake SSL certificates—that is, digital certificates that authenticate a website and enable an encrypted connection. When the Facebook page of opposition journalist Khaled Elekhetyar began posting pro-regime content, I assumed that this was the case, and wrote to my contacts at Facebook to see if they could help.[8] They quickly followed up to say that they had received word of a similar case and were looking into it. By the next day, they had informed me that they had put the account "in a roadblock state," blocking access to it "until the account owner contacts us and proves his or her identity."

I soon learned that Elekhetyar had been detained and forced to hand over his account information—including his password—to security forces, who had used it to post to his account. I informed Facebook of the development, and suggested that they apply two-step authentication to Syrian IP addresses. Two-step, or two-factor, authentication is a method of logging in to a website or app that requires "something you know and something you have"—that is, for example, a password and a code obtained either via SMS or through an authentication app. Today, this login method is common, but in 2011, it was infrequently used, not least by social media platforms.

Facebook's response was tepid—without more data, they didn't want to make any changes that might require their engineering team to be involved. Meanwhile, the arrests kept happening, but no one would give consent to share their information with Facebook.

We were at a standstill. I tried going through other channels, contacting friends of friends who worked at Facebook and wanted to help, but inevitably I ended up talking to my primary contact, who gave me the same answers. My frustration grew. Meanwhile, as the violence on the ground continued, so did the dialogue between me and protesters and Facebook. February turned to March, and more and more Syrians were arrested, the stories multiplied of state security demanding their Facebook accounts. In late March, a Syrian friend that I'd met at a workshop in Beirut—the late Bassel Safadi Khartabil—was detained for questioning. Khartabil was an open-source developer and familiar with security practices. "They said they will arrest me if I change [my] password," he wrote to friends about his experience after being released.

I wrote to Facebook again:

One user (whose name I will share only if you can assure me his account will not be "roadblocked") has informed me that he was detained and questioned, then forced to hand over his login info. Rather than compromising his account, however, they threatened him and told him not to change his password. He gave it to them, and has not updated his account since. I can only conclude that the purpose of this is for security forces to meddle with his account; if they allow him to keep the account, then his friends are none the wiser.

This time, the response from Facebook was more helpful. They offered to investigate the account without placing a roadblock on it. "Of course, we can't guarantee that our automated tools won't otherwise flag any improper access," my policy contact wrote, "but this is something that could happen anyway. The investigation might allow us to identify additional accounts that have been impacted or brainstorm other creative solutions."

Over time, Syrians grew aware of the situation and began creating secondary accounts in case of arrest, but the government was always one step ahead: one activist later recalled security forces asking for her second login. Along with other colleagues, I continued to update Facebook upon learning of new arrests. But as the conflict escalated, the numbers continued to grow, and reports of torture began to emerge.[9] In the absence of meaningful assistance from companies, activists began developing their own strategies to protect their accounts, such as sharing their passwords with friends who could remove anti-regime posts or deactivate accounts.[10]

A harbinger of things to come

As the year wore on and the situation across much of the region grew darker, the media remained caught in a jejune debate about whether the Arab uprisings could be attributed to social media. At the same time, attention toward the field of digital rights was growing: in 2011 alone, I was invited to give at least twenty-five talks on social media and free expression, and now-prominent conferences like RightsCon (then dubbed the "Silicon Valley Human Rights Summit") were launched. It felt as if all of a sudden, a new field had emerged.

Meanwhile, the platforms kept growing. By the end of the year, Facebook had 845 million users, a 40 percent increase from the beginning of the year.[11] Twitter, just five years old at the time, boasted 200 million daily active users by September.[12] With more users came more employees; between 2011 and 2012, Facebook grew from 3,200 to a little over 4,600 employees—a growth rate of 44 percent.[13] Such significant growth brought with it big changes: in May 2012, Facebook, Inc. went public. Its peak market capitalization was over $500 billion, one of the largest initial public offerings in history.

As these platforms grew, the relationships between their policy teams and human rights activists became ever more fraught. At the same time, the monitoring and surveillance of social media was growing too, as governments grew increasingly savvy to what their citizens were doing online. It wouldn't be long before social media companies would be drawn into the cat-and-mouse game, and their power over the world's expression laid bare.

Halfway around the world and less than a month before Tunisians took to the streets in protest, a different sort of battle was brewing. WikiLeaks—then known for publishing national internet block lists, documents from the secretive Scientology cult, and footage from a 2007 Baghdad airstrike—had just released a trove of diplomatic cables. The cables contained diplomatic assessments of world leaders and of their host countries. While many were quite mundane in their revelations, others demonstrated the depravity of certain governments, including Tunisia's. There, they were received with appreciation by activists, some of whom later credited WikiLeaks for pushing their movement forward.[14] The US government, however, did not share in their enthusiasm, and just twenty-four hours after Senator Joseph Lieberman publicly called on companies not to host the site's content, they began booting WikiLeaks content from their servers.[15]

Amazon (which hosted the publication's site on its servers) was the first to comply, followed by Tableau, a software company that was hosting user-created visualizations of the leaks. By the end of the following day, EveryDNS.net—a domain name management service—had terminated the WikiLeaks.org domain, and PayPal, Visa, and Mastercard had barred donations to the project.

The release of the cables was certainly controversial, but WikiLeaks had partnered with widely respected journalists from publications including the *New York Times* and the *Guardian* to prioritize the documents and redact critical information. Just as Daniel Ellsberg had done in the 1970s with the Pentagon Papers, WikiLeaks was blowing the whistle on injustice. But not everyone saw it that way. Pundits were quick to denounce the comparison: Ellsberg, they countered, had a specific target, and furthermore had kept certain documents to himself.[16] Ellsberg, on the other hand, saw the government's persecution of WikiLeaks as evidence that the United States was headed down a repressive path: "Secrecy," he stated at the time, "is essential to empire."[17]

The actions of one company, Twitter, stood out among the rest: the US Department of Justice served it with a 2703(d) court order to hand over user data pertaining to three individuals related to WikiLeaks, giving the company just three days to reply without notifying anyone involved. But instead of complying, Twitter appealed and was granted permission by a judge to inform the users of the demand.[18] "Twitter introduced a new feature last month without telling anyone about it, and the rest of the tech world should take note and come up with its own version of it," wrote tech journalist Ryan Singel. "Twitter beta-tested a spine."[19]

But the actions taken by most Silicon Valley companies against WikiLeaks stood, at least to me, in stark contrast to how they sought to serve Tunisian and Egyptian users. Maybe the pressure from the government was too great, or maybe the companies only feigned support for the protests in the region because they saw potential to grow their bottom line there. Or perhaps it was just the soft bigotry of low expectations. In any case, by the end of 2011, the hope and optimism that had driven the Arab Spring was fading fast, as was the faith activists in the region once had in social media.

Then, in December 2011, the news broke that Kingdom Holding Company, an investment firm owned by Saudi prince Al-Waleed bin Talal, had acquired a 3 percent share in Twitter. Although it was reported that the prince lacked voting rights, some activists were still concerned. "Why silence an opposition, when you can buy it out?" tweeted political analyst Ramy Yaacoub.[20] Others warned that although the prince might not be able to influence the company just yet, he would be able to should the company go public.

But Twitter did not need advice on censorship from a Saudi prince; the company was figuring that out all on its own. By January, Twitter had announced that it had implemented the ability to restrict tweets on a per-country basis, just as its competitors were already doing. In a blog post entitled "The tweets must still flow"—a callback to a post about free expression published during Egypt's internet shutdown one year prior—the company stated:

> As we continue to grow internationally, we will enter countries that have different ideas about the contours of freedom of expression. Some differ so much from our ideas that we will not be able to exist there. Others are similar but, for historical or cultural reasons, restrict certain types of content, such as France or Germany, which ban pro-Nazi content.
>
> Until now, the only way we could take account of those countries' limits was to remove content globally. Starting today, we give ourselves the ability to reactively withhold content from users in a specific country—while keeping it available in the rest of the world.

We have also built in a way to communicate transparently to users when content is withheld, and why.[21]

Many users were up in arms about the policy and called for a boycott. Although Twitter's policy at the time was more transparent than Facebook's, the platform had long been seen as a sacred space for free expression, and this new policy meant that the desires of governments—and not of the users who'd enabled the platform to thrive—would take precedent. Twitter's equating of authoritarian countries to democracies like Germany and France particularly rankled. As I wrote at the time: "We, the users, need to start thinking about how the internet is governed and controlled."[22]

It didn't seem like such a big deal at the time for Twitter to block tweets locally. After all, the company was merely following in the footsteps of Facebook. But years later, it's apparent that this sort of policy copycatting, which became commonplace, is one of the ways in which power has consolidated among just a handful of companies. Just as one company had followed another into the blockade against WikiLeaks, Twitter's move to block tweets locally wasn't a creative solution, but just more of the same.

We soon witnessed this groupthink again and again, first in response to online extremism, then later as companies banded together to block white supremacists and conspiracy theorists. While some have praised this collective response, I see it as dangerous. What authority does Facebook or Twitter have to determine who is beyond the pale? While governments have engaged in this type of collusion for the purposes of, for example, tackling major crimes or foreign terrorism, companies have gone a step further in de-platforming those whose speech in many places would otherwise be protected.

Going public

Twitter's IPO was still more than a year away, but Facebook was already preparing to go public. In February 2012, the company filed its intent with the Securities and Exchange Commission and embarked on a roadshow. CEO Zuckerberg was criticized for his presentation and choice of attire (a hoodie, naturally), but in the end it mattered little: in April Facebook acquired Instagram for $1 billion, and the next month it went ahead with its IPO, with a valuation of roughly $104 billion.

Zuckerberg had previously claimed that Facebook's purchases were "talent acquisitions." In 2010, he said, "We have not once bought a company for the company. We buy companies to get excellent people," and that he wanted "Facebook to be the McKinsey of entrepreneurship."[23] But Instagram was different—the company was quickly gaining popularity, and for Facebook it offered a quick and easy strategy for capturing the attention of the growing number of users accessing the platform via mobile devices. A month after its IPO, Facebook made another big purchase, acquiring Israeli facial recognition startup Face.com for around $60 million.[24] The acquisition of Face.com and its competitor Instagram gave Facebook a serious leg up against its competitors, by enabling the company to help users identify and tag themselves and others in photos, thus improving on their social graph.

The IPO was, by most accounts, a fiasco. CBS News called it "the most famous botched IPO in history," while the *Wall Street Journal* noted that the shares were dropping by $1 a day, putting the company on track to be worth nothing by June.[25] To some close observers, the IPO merely echoed Facebook's infamous internal motto, "Move fast and break things." But to the digital rights community, it signaled something else entirely—that Zuckerberg and co. were woefully unprepared for what was yet to come.

For me, the clues were in Zuckerberg's "Founder's Letter," posted to his Facebook wall. In it, he proclaimed with confidence that "by giving the people the power to share, we are starting to see people make their voices heard on a different scale from what has historically been possible." Furthermore, he predicted,

These voices will increase in number and volume. They cannot be ignored. Over time, we expect governments will become more responsive to issues and concerns raised directly by all their people rather than through intermediaries controlled by a select few.

Through this process, we believe that leaders will emerge across all countries who are pro-internet and fight for the rights of their people, including the right to share what they want and the right to access all information that people want to share with them.[26]

It is worth pointing out his recognition of Facebook's intermediary role. From Zuckerberg's point of view, Facebook is merely a conduit, and the insurance of free expression a matter to be determined by governments and their people. In that framing, when Facebook is ordered by a foreign government to remove content, the company is merely following orders.

In an article for Al Jazeera, I wondered at the time why the company had not shown "more concern about their vulnerable user populations," but in hindsight it's clear: Zuckerberg simply does not see the protection of those populations, and their speech, as Facebook's responsibility.[27] If he had, he might have invested more money in building a just and equitable content moderation system, or invested in the improvement of other technological user tools, instead of acquiring his competitors.

The Founder's Letter is fascinating for just how wrong Zuckerberg's predictions—and his view of the company ethos—turned out to be. He describes hacker culture as "extremely open and meritocratic," an idea that feminists have strongly challenged. He also states that hackers believe that the "best idea and implementation" should always win, ignoring the fact that some of the best ideas are not given a chance to surface in a work culture dominated by white men.

But perhaps most problematic is how Zuckerberg describes Facebook's five core values in the letter: "focus on impact," "move fast," "be bold," "be open," and "build social value."[28] On face, they mostly sound like solid values for a big company to have, but the devil is in the details—and the implementation. Zuckerberg suggests that Facebook focuses on the "most important problems," but doesn't say how, exactly, he defines importance. One might think that "important" would include protecting the privacy or free expression of Facebook users (particularly its most vulnerable), but that has all too often not been the case.

Being bold and open are positive values, but for Facebook, openness has rarely included openness to external consultation or criticism, and boldness is only understood through the lens of one of the company's sayings, "The riskiest thing is to take no risks." It is thus possible to act with great boldness when it is coupled with appropriate caution, though Facebook has rarely heeded its own wisdom.

Similarly, though Zuckerberg states that Facebook staff are expected to "focus every day on how to build real value for the world in everything they do," it's hard to see how the company's failure to protect its users from data mining firm Cambridge Analytica or its co-optation of online news provide real value to anything but Facebook's bottom line.

But it is perhaps Facebook's mantra to "move fast and break things," splashed on posters around its offices and cemented in the Founder's Letter, that has proven most damaging over time. "The idea is that if you never break anything, you're probably not moving fast enough," Zuckerberg wrote. Nearly all of the former employees I interviewed were critical of the mantra. One, who wished to remain anonymous, told me a story about staff having to move quickly on a government blocking request—so quickly that they were not expected to wait for the translation, and accidentally blocked a major protest-related page in a critical country.

"You can't imagine how sometimes when you're so busy, you have this concept at Facebook that you have to move fast and break things, so it doesn't matter if you make a mistake," they told me. "You believe you're making an impact, saving lives; you work so many hours every day, and follow the policies."

Anna, the former operations employee, explained that the mantra, in reality, required staff to move "so fucking fast," and told me that the ubiquitous inspirational posters also included sayings like, "If you can learn, you can learn anything," and "What would you do if you weren't afraid?"—said to be a favorite saying of Sheryl Sandberg's.

Dia Kayyali, a human rights activist—and, for full disclosure, a close friend and erstwhile colleague of mine—sees the mantra as part of a bigger and more insidious problem. Kayyali has worked on corporate policy for nearly as long as I have, but over the past few years, has shifted toward working closely with human rights activists in Myanmar, Palestine, India, and other places where Facebook's impact has been deadly. "Every single one of the major platforms—because they didn't build human rights into their platforms from the beginning, because they weren't people who had any human rights or social justice background—they built corporations," they told me. "And we know that corporations harm people. They didn't think about the potential negative externalities, and now here we are."

Kayyali (who uses they/them pronouns) compares Facebook's rapid growth to the development of Love Canal, a neighborhood in Niagara Falls, New York, infamous in the 1970s for being the site of a public health crisis, the result of a corporation having dumped tons of chemical byproducts into the water supply. Several families were displaced, and numerous cases of leukemia and other severe health problems were attributed to the toxins. Love Canal was described a decade later by New York State Department of Health Commissioner David Axelrod as a "national symbol of a failure to exercise a sense of concern for future generations"—a phrasing that Kayyali says has resonance for how platforms have behaved.[29]

"I guess they just didn't think anyone would find out … or maybe they just decided to 'move fast and break things,' i.e., people's bodies," Kayyali said sardonically. "And frankly, in 2020, Facebook is the same. Facebook is responsible for dozens more deaths that Love Canal was … Unless you specifically build something with human rights or with basic rights in mind, this is where it will always end up."

Despite my early positive interactions with the company's policy staff, what I failed to realize at the time was that those young and at times naive staffers were trying to do what they could to make the world a better place. Their willingness to assist me was not a reflection of corporate policy, but rather a reflection of their own personal values. I did not recognize that, when they appeared eager to help but later returned without solutions, that was the result of Facebook the corporation stopping them in their tracks. In retrospect, it is no surprise that most of those young staffers left in the years immediately after the IPO.

Zuckerberg's prophecy was entirely naive, and willfully so. Had he simply surveyed the vast and growing number of countries censoring online speech, or noticed how his platform was increasingly becoming caught in the middle between the people and their governments, he might have predicted that his company would eventually become the world's biggest censor. Had he recognized how inserting his own moral values—and those of his largely white American staff and all-male board—into Facebook's policies was already stifling free expression, or how employing underpaid and undertrained content moderators was a fatalistic endeavor, he might have changed course. But Zuckerberg's superpower is his ability to ignore his critics, and so onward he forged.

Profit above all

Not long after Microsoft launched its Bing browser in 2009, Helmi Noman—a researcher affiliated with the Berkman Klein Center—noticed something odd: when he changed his location in the browser to the (misnomered) "Arabian countries" setting, certain keywords would fail to return any results. Specifically, Noman found that Arabic-language terms for "breast" (يدث), "gay" (ذاش), lesbian (قاحس), and intercourse (عامج) were being censored. Instead of search results, he was served a message that read: "Your country or region requires a strict Bing SafeSearch setting."

Noman shared his initial findings with me and other colleagues, and we brainstormed a methodology. We created lists of sensitive terms across several categories in both Arabic and English, and a group of participants manually tested them in Bing from four countries: Jordan, the United Arab Emirates, Syria, and Algeria.

What Noman found was that, regardless of which country the tester was based, a significant number of words were blocked from returning search results. Keywords included terms like "sex," "porn," and "nude" as well as LGBTQ-specific terms, innocuous words like "kiss," and words denoting human body parts, including "clitoris" and "penis" but, strangely, not vagina.[30] The blacklist was sloppy—some of the Arabic words were incorrectly formatted and some terms were surprisingly left out—but it did the trick: Arabic-speaking users were effectively blocked from finding content about sex and sexuality, including key information on breast cancer or STI testing. And they weren't the only ones: the SafeSearch function was forcibly turned on in several other locations including India, Thailand, Hong Kong, and China.

What was particularly notable about this instance of censorship was Microsoft's claim that it was a legal requirement. As was noted in Noman's paper, that may have been true for some countries, but in others the blacklist went far beyond existing internet censorship, and in some cases beyond local sensibilities. As a member of the Global Network Initiative, Microsoft had committed to "protect and advance user rights to freedom of expression and privacy, including when faced with government demands for censorship." Specifically, member companies were supposed to work to "avoid or minimize the impact of government restrictions on freedom of expression."[31]

Instead, I later learned through conversations with company executives, Microsoft had based their decision on market research, not legal requirements. That is troubling because the majority of market research is conducted in only a handful of countries in the region—countries that are typically both wealthier and more conservative. Facebook has worked with the market research company Kantar, which has a focus on the United Arab Emirates (UAE) and Saudi Arabia, while Google's reports with Bain show most research being conducted in those countries, as well as Egypt.[32]

Frequently ignored in market research are more socially liberal countries like Lebanon and Tunisia. As a result, people living in those countries are often subject to the values of the region's lowest common denominator. Bing's censorship in the Arab region was merely an early example of how Silicon Valley chooses to serve wealthier users—and their repressive governments—at the expense of others' right to freedom of expression and access to information.

The examples of censorship—sometimes the result of laziness, other times of malice—are abundant. In 2017, five songs from the Lebanese band Al-Rahel Al-Kabir (The Great Departed) that mocked religious fundamentalism and political repression were found to be missing from the iTunes Middle East platform. The band worked with Beirut-based organization SMEX to petition Apple, and learned that the decision to censor had not been made by the company, but by a UAE intermediary, Qanawat, which deemed the songs inappropriate.[33] In this instance, iTunes apologized, restoring the songs and pledging to work with a different intermediary—but in most cases, users are not so lucky.

Twitter, for instance, bans all advertisements of alcohol in the region, claiming that "all alcohol advertising is prohibited in these countries."[34] A reasonable policy, if only it were accurate! As anyone who's visited Beirut will know, it is hard to traverse the city without spotting a liquor ad, and social media is a frequent target of alcohol brands.[35] When in 2014 the northern city of Tripoli sought to ban alcohol advertisements in an effort to curb drunk driving, some online critics called the decision "ISIS-like."[36] Though it is not clear how Twitter arrived at its policy, its regional advertising partner is Connect Ads, a firm based in Egypt—where alcohol advertising is banned.[37]

While Lebanese drinkers will be just fine if they aren't exposed to online alcohol ads, Twitter's lazy policymaking is yet another example of how countries like Lebanon "[fall] through the cracks of so many policies," as Anna, the former Facebook operations manager, put it. "Don't underestimate how careless [the companies] can be."

Though there's certainly injustice in a corporation barring women from learning about breast cancer, or censoring a band's songs in their own country, sometimes Silicon Valley's need to appease governments can have even greater implications at the geopolitical level.

The new cartographers

Some people are good at keeping track of time zones—I'm not one of them. When I have a call with someone halfway around the world, I do what a lot of people do: I turn to Google. So that's just what I did one February morning in 2013 while trying to schedule a call with a lawyer in the West Bank.

"What time is it in Ramallah?" I typed and hit enter.

The answer was a bit surprising. It wasn't the time that surprised me, but the rest of the information returned in the top-level Google "answer box." Under the hour, it read "Time in Ramallah, Israel."

Regardless of one's political position, most readers will be aware that Ramallah is in the occupied West Bank. "West Bank," "Occupied Palestine," or "Palestine" would have been acceptable. A search for Nablus and other Palestinian cities returned the same result. I took a few screenshots and sent them off to a contact on Google's policy team, who replied within five minutes: "Whoa! I have been to Ramallah, and I can definitely say that it is in the West Bank. :)"

My contact shared the screenshots with her team, and within days, Google had implemented a solution: they simply removed the country following the Palestinian cities. Curious, I started Googling the time in other occupied cities around the world, from Dakhla, in Western Sahara to Stepanakert, the capital of the Republic of Artsakh. I found that in most cases, the country was absent, but there were notable exceptions: Lhasa, listed as "Lhasa, Tibet, China," and—unsurprisingly—Jerusalem, listed squarely in Israel. This solution seems positively elegant when you compare it to how Google and its competitors deal with borders.

Border disputes have been around far longer than the modern nation-state, and cartographers have always struggled to accurately depict national boundaries. In the United States, many mapmaking companies have traditionally taken their cues from the State Department, while others (such as National Geographic) have looked for consensus among governments. Still others use dotted lines or other markers to denote areas of conflict.[38]

Today, Google is undeniably the manufacturer of the world's most consulted map, giving the company a unique responsibility to create a product that is accurate and free from local biases. To the former point, the company largely succeeds: only once have I been sent the wrong direction down a one-way street using Google's driving directions (it was in Croatia, and I survived). But on the latter point, Google is known to pander to governments by adjusting the borders of various countries according to where the map is viewed.

Take India, for example: from inside the country, the state of Jammu and Kashmir appears to sit within the country's borders, but from elsewhere the disputed territory is marked with a dotted line, demarcating the contentious international boundary separating India and Pakistan. Similarly, outside Morocco, Google and Microsoft's Bing demarcate the Western Sahara, occupied by Morocco since 1975, with a dotted line.

Neither Kashmir nor the Sahrawi Arab Democratic Republic have wide recognition as independent territories, making Google's job more complicated, but for another territory—Occupied Palestine—it's a different story. The State of Palestine is a de jure sovereign state recognized by 138 members of the United Nations, and since 2012 has held the status of non-member observer state there. But one would not know that from looking at Google, which marks the territories as "West Bank" and "Gaza," using dotted lines and the borders demarcated in the Oslo Accords.

The *Washington Post* has described Google as being influenced "not just by history and local laws, but also the shifting whims of diplomats, policymakers and its own executives."[39] This is apparent in the case of Palestine, but when it comes to Syria, other forces have come into play. In 2012, after the uprising had turned violent, the *Post* documented a different phenomenon: opposition activists utilizing Google's volunteer Map Maker program to rename key spots in honor of revolutionary heroes.[40] While some opposition members praised the tactic, the country's UN envoy accused Google of participating in a foreign plot to undermine Syrian leadership.

That was neither the first nor the last time that corporate digital cartography contributed to conflict. In 2010, Nicaragua essentially invaded Costa Rica, its neighbors turf subsumed into its own, after a Google Maps error suggested the territory was part of Nicaragua. Government officials blamed a Google bug for the error, but Costa Rica was not amused. Google was quoted at the time as saying: "Cartography is a complex undertaking, and borders are always changing."[41]

Cartography is indeed complex, and Google's error was—at least in the case of the Nicaraguan–Costa Rican dispute—an honest mistake. But both cartographic errors and biases can have real consequences, and as such, map creation requires a level of caution and expertise that, at times, the company does not seem to take nearly as seriously as it ought to. Presenting a map differently depending on the location of the viewer might make sense from a profit perspective, but does it serve the public of a country not to know that a given territory is under dispute?

While in some cases (such as Palestine), Google seems bound to major powers like the United States and Israel, the company has explained that in cases where it presents a "local" version of a map, the company "follow[s] local legislation when displaying names and borders." The result of this blending of tactics is a muddled view of the world that becomes even more confusing as one moves throughout it.

Appeasing authoritarians

Just three months after Facebook's IPO, the company opened its first Middle East office, in the shining beacon of democracy, the UAE. Although the country is propped up by the United States and other Western states as a key ally in the fight against terror and plays host to many American and European corporate offices, the UAE is a constitutional monarchy with an abysmal human rights record that covers the gamut from torture to public stoning to application of the death penalty for homosexuality. Women, particularly Muslim women from poorer countries, are treated as second-class citizens, and the legal status of migrant workers is tied to the sponsorship—and whims—of their employers.

There is, of course, no guarantee of freedom of expression in the UAE. The internet is broadly censored, criticism of the government is met with swift legal action, and protests are absolutely forbidden. Those who violate these laws are often held for years without a trial. Although foreigners who break the law are sometimes deported instead of jailed, it seems to depend greatly on the color of the skin and country of origin: in 2014, a US citizen of Sri Lankan descent was sentenced to a year in prison in a show trial after posting a video to YouTube that parodied the wealthy teenagers of the country's largest city, Dubai.[42]

Facebook could be forgiven for thinking Dubai was a smart place to open a regional office; after all, Google beat the company there by four years. Neither company seemed to have much concern about the country's human rights record. When looking out across the city's sparkling landscape, they both likely saw dollar signs. In fact, Facebook was quoted as such back in 2012, calling the decision "purely commercial."[43]

Human rights activists saw the writing on the wall early on, and when news got out in early 2015 that Twitter was to follow in Google and Facebook's footsteps, they were rightly concerned. They feared the company was about to betray its stated mission: "to give everyone the power to create and share ideas and information instantly, without barriers." Just a few months before, the company's general counsel, Vijaya Gadde, had written a *Washington Post* op-ed that seemed to align with that mission. "Freedom of expression means little as our underlying philosophy if we continue to allow voices to be silenced because they are afraid to speak up," she wrote.[44] Although Gadde's point was about the proliferation of hate speech on Twitter, it resonated with activists concerned about the implications of the company opening an office in one of the Middle East's most repressive countries.

Along with Amnesty International and several regional organizations, I joined a call with Twitter in April 2015 to convince the company to reconsider its decision, but as we learned, the office had already been established. We changed tactics, trying to convince Twitter to disclose details on how on a global scale it would ensure due diligence regarding human rights. We asked the company representatives whether they had researched the UAE's human rights record and what their plans were regarding compliance with UAE law, but I recall them giving us no straight answers. A note I scribbled during the call reads: "I'm on the worst call ever. Twitter hemming and hawing over their horrible decision to open an office in Dubai."

By that point, Twitter's decision to open an office in Dubai felt, to me, like a betrayal of ideals. Whether those ideals truly ever existed is a valid question in light of all that has unfolded since, but in its youth—and particularly in comparison with larger platforms Facebook and YouTube—the company had seemed like a rebel. Twitter had stood up to the US government when it demanded information on accounts belonging to people involved with WikiLeaks, and had resisted foreign censorship demands far longer than any other platform.

In retrospect, it seems clear that those decisions can be largely attributed to Alexander Macgillivray, who served as general counsel for Twitter until 2013.[45] A strong supporter of free expression with a willingness to go against the grain, Macgillivray's departure signified a sea change inside the company. Within less than a year, Twitter began to make decisions that failed to comport with human rights frameworks, such as its opaque mass deletion of alleged "terrorist" accounts and its opening of an office in a country that has for many years imprisoned those who speak even mildly against the government. In more recent years, Twitter has joined its competitors in restricting lawful speech at the behest of countries with little regard for freedom of expression and, at times, has kissed up to authoritarian leaders in the pursuit of profit. But one of the most stomach-turning gestures from Silicon Valley is, by far, its continued engagement with Saudi Arabia.

The Gulf country's public investment fund is among Silicon Valley's biggest investors and, in cooperation with SoftBank, is a major shareholder in Uber, WeWork, Slack, and other US companies. Prior to the government's murder of Saudi journalist Jamal Khashoggi inside its embassy in Istanbul, Saudi crown prince Mohammed Bin Salman (often referred to as "MBS") was given a warm welcome when visiting major tech firms, and seen in press photographs with executives of Google and other companies—this, despite his country's brutal human rights track record.[46] Although the image of MBS as a "reformer" was pushed heavily by Western media (in particular the *New York Times*, which in 2017 published a nauseating opinion piece from Thomas Friedman suggesting that MBS was creating a new "Arab Spring"), watchers of the region knew better and stated so clearly.[47] But their warnings fell on deaf ears in Silicon Valley.

One executive I spoke to on background informed me that Saudi visits to tech firms occurred on an annual basis, with some companies rolling out a literal red carpet to government officials. While certainly some of the friendliness was motivated by pure greed, some was born of pure ignorance. One former Facebook employee told me a story about a meeting where, after being briefed on the company's efforts to lobby Saudi Arabia to stop blocking voice over IP (VoIP) on WhatsApp, a senior policy staffer asked "Why are we not lobbying the Saudi parliament?" (It is key to note that Saudi Arabia's consultative assembly has no power to propose or pass laws; that power is reserved for the king alone).

After many years of engaging with policy teams at major social media companies, I'm disappointed but not surprised that a senior policy staffer with a graduate degree would be unaware that Saudi Arabia is a totalitarian absolute monarchy. Companies like Facebook may prize ingenuity when it comes to engineering, but thinking outside the box is no longer valued in policy circles. In fact, policy hires increasingly come from government, law enforcement, or the policy teams of other corporations, which has created a revolving door through which only a certain subset of people can enter.

As such, Silicon Valley policymaking has increasingly come to resemble that of government; and given the absence of any vestige of democratic participation, that means authoritarian government. In 2019, ImpACT International wrote: "If [tech companies] also shape the way businesses, NGOs, governments and ordinary citizens communicate with each other—as the social media giants now do— [interference] or collaboration (depending on the form it takes) can pose extraordinary risks to universal human rights such as freedom of thought and expression."[48]

Even the murder of Khashoggi has not been enough to steer Silicon Valley in the right direction. In October 2019, the Vox Media website Recode stated that "there is little concrete evidence one year after the killing of Khashoggi that Saudi Arabia has suffered any serious consequences from theoretically outraged, socially minded tech leaders."[49] Nor has the appeasement of Saudi Arabia stopped the country from doing further harm: in 2015, a Saudi agent who had infiltrated Twitter as an employee managed to access and export data on thousands of users and share it with the government. Former employees of the company and victims of the breach alike have accused Twitter of not doing enough to safeguard access to user information.[50]

In Silicon Valley years, 2015 feels like a lifetime ago. In the ensuing years, security has surely tightened, but so have the relationships between companies and foreign governments. While we hear in popular media about the pressure governments are applying in countries like France and the United States, insiders tell another tale … of calls from, and sometimes closer collusion with, less democratic countries. They also speak of another insidious development: policy enforcement that, with little to no direct involvement from governments, replicates existing societal power dynamics.

Repression's little helpers

The hope that many across the Arab region felt in the aftermath of the uprisings that so shook in the world in 2011 has, a decade later, dissipated. Although Tunisia has instituted a number of democratic norms and—thanks to continued action from its populace—continues to progress in stops and starts, other countries have not fared so well. Social media has, for better or worse, continued to offer a lens through which to observe the ongoing wars in Syria, Yemen, and Libya, the growing repression in several Gulf states, and the economic collapse and uprising in Lebanon. But that lens is not assured and its persistence not guaranteed—there is no assurance that any given platform will survive. Acquisitions, such as Yahoo!'s purchase of GeoCities in 2009, can lead to the erasure of entire online worlds—as can censorship.

The years following the revolution have been particularly unkind to Egyptians. Not more than two years after brave revolutionaries ousted dictator Hosni Mubarak, the Egyptian military, led by former general and then minister of defense Abdel Fattah el-Sisi, seized power in what seemed to some observers as a second revolution but was to many Egyptians quite clearly a coup. Once the new government had consolidated power, it acted quickly to arrest opponents and install surveillance technologies so that it could monitor a larger number of adversaries on social media.

Keeping in line with its predecessors, the new government continued at first to shy from blatant acts of censorship, instead going after (and making examples of) those who failed to toe the line. By 2019, the Committee to Protect Journalists named Egypt as one of the world's worst jailer of journalists: that year, the watchdog group wrote that the country tied with Saudi Arabia for third place, with each country holding at least twenty-six journalists behind bars.[51] Ordinary citizens were not spared from the crackdown either. In January 2020, British journalist Ruth Michaelson reported an estimated sixty thousand people were being held as political prisoners in Egypt's jails.[52] Michaelson was deported from the country two months later after criticizing the government's response to the COVID-19 pandemic.[53]

In the autumn of 2019, around two thousand Egyptians took to the streets again to call for el-Sisi to be removed from power.[54] The government swiftly cracked down, arresting demonstrators as well as at least one journalist. After the protests, Twitter suspended accounts belonging to a group of Egyptians whose estimated number was between thirty and sixty, most of whom tweeted primarily in Arabic.[55] Many of them had used the multi-layered Arabic term that is often described as meaning "pimp" or "cuckold," but has developed to mean "ass-kisser," 'ars (عرص). Others used a variation of the term. Those that I spoke to said that Twitter provided unclear justification for the suspensions.

Wael Eskandar says that it was no accident. The political commentator and journalist, who along with other Egyptians had once appreciated Twitter for its ability to keep people informed, wrote about the takedowns: "Twitter is no longer empowering its users. Its platform cannot be considered neutral. Twitter's actions suggest it is systematically suppressing voices in the Middle East and North Africa (MENA) region."[56]

"There were two things happening simultaneously [to Egyptian Twitter users]," Eskandar told me over the phone: the flagging and consequent removal of accounts for violating Twitter's hateful speech policy, which had been ongoing for some time before the protests; and the aforementioned bulk suspensions. "The mass suspensions following the protests happened for no particular reason. Some people were banned for using multiple hashtags, and the others were for suspicious activity."

Eskandar chose to focus on the latter, making it his mission to get the accounts restored. "I tried to reach out to George Salama," Twitter's head of policy, government, and philanthropy for the region, he said. But Eskandar didn't have much luck getting answers, even after following up. "I felt like [Twitter] didn't want to listen to new voices. I went public [with my findings] and felt like their MENA office didn't appreciate that."

Eventually, Eskandar scored a meeting with Twitter's trust and safety team, who promised to take a look at the situation. By the end of December 2019, he told me, most of the accounts that had been mass-suspended had been restored, but Twitter gave no explanation as to why they'd been removed, or why others remained banned. "For a long time, people have been complaining about Twitter shutting them down," Eskandar recalled, but their claims were "easily dismissed," even by NGOs that work with the company. "My interactions with [Twitter] helped me understand their structure ... Power is interspersed all over within [the company]." Eskendar's experience matches my own: I've often reached out to different people within the company, only to be given different explanations of the same event. Regional policy staffers such as Salama seem to have minimal decision-making power—instead, that power is concentrated in the hands of a few individuals in California.

While Eskandar believes that structural racism or discrimination was involved in the mass shutdowns, he also feels that it's easier for these things to go unchecked in countries like Egypt, where there are not legal structures to challenge the companies. "If this happened in the U.S., there would be a lawsuit," he said. By ignoring platform censorship, the Egyptian government is effectively letting companies do their bidding, making it easy to "shut people up based on their political inclinations."

Six months later, Tunisian colleagues reported that more than sixty accounts belonging to activists and journalists in the country had been suspended from Facebook without warning. Among those affected was Haythem El Mekki, a journalist and commentator whose blogging played a key role in the 2011 revolution. "It just said that my account had been deactivated and that was my final notice. There wasn't really any negotiation," he told the *Guardian*.[57]

Shortly thereafter, Facebook announced the suspension of hundreds of Tunisian accounts, pages, and groups for "inauthentic coordinated

behavior" following an investigation that had uncovered a sophisticated campaign, dubbed "Operation Carthage", by Tunisian public
relations firm UReputation to influence elections in several African
countries.[58] Local and international rights groups wondered if the
suspensions of activists were related, and penned a letter to Facebook
demanding clarity.[59]

Facebook responded to the letter, but failed to answer most of the
questions, instead blaming the suspensions on a "technical error": "We
were not trying to limit anyone's ability to post or express themselves,
and apologise for any inconvenience this has caused," the company
told the *Guardian*.[60]

Mass suspensions like those that occurred in Egypt and Tunisia are
uncommon, but are becoming less so as companies aim to combat
influence campaigns like Operation Carthage. Preventing such operations from gaining influence is important for the preservation of
democracy, but so too is ensuring that vital voices of activists and
journalists are not silenced.

Less common than mass suspensions is a company being willing
to hold a meeting with an unaffiliated individual; over the years in
my work, most Silicon Valley policy teams have preferred instead to
filter information through established NGOs. And while all the major
platforms consult with NGOs, the degree to which they do so with
transparency differs greatly from one company to the next.

Twitter, for example, developed a trust and safety network after a
sustained anti-harassment campaign in the wake of 2015's GamerGate
targeted the company to take more action against those using the
platform to harass others.[61] The network includes dozens of online
safety and free expression NGOs from around the world, who are
listed publicly on the company's website. Several organizations I've
worked with are members, and have confided that they find the company's consultations useful and generally feel heard.

Facebook, on the other hand, meets regularly with NGOs and other
stakeholders, but remains mum about which ones. The company's
policy team is also deeply susceptible to government pressure, and,
according to more than a half-dozen individuals that I spoke to, it will
often speak openly about it to NGOs when meeting about specific

policies. Facebook, as one person put it, "is prone to false balance"—meaning, in seeking out opinions on a policy on, say, nudity, they might take into equal account the views of religiously bent organizations and those focused on free expression.

Nevertheless, as authoritarianism has crept back across the Middle East and censorship and surveillance are on the rise, Silicon Valley companies continuously make policy decisions that baffle some of the region's fiercest activists and, at times, put people in danger. I asked Wael Eskandar if he thinks that, like Saudi Arabia, Egypt may have found a way to infiltrate Twitter.

"Infiltration and media control are part of any country's intelligence strategy," he told me. "So if they can do that, why not?"

Indeed, the battle for free expression on corporate platforms is often a battle of competing interests brought to the table by outsiders—with governments on one side and advocates of some sort on the other. Of course, corporate and advertiser interests are at play as well, but when it comes to some of the most contentious topics—"terrorism", for example—it often feels as if the companies' policy teams would rather take a step back and let other parties duke it out.

The problem, of course, lies in companies viewing governments and citizens as equals, while in fact governments are, by and large, using their power to implement policies where passing laws is impossible without also changing the national constitution. By remaining neutral, corporations are acting as conduits of the state. They are today's censors, not unlike the religious institutions and governments that came before them.

And although it may seem that governments and citizens (in the form of NGOs or civil society organizations) are given somewhat equal access, the truth is that no citizen, not even a director of a powerful NGO, can simply pick up the phone and dial Mark Zuckerberg to complain about a policy decision the way that Israeli prime minister Netanyahu has been known to do.[62]

In fact, says Eskandar, although companies like Twitter rightfully provide the option to appeal policy decisions, this process has felt broken since before the pandemic sent content moderators home, rendering it mostly moot. While researching the mass suspensions of

Egyptian Twitter accounts last fall, he created a new account of his own, tweeting the words that he suspected to be verboten, and soon found the account permanently suspended. He appealed, and was almost immediately rebuked. He tried again with another account, but the appeal was denied within less than two hours.

Eskandar suspected that the decisions might be automated, so he filed a request using the European General Data Protection Regulation (GDPR) provision on the right to explanation. The explanation that he received was disappointing, to say the least: Eskandar was informed that the decision was made correctly, that he had indeed violated the rules, and that it was made by a human. He would later learn however, from Twitter, that the decision had in fact been made in error.

Processes like the one dealing with the GDPR's right to explanation are intended to provide individuals with due process, similar to what they might have in the event of wrongful state censorship, yet their decision making is entirely reliant on the honesty of the company in question. There is no fact-finding mission, no evidence gathering, just the user's word against that of the corporation.

Once potential forces for good, these corporations have strayed far from their original missions. As Zuckerberg et al. have lined their pockets with income generated from the advertisers preying on the world's citizens, they have increasingly cozied up to power, with apparently little concern for how that power is derived. Whereas corporate leaders once spoke about the power of their platforms to help citizens topple governments, today they meet in secret with authoritarian leaders to create backroom deals that stifle citizen expression.[63]

The fact is, these companies long ago chose profit over people. The ruthless barbarism of the House of Saud matters little to a company like Facebook or Twitter when millions of Saudis use the platforms, potentially generating billions in income.[64] With that kind of money, it should come as little surprise that the companies roll out the red carpet for Saudi leadership, or turn a blind eye to the ways in which governments are manipulating their systems.

In an increasingly global world, we as citizens are up against not just our own governments, but any and all of those with influence over corporate policies. If Facebook's ban on nudity is the result of pressure from conservative governments, we all suffer for it. When Saudi Arabia infiltrates Twitter and accesses user data, there's no country to which a Saudi user can safely escape. When the Syrian government demands a user's password, that user has nowhere that they can file a complaint. And when the European Union exercises its power to ban hate speech or regulate copyrighted content, we are all subject to its rulings regardless of where we live.

5

Extremism Calls for Extreme Measures

Every tweet has the potential to radicalize vulnerable people.
—Commander Dean Haydon of the Counter Terrorism
Command, Metropolitan Police Service (UK)

On an unusually hot spring day in 2019, I sat in a small but fantastically appointed room at the Organisation for Economic Cooperation and Development in Paris, listening intently as New Zealand's prime minister, Jacinda Ardern, described the impact of the right-wing attack on two mosques in Christchurch two months prior. The shooting, which killed fifty-one people and left fifty more injured, had devastated the city's close-knit Muslim community, and Ardern's government had moved quickly to enact reforms, banning military-style semi-automatic and assault rifles within a month.

The shooter—a twenty-eight-year-old white supremacist of Australian nationality—had live-streamed footage of the attack to Facebook, which was quickly shared across numerous platforms. The video, shot from the perspective of a first-person video game, was designed to be performative, to terrorize those who inadvertently stumble upon it and titillate those who share the killer's poisonous ideology.

In the immediate aftermath, three of New Zealand's major ISPs had blocked access to sites found to be hosting the video, and the country's Office of Film and Literature Classification had classified the video as "objectionable," effectively criminalizing its distribution, with penalties of up to fourteen years' imprisonment for individuals or six-figure fines for corporations. Facebook, YouTube, Reddit, and other companies removed the footage from their platforms, though it quickly cropped up elsewhere across the Web.

Although social media companies worked to self-police the video and related content, New Zealand's government acted swiftly to convene an international meeting in Paris, inviting officials from other governments, tech companies, and civil society. There they launched the Christchurch Call, aimed at eliminating violent extremist content online. It opens with the statement, "A free, open and secure internet is a powerful tool to promote connectivity, enhance social inclusiveness and foster economic growth," and it outlines a set of voluntary commitments for governments and online service providers, from strengthening the resilience of societies to ensuring the effective enforcement of existing laws. At the time of its publication, the Call's supporters included eighteen governments and more than half a dozen tech companies.

Before the prime minister's arrival, I had gazed around the room of Western academics and anti-terrorism advocates, listened to a series of unexceptional remarks by government officials, and resigned myself to the idea that this might be yet another meeting filled with hand-wringing over the specter of online extremism and proposals that could, undoubtedly, have a deleterious effect on free expression. I scribbled thoughts in the margins of my notebook, anticipating another dog and pony show like the one that had followed the attack on the *Charlie Hebdo* office four years before.

But the moment Ardern entered the room, the atmosphere shifted. She waited quietly at the side of the room until others had finished their addresses, then joined the officials at the center of the room to give her own. She pulled no punches: condemning the attack in the strongest of terms, she described her own experience of stumbling upon the killer's footage on her social media feed, and shared harrowing statistics on how many New Zealanders had called the country's mental health helpline in the days following the massacre. She spoke boldly and earnestly, admitting to not knowing all the answers but with the conviction that something must be done to stem the tide of online extremism.

After her formal address, Ardern took over moderation of the session, asking the room to weigh in on the Call. She sat attentively, legs crossed, her hand resting on her chin as she listened to researchers critique the proposal. Surprisingly, the forty or so us gathered in that room found ourselves in overwhelming agreement: while everyone recognized that social media is increasingly being used to recruit and radicalize people into extremist ideologies, precious few believed that internet companies were going to solve the problem, and almost no one expressed a belief that censorship was an effective solution.

Ardern's actions that day felt unprecedented. Over the past decade, I have watched as countless governments have cynically utilized terrorist attacks as a pretense to enact ever-more-repressive measures against their citizens. From the United Kingdom's obsession with closed-circuit television monitoring systems to the cynical "Paris unity march" that brought together democrats and tyrants alike to proclaim "*Je suis Charlie*," the specter of terrorism has all too often served as cover for governments seeking to exert more control.

Ardern's honesty about how the video had affected her disarmed me, as did her willingness to admit frankly that she did not have all the answers. And yet, despite her sincerity, I was struck by the feeling that the Christchurch Call was not all that different from previous efforts—driven by emotion and the urge to "do something," leading to the same blindness toward civil liberties that had defined the majority of responses to terrorist attacks over the past decades.

Those who use terror to advance their ideologies have always sought an audience because, without one, their attacks lack meaning. Television once provided terrorist actors with a medium to spread their message and provoke sympathy or fear: images from the 1972 Munich Olympics, viewed by an estimated 900 million viewers worldwide, or the 9/11 attacks, shown over and over on international broadcasts for days, are indelibly stamped in our brains, reminding us of humankind's potential for evil. But while television requires the cameras to be rolling and aimed properly, social media provides any extremist with their own free platform.

The logic pushed by state actors and tech companies, then, is that by taking away the tools, we deprive extremists of their reach, thus disabling their ability to gather, to recruit, and, heaven forbid, to broadcast their attacks for the world to see.

The widespread recognition of a correlation between terror attacks and social media came in 2008 when, after an attack in Mumbai, the media took note of how locals were using Twitter to share information about the attack and send pleas for people to donate blood to local hospitals. CNN even quoted one Twitter user as saying, "Mumbai is not a city under attack as much as it is a social media experiment in action."[1]

But while ordinary citizens were using the medium for good, terrorist groups had also taken notice of social media's potential for amplifying their messages, and by the end of the aughts, politicians had as well. In a 2008 letter to then Google CEO and chairman Eric Schmidt, US senator Joseph Lieberman wrote:

> According to testimony received by our Committee, the online content produced by al-Qaeda and other Islamist terrorist organizations can play a significant role in the process of radicalization, the end point of which is the planning and execution of a terrorist attack. YouTube also, unwittingly, permits Islamist terrorist groups to maintain an active, pervasive, and amplified voice, despite military setbacks or successful operations by the law enforcement and intelligence communities. YouTube posts "community guidelines" for users to follow, but it does not appear that the company is enforcing these guidelines to the extent they would apply to this content.[2]

The senator further implored Schmidt to take action, claiming that in doing so, Google would be making "a singularly important contribution to this important national effort."[3]

YouTube responded publicly on its company blog, explaining to readers that "hundreds of thousands of videos are uploaded to YouTube every day" and that "because it is not possible to pre-screen this much content," they rely on their users to flag anything that could be in violation of the rules. The company stated that they removed videos Lieberman had identified that contained graphic violence, hate speech, and other forbidden content, but that "most of the videos, which did not contain violent or hate speech content, were not removed because they do not violate our Community Guidelines." It further noted: "While we respect and understand [Lieberman's] views, YouTube encourages free speech and defends everyone's right to express unpopular points of view."[4]

Lieberman's entreaty to Schmidt was his first, but was not his last. The senator soon made a name for himself appealing to social media platforms to censor otherwise constitutionally protected speech. Less than a year later, his staff famously pressured Amazon to cut off services to WikiLeaks, but for the most part, Lieberman's focus remained on terrorism. In 2011, a year after an attempted car bombing was thwarted by New York authorities and the attacker found to have had a Blogger account, Lieberman called for Google to add a system for users to flag content as "terrorist." Not long after that, the senator appealed to Twitter to remove accounts belonging to the Afghan Taliban.

The decision to go after the Taliban was particularly notable: unlike al-Qaeda, the Afghan Taliban isn't officially considered a terrorist group by the US government. This may seem odd, given its history of violence, but the process through which a given group receives such a designation may provide an explanation.

In accordance with Section 219 of the Immigration and Nationality Act of 1965, the US Department of State keeps a list of designated foreign terrorist organizations, or FTOs. The criteria are clear: an organization must be foreign, engaged in terrorist activity, and that activity must threaten the security of the United States or its nationals. The manner in which a group lands on the list is inherently political: the secretary of state, who is appointed by the president, can name any group to the list that fulfills the criteria. They must then notify relevant members of Congress, and the designation must be published in the Federal Register. After 9/11, additional regulations contained within the Patriot Act meant that those deemed to be providing "material support" to terrorist groups on the list would be subject to criminal sanctions.

Congress or the secretary of state can revoke a designation, however, and in 2012, following a lengthy and expensive lobbying campaign that included payments to journalists and elected politicians, support from Congress, and a lawsuit from the group in question, Secretary of State Hillary Clinton did just that.

The Mujahedin-e Khalq, or MEK, is an Iranian militant organization that advocates for the overthrow of the Iranian leadership and is one of the country's largest and most active opposition groups. Its members also have a sordid history of violence that includes the killing of two US air force officers in 1975; the bombing of the headquarters of Iran's ruling party in 1981, killing seventy-four people; and an alliance with Saddam Hussein during the Iran-Iraq War. They have been called a "cult" by former members, and Human Rights Watch has extensively documented abuses inside the group's camps.[5] They're also known for trying to sue their critics into silence.

In the mid-aughts, the MEK began campaigning to be removed from terrorist lists, and in 2007, they achieved their first success when a London tribunal ruled for their removal. In 2008, they were officially removed from the UK's national list, and a year later, from the European Union's. Getting removed from the US list took a bit more effort—and money.

In 2006, in a piece that dubbed the MEK "the monsters of the left," the editor of the right-of-center *Middle East Quarterly* suggested that it was an "anti-Semitic and partisan-driven" conspiracy theory to suggest that the MEK had support in Washington's power centers.[6] And yet, in the very center of power, the White House, then vice president Dick Cheney had already shown support for the group, arguing along with the secretary of defense, Donald Rumsfeld, that the MEK should be used as a pawn against the Iranian government.

As neoconservatives ramped up their fervor against Iran, the MEK worked to improve their image in the United States. In the years leading up to the group's de-listing, Iranian American groups paid hundreds of thousands of dollars to lobby groups to advocate for human rights in Iran—and that request included the de-listing of the MEK from the FTO list. One leader of Colorado's Iranian American community paid nearly $1 million to Washington firm DLA Piper to get the group unbanned, while his brother paid to fly a member of Congress, Bob Filner, to meet with MEK leaders in Paris. Former

New York City mayor Rudy Giuliani—who, it should be noted, made his name by condemning terrorism in the wake of 9/11—accepted money to speak at an MEK event. Journalists from the *Washington Post* and the *Chicago Tribune* reportedly received money from the group. While some individuals faced scrutiny and legal charges from the US government for this work, most escaped notice.

Between 2007 and 2012, five Iranian nuclear scientists were assassinated using sophisticated methods that experts said pointed to Israel. The Iranian government claimed that MEK members were receiving training from the Israelis, while two anonymous US officials confirmed the MEK's involvement to NBC News. While, under normal circumstances, this might be cause for condemnation, numerous conservative pundits praised the assassinations and the unsavory alliance, their hatred for and opposition to the Iranian government so great as to throw all moral conviction out the window.

In the end, the MEK and its allies in Washington won out. Although for some the group's removal from the list was a just end, for many it demonstrated the political and at times arbitrary nature of the FTO list and the prosecution of those whose actions are deemed to be material support. In the wake of the MEK's de-banning, journalist and pundit Glenn Greenwald decried what he saw as the "separate justice system in the US for Muslim Americans," stating that "it is hardly an exaggeration to say that any Muslim who gets within sneezing distance of such a group is subject to prosecution." He further called the act of de-listing "simply a way the US rewards those who comply with its dictates and punishes those who refuse."[7]

Terrorism, as scholar Lisa Stampnitzky has documented, was once viewed as the product of grievances, a tool, and one that could be used both by opposition forces and established regimes. But within a short period that definition shifted within the US government to one that cast terrorism as purely an activity of sub-state actors. "The discourse of counterinsurgency was based upon a mode of knowledge production in which moral, political, and rational evaluations of insurgents and insurgency were (at least in theory) separable from expert/scientific analyses," writes Stampnitzky. "Within the new discourse of 'terrorism,' however, the morality, politicality, and rationality of political violence would come to be strongly intertwined with the production and evaluation of experts and expertise."[8]

So what expertise do internet companies have or rely upon to make decisions about terrorist content? Do they rely on lists issued by the United States or other governments, or do they create their own guidelines? And how do external actors play into their decisions about what constitutes a terrorist organization?

The answer, it turns out, is not so clear. Over the years, as pressure has mounted from politicians, terrorism "experts," and even the State Department, tech companies have modified their policies to adapt to the changing environment. Whereas once upon a time, YouTube defended the free speech rights of al-Qaeda, today the company's policy is to remove any content produced by government-listed terrorism organizations—even if the public might have an interest in seeing that material.

What might seem like an implausible consideration today was, in the not-so-distant past, an important one for companies trying to balance free speech considerations with concerns for their own legal, ethical, and moral responsibility.

"I remember going through the process of looking through [videos] and there are men in fatigue running around the desert with guns, and they look identical to US army recruitment videos," recalls Nicole Wong. "Sometimes [both] would show them blowing things up. Sometimes it's not clear to me where the call to action is but also where I make this distinction based on the content alone. Ask someone who's not a trained lawyer to make that distinction in a way that will be consistent, principled, in the long term …," she said, trailing off, as if acknowledging the impossibility of the task.

In 2011, Twitter was forced to grapple with such questions amid a spate of violent attacks—and tweets—from Somali group al-Shabab.

Unlike its contemporaries, Twitter began as something of a lawless Wild West. The company's earliest terms of service were remarkably brief; the only verboten content was spam, and the sole admonition was not to "abuse, harass, threaten, impersonate or intimidate" other users. A subsequent version of the terms released in 2010 listed just a few more limitations, including impersonation, "direct, specific threats of violence," and illegal activity. Pornography was implicitly allowed—though banned from use in profile photos or background images—and the terms further included pithy "tips" like, "What you say on Twitter may be viewed all around the world instantly. You are what you Tweet!" Because of this—and, no doubt, because of the platform's simplicity and open architecture—a number of groups on the FTO list, including al-Shabab, took an early shine to it.

Al-Shabab was formed when Somalia's Islamic Courts Union—which had once controlled large swaths of southern Somalia—splintered into several factions after its defeat by the country's transitional federal government in 2006. Two years later, the group was added to the FTO list and by 2010, US officials were claiming that al-Shabab had recruited more than twenty Americans. With native English speakers among their ranks, al-Shabab's use of Twitter proved to be savvy. As the group battled for control of Somalia, it used the platform to disparage oncoming troops and to spar with a major in the Kenyan military. The *New York Times* was confounded, calling the group's use of the platform an "almost downright hypocritical move" and writing that "the Shabab have vehemently rejected Western practices … only to embrace Twitter, one of the icons of a modern, networked society"—but recognized that the group's shrewdness was part of a growing trend.[9]

That trend, which had begun with al-Qaeda and spread to its affiliates in Africa, soon found its way to Syria, Libya, and beyond as the hope that had just a few years before spread throughout the region was replaced with overwhelming violence.

Google takes a turn

Less than two months after Syrians began protesting in 2011, the media started to predict civil war. Demonstrations in Daraa were met with government violence, captured on video and uploaded to the internet for the world to see. The escalating violence in Syria—as well as in Libya—received only sparse coverage from global media, and as a result, Facebook and YouTube became the lenses through which the world viewed the conflicts.

Despite having defended the right to host content uploaded by terrorist groups, YouTube's parent company Google had historically drawn the line at graphic violence. But in light of the minimal access and coverage from traditional media and calls from the public to keep content online, the platform made an exception. In May 2011, You-Tube's manager of news, Olivia Ma, stated that despite many videos violating the platform's policies, "we have a clause in our community guidelines that makes an exception for videos that are educational, documentary, or scientific in nature … So, we will actually adjust our policies in real time to adapt to situations."[10]

The policy shift was welcomed by human rights activists, but its subjective nature meant that not all videos were kept online, at least not without a fight. One such video to emerge from Syria early on documented the alleged torture of slain thirteen-year-old Hamza Ali Al-Khateeb, whose face became a symbol for opposition activists in the country.

The video, which was posted to YouTube and immediately went viral, showed Al-Khateeb's battered remains, while a narrator describes in graphic detail the damage to his young body.[11] The footage was broadcast on Al Jazeera and into Syria, but it didn't last long on YouTube. Just a few days after the video was uploaded, the plat-form removed it, citing its policy against "shocking and disgusting content."[12] The video was restored after the *Nation* contacted YouTube. I was quoted at the time saying: "I think it often takes a high-level complaint to get their attention. I don't totally blame them, as I imagine they're flooded with appeals."[13]

In 2011, there were "less than 100" content reviewers at YouTube, according to Alex, one of the handful of people I interviewed who worked there at the time. According to former employees, the com-pany's trust and safety team, internally called "the Squad," managed both legal and policy complaints, and employed a number of language specialists to handle requests from around the world. "The volume [of flagged videos] at that time meant that every single video that was flagged and needed review could be reviewed by a native Arabic speaker," Alex told me.

When Alex joined YouTube in 2011, the company had recently

reversed its stance on allowing speech from US-designated terrorist groups. In the wake of calls to remove videos of American-born Yemen-based cleric Anwar al-Awlaki, YouTube's then director of global policy Victoria Grand (who later held similar roles at Facebook and WhatsApp) stated in an email to the *New York Times* that the company had removed videos "'registered by a member of a designated foreign terrorist organization,' or used to promote such a group's interests."[14]

Before 2011, enforcing YouTube's policies against violent extremist and "terrorist" content was not so difficult. Most of the content being posted by members of al-Qaeda, al-Shabab, and other designated terrorist organizations was in general clearly identifiable as such. Although identifying "newsworthy" graphic violence was more complicated, before the Arab uprisings, such content was far less common on the platform. But as mobile phones with video capabilities became more ubiquitous, so too did the amount of violence caught on camera.

That year for YouTube represented "an inflection point of, 'Oh, we're not just a home video platform, we can't just take this stuff down,'" said Alex, who saw videos coming out of Syria during their early days at the company. "There was so much content. I saw a lot of awareness in the videos," they recollected. "The camera person would be saying, 'Here we are in Deir Ezzor' and [showing] the date … it was easy to decide to leave that content up."

But as for the content being taken down, Alex recalled being less worried about censorship and more concerned that important content was disappearing into a black hole. "When companies remove child sexual abuse imagery, it goes to NCMEC [National Center for Missing and Exploited Children][15] and someone can follow up, but with [these videos], there's nobody that decides, 'This is a human rights violation, someone should have this.'" Alex described one video from Syria in which a teenage boy's face was unrecognizable after a bombing. "You'll remember that for the rest of your life."

During that period, human rights groups began meeting with YouTube's policy staff about building a clearinghouse to ensure some means of preservation for the human rights–oriented content that was removed from the platform. There was also talk of creating a vetted channel specifically for human rights content. Neither ever materialized. "I don't know ... if anything ever came of [the human rights repository], but I hope that it does someday," said Alex. They described their experience with the violent content as lonely. "[You can] feel that you're the only one and that nothing's happening."

This is where the system breaks down. In its early days, a social media platform instituted a basic set of rules for how to behave, and the relatively small number of people posting to it *do* behave, mostly. Those who do not are quickly identified, and action is taken against their content or account. But as a platform grows—slowly at first, then exponentially—it becomes more and more difficult to police every item, every action. Eventually, it becomes impossible to moderate content at scale.

Companies are by now aware of this, but continue even now to fight a losing battle by instituting new policies, processes, and technologies —a strategy that has often appeared to me like throwing spaghetti at a wall and hoping it will stick. Users, including extremists, saw the writing on the wall much sooner, and reacted faster. They began tagging controversial content using popular but unrelated hashtags and re-uploading videos that were taken down under different names, and then repeating the process multiple times in a cat-and-mouse game that the companies didn't seem agile enough to win. The posters' grasp on social media was simply better than that of the government and corporate executives.

This was made abundantly clear in 2013 when, following its attack on a Nairobi shopping mall, al-Shabab turned to Twitter to boast about the attack, taunt the Kenyan military, and threaten more mayhem. Twitter repeatedly shut down the group's accounts, but as in a game of Whac-A-Mole, new ones simply sprang up in their place. Astute observers noted the difference between the group's tweets in English—clearly designed to grab headlines—and those in Somali, which were tailored to a domestic audience. Critics also noted the Kenyan military's poor online communications, which were ripe for al-Shabab to undermine.[16]

The Somali group—today an afterthought in the global media— undoubtedly paved the way for what was yet to come. Its use of social media to grab headlines, recruit new members, and shock the populace undoubtedly drew the close attention of other groups with similar goals.

In late June of 2014, Jama'at al-Tawhid wal-Jihad—which had emerged in the late 1990s, had pledged allegiance to al-Qaeda after the US invasion of Iraq, and was operating primarily in that country—proclaimed itself a worldwide caliphate, declaring religious and political authority over Muslims worldwide and rebranding as the Islamic State (ISIS).[17] The group was already organized and internet-savvy, publishing annual reports detailing its operations. The *Financial Times* compared ISIS to a corporation in its "level of precision," noting that the aim of the reports "appears to be to demonstrate its record to potential donors."[18]

Even before the caliphate's official launch, the media took notice of its online acumen and pieces with titles like "ISIS Fighters and Their Friends Are Total Social Media Pros," and "The Sophisticated Social Media Strategy of ISIL," in which the reporter described how "extremists of all stripes are increasingly using social media to recruit, radicalize and raise funds, and ISIS is one of the most adept practitioners of this approach."[19]

"One day, we woke up and there were millions of pieces of ISIS content," recalls Maria, who worked at Facebook at the time. A piece from the *Guardian* explains why:

> Thousands of their Twitter followers installed an app—called the Dawn of Glad Tidings—that allows Isis to use their accounts to send out centrally written updates. Released simultaneously, the messages swamp social media, giving Isis a far larger online reach than their own accounts would otherwise allow. The Dawn app pumps out news of Isis advances, gory images, or frightening videos like Swords IV—creating the impression of a rampant and unstoppable force.[20]

Although the app gave ISIS's following an inflated appearance, the group was nevertheless actively working to attract new followers using social media, employing techniques such as utilizing clips from the popular, and extremely violent, video game *Grand Theft Auto* in recruitment videos.[21]

At first, companies appeared to be floundering, with no consistent strategy for countering the dizzying amount of ISIS propaganda popping up across social media—that is, until one event changed everything ... the beheading of James Foley in northwestern Syria by ISIS, broadcast across social media for the world to see.

Foley, a journalist working with Agence France-Presse and GlobalPost at the time of his death, grew up just a few towns away from me, and news of his death hit our home state hard. Foley had been captured in late 2012, and his captors had demanded a multi-million-dollar ransom for his release. While GlobalPost reportedly spent millions trying to secure his release, the United States government refused to negotiate, instead attempting a military rescue.[22] That attempt failed, as ISIS had moved their captives, and on August 19, 2014, ISIS brutally beheaded the journalist on camera.

Like YouTube, Facebook had previously made the controversial decision to allow beheading videos to remain up, provided there was sufficient context.[23] Until Foley's murder, most videos of that variety had been filmed in faraway places, with unknown victims—perhaps making it easier for policymakers to justify allowing them to remain online. Now, calls from the public—as well as from Foley's family— caused them to reconsider. Faced with significant public pressure, Twitter and YouTube caved and banned the video from being shared.[24] A Facebook spokesperson stated that policy already did not permit terrorist groups, or any person or group, to "promote terrorism or share graphic content for sadistic purposes."[25] Mainstream media outlets also shied from publishing stills.

While public sentiment largely favored this outcome, some experts dissented. Walter Reich, the former director of the United States Holocaust Memorial Museum, expressed the importance of bearing witness, arguing for intermediate measures by companies: "Warnings should be posted about the violence; the public should have the choice of watching or not watching. But if they want to watch, they should be able to do so—and learn something important in the process."[26] *Boston Globe* columnist Jeff Jacoby concurred, writing: "The least we can do is bear witness to the courage and dignity with which he met his awful end."[27]

Alex, who worked at YouTube, said they went "back and forth" on where the company should land. Among their concerns was the fact that, while Foley's story would be covered regardless, many of the graphic videos being uploaded to the platform depicted executions of victims who were not readily identifiable. This fact weighed heavily on Alex.

"When no one knows, what do you do?" they lamented. "There was this one seventeen-minute video that wasn't famous and wasn't a white person being beheaded. There were five people brutally beheaded. It was one of the ones where if we took it down, no one would know. You think, 'If I'm hit by a bus tomorrow, this piece of history will just be lost forever.'"

And therein lies one of the core problems with how Silicon Valley policymakers have dealt with graphic and extremist violence. When videos of beheadings began to emerge from Syria in 2011, with nameless victims, keeping them up was deemed "newsworthy." But when an American's death was broadcast to the world, that calculation changed. The fact that Foley's family had spoken out in favor of banning the video from being shared certainly matters; but what about the Syrian victims whose families had no way of reaching YouTube, let alone mainstream media?

More importantly, the shift in policy was not coupled with any real effort to preserve content by developing a sealed-off archive on the site. That too weighed heavily on Alex, who said: "When companies remove child sexual abuse imagery, it goes to the National Center for Missing and Exploited Children and someone can follow up, but [with these videos], there's no body that decides, 'This is a human rights violation, someone should have this.'"

Alex and I discussed YouTube's aborted attempt to create a clearing-house for such content and their disappointment that nothing came of it. Said Alex: "I hope it does someday. Even from a content reviewer's perspective, it's horrible to know [that something has happened], and feel that you're the only one and that nothing will come of it."

* * *

As the conflict in Syria wore on, YouTube filled up with hours upon hours of video uploaded from inside the country, much of it key documentation in the absence of professional journalism. As one staffer from a big tech firm stated in a 2018 talk: "You have more hours of footage of the Syrian civil war on YouTube then there actually are hours of the war in real life."[28]

Of course, among the documentation of chemical weapons attacks and barrel bombs, first-person narratives, and community protests were countless videos from ISIS and other extremist groups, showcasing their brutality or urging young people to join them. The decision making around the James Foley video, difficult at the time, was undoubtedly comparatively simple for Silicon Valley's policymakers: it concerned a single, easily-identifiable video of a clear crime.

One 2017 opinion piece from Washington D.C. daily the *Hill* accused US efforts to monitor and counter ISIS's use of social media of being "tentative, hesitant and amateurish," and recommended that the government "immediately move to hijack ISIS's own narratives and create alternatives."[29] But President Trump was far too busy waging war on his country's own media, leaving Silicon Valley with the Herculean task of countering and combating ISIS online, alone.

Nonetheless, as demands from the public and media to *do something* about ISIS grew, Facebook took initiative. In June 2017, the company announced that it was going to introduce artificial intelligence to help remove extremist content. The *New York Times* reported: "Artificial intelligence will largely be used in conjunction with human moderators who review content on a case-by-case basis. But developers hope its use will be expanded over time, said Monika Bickert, the head of global policy management at Facebook."[30]

I was quoted in the same piece, and in it I raised some questions: "Will it be effective or will it overreach? … Are they trying to discourage people from joining terrorist groups to begin with, or to discourage them from posting about terrorism on Facebook?" As it turns out, Facebook's strategy—using artificial intelligence to identify and remove videos and imagery posted by or in praise of extremist groups like ISIS—was more attuned to the latter.

Of course, moderating images and video is simply much easier than moderating text, particularly the kind that occurs in more closed-off spaces like Facebook groups or private messages. In order to identify an inappropriate image, a machine learning algorithm is trained using similar images. For example, such an algorithm, provided with enough photographs of flowers, will be able to identify other images that contain flowers with ease. But "extremist imagery" doesn't entail pictures of flowers; context is everything. An image of a beheading is obvious, but a picture of an explosion could be the boasting of a terrorist group or a key document of human rights abuse. And when Facebook—followed by YouTube and others—began using artificial intelligence to combat extremism, says Dia Kayyali: "People started seeing hundreds of thousands of videos erased."

Kayyali (who uses "they" as a pronoun) works for WITNESS, a non-profit organization with a mission to help people "use video and technology to protect and defend human rights." In 2017, Kayyali became aware that the same algorithms being used to tackle extremism were also taking down vital documentation of the Syrian conflict: "There's been a large range of content actually removed ... that includes videos of protest, videos of chemical weapons attacked, videos filmed by perpetrators of human rights abuses—for example, a video filmed by ISIS showing them killing people," they told me over coffee at their Berlin office.

Human rights groups like WITNESS were among the first to take notice that essential documentation was disappearing. Just a few months after companies began using artificial intelligence to tackle extremism, the *Intercept* published a lengthy piece that accused Facebook and YouTube of removing evidence of atrocities and jeopardizing cases against war criminals. The piece quoted Kayyali as well as experts at Human Rights Watch, UC Berkeley's Human Rights Center, and a group, little known at the time, called Syrian Archive, with whom Kayyali and I would later co-author a paper. All these groups stepped in to do the thing these companies failed to do: preserve evidence.[31] Since the YouTube plan for a multi-company clearinghouse to preserve human rights content never came to fruition, frustrated Syrians had no option but to build their own.

Syrian Archive was founded to document and preserve evidence of war crimes, but its staff soon found themselves spending an increasing amount of time battling YouTube. Thanks to their connections with human rights groups, they were able to make contact with the company early on to send it information on videos that should be restored—and although YouTube was responsive in most cases, the videos would soon be removed again.

In some cases, Syrian Archive struggled to get videos restored at all. Hadi Al Khatib, one of the group's founders, told the *Intercept*, "Some of what we collect is the only thing that is left indicating that a crime took place." As one of his examples, he described video evidence of a Russian airstrike on the countryside near Idlib that he said targeted civilians. "This was quite crucial," he said. "It was a violation of international law and, until now, we can't get it restored."[32]

Social media evidence can be a key asset for prosecuting war criminals. In 2017, the International Criminal Court issued an arrest warrant for Libyan military commander Mahmoud Mustafa Busayf al-Werfalli that was based on video evidence plucked from Facebook.[33] Al-Werfalli was accused of directly ordering the execution of thirty-three people. His arrest warrant states that evidence for seven of those incidents is based on video and transcripts of video posted to his social media profiles.[34]

Human rights organizations have rightly expressed their frustrations with platform policies that contradict how platforms have been promoted in the past. Alexa Koenig, the executive director of UC Berkeley's Human Rights Center, has pointed out that, after the 2011 uprisings, companies encouraged people to use their platforms for documentation. "They held themselves up as arbiters of social good," said Koenig, "and at that point of creating dependency, I would argue they acquired a heightened responsibility."[35]

It is not just documentation of crimes that we're losing, as Kayyali points out: it's also history. "The impact we talk about less is cultural and psychological," they told me. "I'm Syrian, and I've also heard many other Syrians talk about the feeling that people don't care about what's happening and that we have to preserve documentation of what's happening because it is the only record. So there is a very real impact ... of knowing that this stuff's being deleted and feeling like our history is being deleted and adding to this feeling that the world doesn't care about Syria and the world doesn't care that these videos are deleted."

Three years later, Syrian Archive is still fighting with YouTube and Facebook, while smaller, lesser-known groups are rarely able to even reach the companies. In the face of rising extremism, Silicon Valley has turned inward, become even more opaque.

Jacinda Ardern's Christchurch Call, issued in response to an attack by a white supremacist terrorist, could have worked with civil society to develop new and innovative solutions, but instead turned to the usual suspects—in this case, Facebook, Google, Microsoft, and Twitter, the four companies that make up the Global Internet Forum to Counter Terrorism, or GIFCT.

The GIFCT emerged in the summer of 2017 as an industry-led initiative started with the objective of "disrupting terrorist abuse of members' digital platforms."[36] The group's work is organized into three pillars: joint tech innovation, research, and knowledge sharing. Among the knowledge-sharing efforts is perhaps the most controversial and opaque GIFCT initiative: a shared "hash" database of "violent terrorist imagery and propaganda."

The database collects hashes—unique digital fingerprints—for videos or images that member companies have defined as terroristic under their own policies. Other member companies can then utilize the database to identify and block the same content on their services. In short, if one company decides that a particular video constitutes violent extremist or terrorist content and takes it down, any other company using the database will also remove that same video—without being able to see what it contains.

Free expression and human rights organizations have been critical of the GIFCT from its inception, and have repeatedly asked for more transparency about the database from the initiative and its member companies. In a February 2019 letter to the European Parliament, more than 35 organizations and individual experts wrote that lawmakers and the public 'have no meaningful information about how well the Database or any other existing filtering tool serves this goal, and at what cost to democratic values and individual human rights," and urged the Parliament to reject proactive filtering requirements such as those laid out in the proposed EU terrorism regulation.[37]

In late 2019 the GIFCT announced that it would be establishing itself as a non-profit organization, independent from the companies that founded it, and would establish an independent advisory committee (IAC) inclusive of "civil society, government, and inter-governmental entities."[38] Prominent digital and human rights organizations—including Human Rights Watch, the Electronic Frontier Foundation, ACLU, and the Center for Democracy and Technology—balked at the inclusion of governments in the IAC as well as the lack of concern for human rights expressed in its mandate and in February 2020 submitted a private letter to the GIFCT's interim leadership detailing their concerns, including the risk of extra-legal censorship from government participation in the IAC, increasing use and scope of the hash database, "persistent lack of transparency around GIFCT activity," and a lack of focus on the protection of human rights.[39]

When the response from the GIFCT failed to address the groups' concerns, they published another letter, this time stating "GIFCT's prior lack of responsiveness to our critiques informed our decision to not apply to join the IAC, thus leaving the IAC composed almost entirely of government officials and academics."[40] Chief among the groups' apprehensions stated in the second letter were the increasingly blurry lines between counter-terrorism and content moderation, the companies' high error rates, and the reality that the GIFCT operates "in a complex global environment that lacks internationally agreed upon definitions of terrorism or extremist violence [and] where [right-wing violent extremism] is by and large not legally recognized."[41]

Indeed, the priority of the GIFCT database remains ISIS and al-Qaeda propaganda, meaning that it will have little effect on the kind of extremism the Christchurch Call was set up to counter. Furthermore, the opacity of the database prevents civil society from ensuring that the human rights of those most affected by both terrorism and counter-terrorism—that is, Arab and Muslim communities—are not doubly violated.

But the chief concern of an industry-wide database should be the inequity and bias with which "terrorist" content is already discovered and determined by companies. By and large, Silicon Valley tech companies rely on the US government to define "terrorism," and remove content from groups on the State Department's list of foreign designated terrorist organizations (FTOs). While I've heard staffers from Facebook suggest that doing so is a legal obligation, numerous lawyers I consulted with disagree. Just as the leader of a designated foreign terrorist organization can publish an opinion piece in the *New York Times*—they can and they have—so too can they publish a page on Facebook. There are exceptions to this rule—that is, if a group or individual also appears on the Treasury Department's Office of Foreign Asset Controls list of "specially designated nationals"—but this list is short.

Each company's policy differs slightly, but by and large, most platforms remove content from groups on that list (or that is in praise of them), while generally avoiding the word "terrorism" in their written policies.

Facebook's policy, for instance, makes use of the term "dangerous groups and organizations," a designation that includes terrorists, but also those participating in organized violence, human trafficking, and other destructive acts. In addition, the company's policy against depictions of graphic violence covers a broader range of potential content. YouTube's policy makes no mention of terrorist groups per se, but bans graphic violence. Both companies, however, regularly remove non-violent content from even lesser-known groups on the FTO list.

Interestingly, the Twitter Rules ban terroristic threats or the promotion of terrorism and violent extremism, noting that under the rules, "you can't affiliate with and promote the illicit activities" of terrorist groups—but notably, the rules also specify that there are "limited exceptions for groups that have reformed or are currently engaging in a peaceful resolution process, as well as groups with representatives who have been elected to public office through democratic elections. We may also make exceptions related to the discussion of terrorism or extremism for clearly educational or documentary purposes."[42] Twitter's policy seems to confirm the legality of hosting such speech.

That the speech of FTOs is legally protected matters little to US politicians, a number of whom have called on companies to deny them a platform, citing their status as FTOs. Senator Lieberman may have been the first, but he was by no means the last. Over the years, lawmakers in several countries have implored tech companies to go above and beyond the law to remove certain designated groups, in particular Hamas and Hezbollah—calls which have at times succeeded.[43] Most recently, a 2019 letter from sixteen members of US Congress to Twitter to ban Hamas resulted in the company caving, after first pushing back, and banning accounts from both groups.[44]

Whether these politicians lack understanding of the law or simply seek to circumvent it by using corporate regulations instead is unclear. But in the case of both Hamas and Hezbollah, we need to ask: What is the impact in Palestine and Lebanon, where these groups are powerful players in local politics—local politics that have no shortage of violent actors?

Azza El Masri is a media researcher from Lebanon who, for the past several years, has studied content moderation. "Is Hezbollah's involvement in Syria, Iraq, Yemen and its participation in the Iran-KSA proxy war tantamount to terrorist activities? Yes," she told me in a text message. "However, this doesn't absolve the fact that Hezbollah today is the most powerful political actor in Lebanon."

Lebanon's political scene is, to the outsider, messy and difficult to parse. After the fifteen-year civil war that killed hundreds of thousands, the country's parliament instituted a law that pardoned all political crimes prior to its enactment, allowing the groups that were formerly militias to form political parties. Only Hezbollah—an Iran-sponsored creation to unify the country's Shia population during the war—was allowed by the postwar Syrian occupation to retain its militia. The United States designated Hezbollah (which translates to "Party of God") a foreign terrorist organization in 1995, more than a decade after the group bombed US military barracks in Beirut. Other countries, such as the United Kingdom and the European Union—as well as Twitter—make the distinction between Hezbollah's military wing and its political arm—putting only the former on their blacklists—while still others do not list Hezbollah at all.

For better or worse, Hezbollah remains a major player in contemporary Lebanese politics, as El Masri points out, and the willingness of tech companies to cave to US pressure has an immeasurable impact on the country's political scene. "With all of these platforms having their headquarters in the West and their reliance on those lists to inform their policies related to extremist and dangerous groups, applying a universal view of terrorism to local complex contexts such as Lebanon's allows for the weaponization of these policies in the interest of one side of the political equation," she says. "The [de-platforming] of the group presents Hezbollah within a Western lens—as a terrorist group—and erases the political history of this group and its current participation in local and regional politics. This doesn't just mean in its dealing with Iran, but also in the context of representation at a governmental, parliamentary, and municipal level as well as in unions and syndicates."

Corporate policies often result not only in the removal of such groups, but also anyone who dares speak their name, says El Masri. "An alternative independent media platform has had several of its videos taken down on Facebook and YouTube for featuring [Hezbollah leader Hassan Nasrallah]—although they were not praising Hezbollah at all. The implications of these policies, which take on a Western purview, also pose a threat to the free speech of alternative media and independent actors."

Imagine, for a moment, an election scenario where every group except one is able to campaign on social media. Although El Masri says that social media currently plays a minor role in Lebanese electoral politics, the fact that it might in the future seems not to have been considered by Silicon Valley—or worse yet, dismissed. By banning certain violent groups and allowing others, Facebook will be able to effectively determine the outcome of an election in a sovereign nation.

That is, ultimately, what is so troubling about the increasing reliance by governments on corporate policies to accomplish what existing laws cannot. The US list is certainly political—and by many accounts deeply problematic—but what happens when less democratic countries start exerting authority within processes like the GIFCT? Will their definition of "terrorist" hold up in the court of international opinion?

As journalist Tom Risen pointed out back in 2014: "Another hurdle for social media sites working to remove objectionable posts is that governments of the different countries where they operate can vary in their motives when pushing for the content's removal."[45]

Indeed, we know that companies are responsive to the demands of authoritarian countries like Saudi Arabia, which in recent years has used anti-terrorism statutes to stifle dissent.[46] It is not difficult to imagine a scenario in which the country could effectively exert influence over a group like the GIFCT.

Today, the moderation of "terrorism" on social media exists far outside of existing norms around speech governance. Politicians who would otherwise cry "free speech!" in the face of content takedowns take no issue, without any sense of due process, of the speech of individuals who so much as mention a terrorist organization. Companies that otherwise participate in transparency initiatives regularly remove, en masse, alleged "terrorist" accounts on the basis of criteria they refuse to share. And while both companies have, in the past, have been criticized for defending the right of right-wing conspiracy theorists to spew misinformation and hate on their platforms, no one blinks when Twitter announces that it has banned another half a million so-called terrorist accounts.

While in general the governance of speech on social media has been on a trajectory of increased transparency and accountability, the policing of so-called terrorist speech is becoming more and more opaque, and decisions about policies are being made by elites, behind closed doors, absent the meaningful inclusion of civil society … and the communities likely to be most affected by such decisions.

6

Twenty-First-Century Victorians

For an entire generation of power-hungry, rich, straight white men, this is the way it goes then, in art as well as life: the female form exists as something to be viewed; to be controlled. It does not belong to a woman— it belongs to the men who line up to view her; to paint her; to possess her.

—Charlie Arthur

We restrict the display of nudity or sexual activity because some people in our community may be sensitive to this type of content.

—Facebook Community Standards (July 2019)

Michelangelo's marble sculpture of *David* is a masterpiece to behold. Stand below it, inside of Florence's crowded Galleria dell'Accademia, or underneath its replica outside the Palazzo Vecchio, and you will feel dwarfed by its towering presence. Your eyes will gaze up toward the chiseled figure, resting perhaps on David's perfect shoulders or abdominal muscles. You will likely glance quickly past the unremarkable genitalia, as your eyes are drawn to the perfection of David's veined hands or the musculature of his legs.

The statue, which took the young Michelangelo more than two years to finish, was first installed outside the entrance of the city's town hall in 1504. Almost immediately, some historians say, the local authorities covered David's genitals in a wreath of gold leaves.[1] Less than forty years later, the Catholic Church sought to censor Michelangelo's famous fresco, *Last Judgment*, eventually succeeding after his death when, after the Council of Trent, the Church hired Daniele da Volterra to cover the genitals of the men in the painting. Thus marked the beginning of the "fig leaf campaign," in which the genitalia of famous works of art—particularly statues—were sometimes chiseled off or simply covered with plaster fig leaves, a nod to the coverings used by Adam and Eve in the biblical Book of Genesis.

As the story goes, Adam and Eve were not ashamed when they entered the world. ("And they were both naked, the man and his wife, and were not ashamed.") Rather, it was only after eating the forbidden fruit that they became aware of their nakedness: "The eyes of them both were opened, and they knew that they were naked; and they sewed fig leaves together, and made themselves aprons." For non-believers, the story of Adam and Eve represents the beginning of shame as a culturally manufactured concept. Most intepretations of the parable believe it serves to teach believers to feel ashamed of their bodies, and view expressions of nudity as sinful.

The earliest photographs of David in Florence, from 1873, include the fig leaf. In 1857, a replica of the statue was presented by the Grand Duke of Tuscany to Queen Victoria, who placed it in the South Kensington Museum—adding a plaster fig leaf to "spare the blushes of visiting female dignitaries" (and, more likely than not, herself).[2] In more modern times, the statue or depictions of it have been covered up in places as far-flung as California, Sydney, and Jerusalem. Poor David has suffered the indignity of censorship many times over the course of the last several centuries.

One entity that seemingly has not censored David is Facebook, though anyone who remembers differently might be forgiven for thinking so. Over the years, the company has taken down works by some of the world's most renowned artists as a result of its restrictive policies barring nudity and other "adult" content, often in direct contradiction to written policy. The removal of artistic works from an online platform may be analogous to fig leaf censorship in some ways, but differs in one key aspect: whereas the fig leaf covers just a portion of a piece of art, modern censorship disappears it entirely.

It is impossible not to pause and note a unique parallel between Queen Victoria—the "Grandmother of Europe"—and Mark

Zuckerberg. The pervasive censorship and prudish morals of the Victorian era were not the result of one woman's particular disposition, as were the laws created during her tenure. Just as Queen Victoria is falsely attributed as setting a moral standard for an era, so too could Mark Zuckerberg be accused of the same, his childlike prudishness leading to a set of rules that are now accepted as canon by users of his platform, and copied by leadership of other companies.

David gets to stay on Facebook precisely because he has literally been canonized in the rules, recognized as a legitimate expression of nudity. The first iteration of Facebook's Community Standards, launched in 2011, read: "Facebook has a strict policy against the sharing of pornographic content and any explicitly sexual content where a minor is involved. We also impose limitations on the display of nudity. We aspire to respect people's right to share content of personal importance, whether those are photos of a sculpture like Michelangelo's David or family photos of a child breastfeeding." The naming of David in these early policies is what spared him from content moderators, who were undoubtedly trained with his image in mind, but other works of art have been less fortunate.

In 2011, an administrator at the New York Academy of Art was surprised to receive a stern warning notifying the school that its Facebook page was subject to a seven-day ban from uploading content. The reason? An ink drawing of a woman's nude upper body by one of the academy's graduate students, Steven Assael, had apparently run afoul of the company's standards. The message the academy received from Facebook stated that the company's policies are designed "to ensure Facebook remains a safe, secure and trusted environment for all users, including the many children who use the site."[3]

The academy blogged about the incident, writing that they "find it difficult to allow facebook to be the final arbiter—and online curator—of the artwork we share with the world."[4] In response to the press coverage, Facebook reversed the ban, with representatives referring to an "unwritten policy that allows drawings or sculptures of nudes." Company spokesperson Simon Axten further congratulated the artist on his "lifelike portrayal that, frankly, fooled our reviewers."[5]

The following year, the *New Yorker* ran afoul of the company's guidelines when editors posted a cartoon of Adam and Eve seated nude beneath a tree, their knees drawn up to their chests, with the caption, "Well, it *was* original." The nipples of both figures were quite literally pen dots, but Facebook temporarily banned the magazine's account on the grounds that the cartoon violated it policy on sexual content, in an incident the magazine's cartoon editor, Robert Mankoff, called "Nipplegate."[6]

In a piece on the incident, Mankoff quotes from a training document entitled "Abuse Standards Violations." A Moroccan employee of oDesk, an outsourcing firm and service provider to Facebook, had leaked the document to *Gawker* just half a year before. It offers internal guidelines for adjudicating all types of content. Under the heading "sex and nudity," the following restrictions are listed alongside ten others:

- Naked private parts, including female nipple bulges and naked butt cracks; male nipples are ok.
- Digital/cartoon nudity. Art nudity ok.[7]

A moderator viewing the *New Yorker*'s cartoon would have to parse through a set of twelve bullet points, each containing a handful of banned (or acceptable) items, and quickly determine whether the cartoon violates the rules. This list clearly bans cartoon nudity, but do the two dots really depict "bulging female nipples"? Mankoff didn't think so, and in the end, neither did the company—the magazine's ban was overturned.

Anna,* a longtime Facebook community operations staffer who has since left the company, told me that although the rule-making department is "moving to become more nuanced," a lot of the decisions made in the early part of the decade were, she says, "stupid." "[Training manuals] should be treated with more attention," she told me, "but there's very little time dedicated to this. [Community operations is] very much a department that functions in permanent chaos."

Although the decision that was handed to the New York Academy of Art should have set a precedent to prevent further censorship of artistic nudity, Facebook and its counterparts don't operate like courts; there is no case law, no checks and balances, and—until recently—no due process. The judges (content moderators) are not appointed or elected by voters, unlike in well-functioning democracies. There are simply no systems of accountability to the process and, as such, the same image that might be banned for one user can be allowed for another.

In 2011, *Le Monde* reported that a Danish artist had been banned from Facebook for posting a copy of Gustave Courbet's famous painting *L'Origine du Monde*, which depicts the lower half a woman's supine body, legs slightly spread to reveal just a hint of her labia beneath a puff of pubic hair.[8] As Victoria and the Church before her might have done, Facebook repeatedly deemed the painting inappropriate, and many users who posted it reported being banned.

For Parisian instructor Frédéric Durand-Baïssas, the ban on Courbet was a step too far. Like the Danish artist, Durand-Baïssas decided to signal boost *L'Origine du Monde*, only to find himself banned from Facebook—permanently. The primary school teacher decided to take the matter to court, accusing Facebook of having engaged in censorship and requesting the restoration of his account and 20,000 euros in damages. The case took seven years to resolve, and although the French court ruled that Facebook had failed to fulfill its contractual obligations by closing Durand-Baïssas's account without notice, the teacher lamented that the court had avoided the question of whether the takedown had violated his freedom of expression.[9]

A year before the resolution of the case, a set of leaked documents on Facebook's policies dealing with sex and nudity in art demonstrated the mental gymnastics involved in attempting to devise a coherent policy. Internally, the company distinguished between "handmade art"—in which depictions of both nudity and sexual acts were permitted—and digital art, in which only nudity and the "contours" of genitalia are permitted visibility.

The incongruity of the company's policies was finally laid bare. As one art journalist lamented, "Indeed, the nonsensical sense of Facebook content moderation takes shape in a set of art guidelines that consider painting, but not photography or video, 'real world art' and would, in theory, find Courbet's 'The Origin of the World' acceptable but not a digital print of a woman's butt."[10]

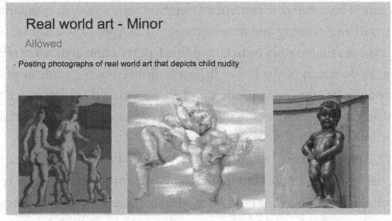

Source: *Guardian*

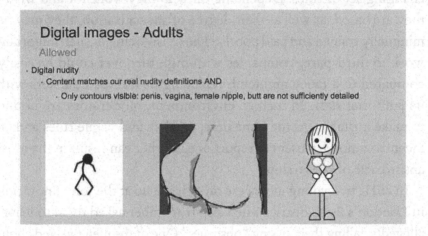

Between the time that Durand-Baïssas filed his case and when he received the final ruling, Facebook amended its policy to explicitly allow more artistic depictions of nudity—that is, "photographs of paintings, sculptures, and other art that depicts nude figures."[11] But in March 2018, Durand-Baïssas was dealt another blow when a higher court in France overturned the ruling. Still, the court reprimanded Facebook for not notifying the teacher with a full explanation as to why his account had been closed.

Mistakes will be made

Although US social media companies operate in a diverse set of global communities, moderating content in around fifty languages,[12] the amount of investment in content moderation teams pales in comparison to that of engineering and development, or mergers and acquisitions. This means that mainly outsourced third-party contractors are relied upon to do much of the heavy lifting to police the foundation of the companies' major innovation: a global, networked communications platform. This is not a coincidence, but rather a deliberate decision to prioritize expansion over core services.

These commercial content moderators are forced to make rapid-fire decisions about the content that comes through their queue. It's a grueling job: the average content moderator sees thousands of images every day and is forced to keep up with what seems like a constantly changing set of rules. Depending on who they work for and where they are based, as well as their degree of specialization, they may be minimally trained and paid poorly. The outsourcing of such important work to third-party companies with high turnover could be easily compared to a fancy nightclub replacing its trained bouncers with its janitorial staff. In such an environment, moderators are bound to make mistakes. At the same time, prudish and vague rules and an incentivization for users to report one another can result in the most absurd acts of censorship.

In 2011, two young men were on a first date at the John Snow pub in London's Soho district when a staff member asked them to leave, allegedly calling their kissing "obscene." One of the men tweeted about the incident, drawing the attention of national media. In response, a "kiss-in" was organized, with posts about it on Facebook drawing hundreds of attendees.

Richard Metzger is the former host of a television show on the UK's Channel 4 called *Disinformation* and blogs for the site *Dangerous Minds*. When one of his fellow bloggers posted about the kiss-in, including an image, he shared the event on his own wall. The image that he shared was a still from the BBC soap opera *EastEnders*, featuring two men sharing a tender kiss. In it, one man's hand grasps the other's cheek, their lips lightly touch … but that's about it. The other man's hand can be seen off to the side, palm open. There are no wayward hands, nothing scandalous or sexual about it. And yet, as Richard recalled in a blog post, when he awoke the next morning, the post was gone.

"I didn't really pay that much attention to the matter," he wrote, "but before we went to sleep that night, my wife ... mentioned that this heavy metal kinda guy 'Jerry' had written a bunch of childish and homophobic things about this picture on my Facebook wall, saying that he found it disgusting. The next morning I woke up around 6am to find a note from Facebook waiting for me with the ominous subject 'Facebook Warning' informing me that I had posted "abusive material" which they had removed."[13]

That warning, like so many others I've seen over the years, was incongruous with the actual rules at the time. It read:

Hello: Content that you shared on Facebook has been removed because it violated Facebook's Statement of Rights and Responsibilities. Shares that contain nudity, or any kind of graphic or sexually suggestive content, are not permitted on Facebook. This message serves as a warning. Additional violations may result in the termination of your account. Please read the Statement of Rights and Responsibilities carefully and refrain from posting abusive material in the future. Thanks in advance for your understanding and cooperation.[14]

The Statement of Rights and Responsibilities, replaced with the first iteration of the Community Standards later that same year, was a lengthy document created to complement the Terms of Service. It condensed, in the words of a Facebook Newsroom blog post, "40 pages of legal jargon into fewer than six pages."[15] At the time Metzger's post was removed, there was no mention of "sexually suggestive" content, just this sentence: "You will not post content that: is hateful, threatening, or pornographic; incites violence; or contains nudity or graphic or gratuitous violence."

But the kiss contained no nudity, and certainly no pornography. It was not violent, hateful, or threatening, nor was it "abusive." And, according to the document leaked to *Gawker*, it was not even in violation of Facebook's guidelines. At the time, reports suggested that if the kissing couple had been straight, the image would not have been taken down. In an interview with culture blog *Boing Boing*, Metzger noted that he did not believe the company to be homophobic, but blamed the system of community policing for the takedown. "The more I thought about it, the more this minor act of censorship bothered me," he said. "It seemed so small-minded. I wondered why Facebook would remove this rather innocuous photo and I was also pissed off that this 'Jerry' fellow … should be able to get something taken down from my wall simply because he's *a whiner*."[16]

Metzger's instinct of how it all went down is likely accurate: Jerry the homophobe likely clicked a button to report the content. Back then, he would have been offered a set of choices beginning with the option to "unfriend" or block Metzger, followed by a series of options for reporting the content that included "inappropriate wall post." Selecting that option would have taken Jerry to a second page asking "What best describes this?" and providing him with five options, one of which was "nudity, pornography, or sexually explicit content."

Jerry probably clicked that button, sending the report to a human content moderator. As we've seen, the public-facing rules at the time differed significantly from both the reporting options and the explanation that Metzger received—only the latter mentioned sexually *suggestive* content. And the content moderator, as we've learned, may have been looking at a different framing of the rules entirely.

As in the cases of the New York Academy of Art and the *New Yorker*, Metzger was able to use his public profile to attract media attention. Eventually, Facebook restored the photo of the kiss, apologizing, in a statement provided to a popular gay blog, for the "inconvenience" and clarifying that the decision was made in error.[17] However, over the years, the casualties of overzealous content moderation have ranged from run-of-the-mill to the utterly absurd, and include breastfeeding mothers; cupcakes iced to look like vulvas; a prehistoric statue of Venus and a sixteenth-century one of Neptune; Evelyne Axell's 1964 painting *Ice Cream*; Copenhagen's famous *Little Mermaid* sculpture; and a spoof of a classic advertisement for Coppertone sunscreen.

Among the more illogical, and ironic, casualties of social media in recent memory involves the young Canadian poet Rupi Kaur, who rose to prominence by sharing her art on Instagram. Kaur's poetry often addresses themes including abuse, femininity, and self-care. In 2015, as part of a final project for her undergraduate studies, Kaur, who has written poetry addressing the taboos of menstruation, posted to Instagram a series of photographs of herself with menstrual blood staining her clothes and sheets. Although the reaction from her online community was supportive, within a day the photos had been reported and removed.

In a 2016 interview with the Canadian Broadcasting Corporation (CBC), Kaur lamented: "How did somebody, like, a human being that came from a womb … how did this person sit there and think that this is unsafe? Instagram is like, full of pornography and visuals that are so unintelligent sometimes, that are so horrific and so harmful to us, and you're going to tell me that that's harmful?"

Kaur reposted the images, but they were removed again within eight hours. She then shared a screenshot with her followers of the message she'd received from Instagram, and posted angrily to Instagram, writing: "Thank you Instagram for providing me with the exact response my work was created to critique."[18] When she awoke the next morning, she recounted in the 2016 interview, the post had more than 4 million "likes" and her images had been restored to Instagram.

Kaur's persistence, as well as her public profile, prompted a response from the company, but most users are not so fortunate. As Sarah Myers West has observed, celebrities and other public figures are able to attract the attention of company executives through media attention. In one instance, Rihanna, participating in the #FreetheNipple campaign, posted a series of nude images of herself, each resulting in a temporary suspension from Instagram. Because of Rihanna's popularity, the suspension quickly drew media attention, and Instagram issued an apology to the singer, stating: "This account was mistakenly caught in one of our automated systems and very briefly disabled. We apologize for any inconvenience."[19] Sometimes the decision not to censor is simply a calculated business decision.

West recounts a similar story in which the subject was a maternity photographer, Heather Bays, whose account was disabled over a photo she'd posted of herself breastfeeding her young daughter. Bays "initially lacked the public platform to attract attention from the company to her case. Her account was only reinstated after she used other social media accounts to draw attention to the issue."[20]

These stories, as frustrating as they are to each individual they affected, are all the result of content moderation errors; they're mistakes, likely to be arbitrated today by utilizing the appeals processes offered by most companies. The majority of these stories have happy endings, but in nearly every case, those outcomes are owed to media or other attention. Most users, as West observes, lack such channels for resolution: "[Users] have relatively little recourse to seek accountability from the company within existing channels. Many social media platforms do offer some form of appeal to users when their content is taken down, but users often report they are unaware of this or are unsuccessful in seeing the content restored after appealing."[21]

Indeed, although appeals processes are now common, they rely on the same commercial content moderators for quick review and are not always an effective means of remedy. As Kate Klonick wrote after experiencing a Twitter suspension: "Despite all the shininess of new technology, so often getting suspended accounts or deleted posts restored works the good old-fashioned way: via influence, power, connections. It's an unfair system that favors elites and disfavors the average user who doesn't know someone at a technology company, or a government official, or someone with 100,000 followers."[22]

Nevertheless, the *New Yorker*, Metzger, Kaur, and the others had cause to accuse Facebook of prudishness, and they were not entirely wrong. Indeed, in every instance, it appears that personal bias resulted in the moderation errors. As Klonick articulates, "Content moderators ... came with their own cultural inclinations and biases."[23] In the early days, Facebook sought to mitigate bias through intensive in-person training of moderators. Klonick, a lawyer, notes that "training moderators to overcome cultural biases or emotional reactions in the application of rules to facts can be analogized to training lawyers or judges."[24]

Bias in content moderation is a difficult problem to overcome, whether stemming from the puritanical mind of a moderator or a lack of clarity in internal rulebooks and guidance. Companies cannot ask potential hires about their political proclivities or beliefs, nor can they necessarily share information that would help users understand why a particular error occurred. What they can do, however, is ensure that their internal rulebooks match their public-facing policies, be more transparent about their training processes, and release data on the number of false positives that occur across each subject area of their rules.

Censors and sensibilities

While Facebook's moderation of a gay kiss or a woman's menstrual blood might strike many users as censorious, the stance that Facebook and many of its contemporaries have taken when it comes to sexuality and the human body may be seen simply as a reflection of American values.

Courtney Demone grew up in the era of social media. The native of western Canada came out as trans in her early twenties while working for a web app company and writing the occasional freelance article. One afternoon, she recalled to me over Skype, she was sunbathing topless in her yard when one of her roommates said, half-jokingly: "Now that you're a girl, I shouldn't be able to see your nipples." In a now-famous piece for *Mashable*, she recounted how the incident stuck in her mind, prompting her to feel shame for her body that she hadn't felt before. "When people start to consistently see me as a woman," she wrote, "my privilege to be comfortably topless in public will be gone for good."[25]

The policing and sexualization of women's bodies is by no means a new phenomenon. In much of so-called Western society, the conflation of nudity with sex begins at a young age. We're taught that nude bodies are meant to be kept private, to be shown only at home, in front of our partners or perhaps our families. When skin is on display, whether in an advertisement for beer or in bikinis on the beach, it's most often sexualized. In the United States, women's semi-nude bodies are most often seen when they're being used to sell something.

This is not the case everywhere. For instance, in Germany, land of Freikörperkultur (free body culture), there are acceptable occasions for casual public nudity: at the sauna, in parks and at the lake, at the annual

Christopher Street Day parades. Calendars with sexualized (yet still relatively innocent) images of topless women are displayed in shops openly, sometimes at the eye level of children. At certain nightclubs in Berlin, men and women grace the dance floor clad only in shoes. Bodies are sometimes allowed to just be bodies, regardless of gender.

But not on Instagram, where Demone decided to try a little experiment to see how her changing body might be perceived. "We did a photoshoot and wrote [the *Mashable* article] and then I kept on posting as regularly as possible to see what would happen. It didn't last that long, it was about two or three months, and then Instagram and Facebook decided to pull everything—including the earliest ones before I'd started hormone therapy and didn't have any breast development ... they just pulled it all down."

At the time of Demone's experiment, Facebook's (and Instagram's) policy was to "restrict the images of female breasts that include the nipple" with exceptions for acts of protests, breastfeeding imagery, and photos of post-mastectomy scarring—as well as non-photographic art that depicts nude figures. "The current policies are obviously very hypocritical," Demone told me. "One of the goals [of my photos] was not to be sexualized ... and yet all of those got taken down as the project went on. Now, the tone of my social media pages is far more sexual, but because I don't post nipples, I'm not getting kicked off."

Demone was well aware of the company's restrictions and violated them knowingly,

but they have not always been so clear. Like Durand-Baïssas, Metzger, and all the others, breastfeeding mothers were among the early victims of Facebook's inconsistent application of the rules, which did not, until 2015, provide the much-needed clarity that breastfeeding images were in fact allowed.

#FreeTheNipple

In 2007, a new mother named Kelli Roman discovered that a photo she'd posted of herself breastfeeding her daughter had been deleted. Roman wrote to Facebook to ask why the photo had been removed, but received no response, prompting her to start a group on the platform entitled "Hey Facebook, Breastfeeding Is Not Obscene." The group grew quickly, and it spawned several offshoots, one of which—the Mothers International Lactation Campaign (MILC)—held a protest of the policy, which was reported in the *New York Times*. The 2008 online protest, in which more than eleven thousand Facebook users changed their profile image to images of mothers nursing their children, led to others, including a 2009 protest in front of Facebook's Palo Alto headquarters.

At the time, a spokesman for the company said that banning nudity was "a clear line to draw." The company clarified that while breastfeeding imagery was acceptable, photos that displayed visible nipples were in violation of the policy. "We think it's a consistent policy," said the spokesman.[26] Left unsaid was that only *women's* nipples were considered nudity.

As scholar Tarleton Gillespie has written, breastfeeding images might seem trivial to many, but are "part of the problem for social media platforms and how we think about them." Expanding on that, he writes that the debate is "woven into a larger set of questions about Facebook's comparatively strict rules against nudity: what are the reasonable exceptions to such a rule (accidental, artistic, nonrepresentational), how consistently is the rule applied, and how does a rule against nudity run up against the interests of users who find it reasonable, even empowering, to display their own bodies."[27]

The dichotomy between those who would find the display of nudity empowering and those who would be scandalized is clear, but Facebook's double standard on gender—and the reasoning behind it—is less so.

This hypocrisy is rooted in surprisingly recent American norms. Until 1936, it was illegal in most states for men to go topless. It took several protests and dozens of arrests before men won the right, in 1936, to bare their nipples on New York's beaches, a right that soon extended to other states. New York's Supreme Court decriminalized female toplessness in 1992, but even today only thirteen states allow women to sunbathe nude, and women who try might find themselves arrested anyway. Although men are often seen shirtless in advertisements or city basketball courts, it's a rare sight in the United States to see a woman's bare breast outside of a sexualized context. I've never seen a topless woman in a magazine or in the news, and I can't remember the last time I saw breasts on mainstream American television.

And it's in those industries, as well as state and local laws, where the roots of social media companies' policies seem to lie. The Federal Communications Commission (FCC) restricts to the period after midnight the broadcasting of "indecent" television programming— defined as "language or material that, in context, depicts or describes, in terms patently offensive as measured by contemporary community standards for the broadcast medium, sexual or excretory organs or activities." Nudity is not specifically mentioned, but "Nipplegate," the incident in which Janet Jackson's nipple was exposed during the 2004 Superbowl halftime show, provoked more than half a million complaints to the FCC and resulted in large fines to broadcaster Viacom.

The film ratings system, though voluntary, is even more opaque. Ratings are doled out by an industry trade group, the Motion Picture Association of America (MPAA), which has been criticized over the years for its double standards when it comes to sex and violence. The 2006 documentary *This Film Is Not Yet Rated* addresses this double standard directly, demonstrating how violence typically garners adolescent-friendly ratings while nudity and sex are nearly always restricted to R or NC-17 ratings. Similarly, the film accuses the MPAA of unfairly classifying films that depict homosexuality with harsh ratings. In response, the association notably placed the blame on the public, saying "We don't create standards; we just follow them."[28]

Legally, in the United States, the female nipple has also been held to represent nudity. In *Barnes v. Glen Theatre, Inc.* (1991), the US Supreme Court found that the state of Indiana could regulate nude dancing without violating the First Amendment. The decision hinged on the state's interest in upholding "moral standards." Indiana's public indecency statute describes nudity as the "showing of the human male or female genitals, pubic area, or buttocks with less than a fully opaque covering, the showing of the female breast with less than a fully opaque covering of any part of the nipple, or the showing of covered male genitals in a discernibly turgid state."[29]

While a majority of US states allow exotic dancing or strip clubs, most maintain laws requiring strippers to cover their nipples. But why? In her book *Naked Truth: Strip Clubs, Democracy, and a Christian Right*, Judith Hanna argues that the desire to keep women's nipples—but not men's—covered stems from America's uniquely Puritan roots. "What the breast means to the bearers and beholders has cultural and personal resonance," she writes, noting that a survey of 190 societies found that few insisted on women's breasts being concealed. "People need scripts to define a situation as being potentially sexual."[30]

California, from where all the social media companies emerged, is relatively liberal, particularly when it comes to the exposure of skin. The state's indecent exposure law does not prohibit the baring of female nipples, and full nudity is allowed in some strip clubs, provided they don't serve alcohol.

The state is also relatively progressive when it comes to gender issues, and transgender rights in particular. Home to one of the first queer uprisings in the United States (the 1959 Cooper Do-nuts Riot) and some of the nation's first openly trans women, California was a bit of a refuge for trans individuals, who faced far more severe persecution elsewhere in the country. California has also been more legally progressive than many geographies when it comes to recognition of trans and non-binary identities. It is there that the first law protecting trans students was codified, in 2013, and in 2014, the use of "trans panic" as a defense in murder trials was abolished.

Then, in 2017, California became one of several states (along with Oregon, New York, and a handful of other jurisdictions) to allow transgender and non-binary people to change their legal gender on the basis of self-identification, a process that previously had been medicalized. By enacting that policy, the state functionally blurred the lines of what, when it comes to the human body, is male and what is female.

But these advances remain outliers and on social media platforms, progressive notions about transgender and non-binary people have by and large failed to take hold. In other words, a person of any gender (or no gender) can have large breasts, but either by policy or process is classified by moderators as a woman.

The absurdity of creating and enforcing nudity bans along gender lines is perhaps best exemplified by streaming platform Twitch's poorly worded April 2020 policy, which reads: "For those who present as women, we ask that you cover your nipples."[31] Or, by Tumblr's 2018 policy, which banned "female-presenting nipples" from view.[32]

The irony of these trans-ignorant policies is that most of these companies have otherwise been (again, relatively) progressive when it comes to providing features for queer individuals. Facebook, for instance, began offering a multitude of gender identity options back in 2014—more than fifty at the time of the announcement—and in the past has offered fun features like a rainbow reaction button during Pride Month. That feature was, however, notably absent in a number of countries where homosexuality is illegal, something that Facebook refused to comment upon.[33]

The fact is that the policies of many Silicon Valley companies— including Facebook—remain reflective of large swaths of US culture … particularly those with the loudest voices. Facebook and Google staff might therefore argue that they too are just following existing cultural standards, but that begs the question: Whose cultural standards, exactly, demand that women be covered?

Silicon values

Early policies at most major companies, as we've learned, can be attributed to the values of the small teams—or, in some cases, individuals —that created them. As Dave Willner, a policy staffer in Facebook's early years, pointed out, the company's first Community Standards were created by "a bunch of twenty-six-year-olds who didn't know what they were doing." Still, he says, "the fear, in my understanding, is that if [in 2006–2007] you didn't draw a pretty hard line on nudity, you rapidly became a porn site, which drives away other users."

"Like Disneyland," he argued, Facebook sought to "create a demarcation of space." In other words, Facebook sought to carve out its own tidy little space in the vast, messy web by creating a design and a set of rules that would force users to conform to certain standards. But he pushed back against my hypothesis that the company's early policy creators were mainly young American men: "The early group of us doing the drafting were [something like] four women, two men. One was German, one was from India, one was Irish, three were American."

Nevertheless, the gender composition of these companies as they grew has become increasingly skewed. Today, the Valley's top companies are predominantly staffed by men. Men make up 68 percent of Google's global staff, 64 percent of Facebook's, and 58 percent of Twitter's. At the leadership level, where policy is made, the numbers are even more dire: women make up only 25.9 percent of Google's senior leadership and 30 percent of Facebook's. We know that among the companies' engineers, some racial and geographic diversity exists, but the top policymakers at both Facebook and Google are overwhelmingly American-born and white.

Mark Zuckerberg dropped out from Harvard, but his company's top policy staff did not. A Reuters report published during a spate of company controversies in 2016 noted that all five of the top executives involved in controversial content decisions studied at Harvard, and "four of them have both undergraduate and graduate degrees from the elite institution."[34] Similarly, the LinkedIn profiles of policymakers I have communicated with over the years list Princeton, UC Berkeley, and Stanford as alma maters; many of the conversations we have had on the sidelines of conferences betray the worldliness that is supposedly conferred on someone who has attended such respected institutions.

As the Reuters article notes, and as I have been told time and time again, a diverse array of policy staff and mid-level managers weigh in on Facebook policy changes, but as Maria,* a former community operations staffer based in one of the company's regional offices told me, their expertise didn't always get taken into account. "It's like a one-man team; when shit hits the fan, it's only one person's decision and it's always very high up," she told me. "Even if there were hundreds of people working on something, [Zuckerberg] would wake up and say, 'This was my decision.'"

So it's not American values, per se, that are being exported to billions of users around the world, but the values of a very particular demographic—perhaps not incidentally the same demographic that made up Facebook's first set of users. These elite executives are making policies that are undoubtedly shaping the values of a generation of users, many from cultures that have a more lax or positive outlook toward nudity and the human body. It begs the question: If Facebook had been founded in Germany or the Netherlands (which famously issues a tolerance test to would-be residents that includes questions gauging their comfort with nudity), or by an Indigenous community like the Caiapó of Brazil or the Arrernte of Australia, or, for that matter, by a woman, how different would the rules be?

There is plenty of evidence to show that, even in the United States, attitudes toward nudity are not as puritanical as the men who founded these companies might have thought. One 2019 survey showed that seven out of ten Americans are comfortable with a woman breastfeeding next to them in public.[35] And a 2015 poll found that 65 percent of US respondents were comfortable with nude sunbathing, provided it took place in a designated area.

For nearly a decade, I wondered why Facebook bothered to maintain a policy that so clearly vexed many of its users, that was the cause of protests and scorn. Was it because nudity was difficult for humans and machines to distinguish from pornography? Was it maintained so the company wouldn't risk its products getting blocked by governments such as Saudi Arabia's? Could it really be that Zuckerberg and his fellow executives were that prudish?

I asked numerous policy staffers over the years, and more often than not, the question went unanswered. One now-former regional director told me that the company had received pressure from some governments to keep the policy (and from Sweden's to reverse it), but they did not think that was the reason it remained in place. Monika Bickert, Facebook's head of global policy management, has stated publicly that it is a matter of safety, because it ensures that topless images are not shared without consent. It was only recently that a Facebook employee casually let what she believes is the real reason slip in the middle of a broader conversation: "Because there would be boobs all the time," she told me nonchalantly over the phone.

The company's policy toward women's bodies is only the tip of the iceberg because, for Facebook's rulers, nudity, pornography, and sex seem interchangeable. Notably, the company's community standards have never contained the word "pornography," only the words "explicit sexual intercourse" and "sexual activity." However, until very recently, users attempting to report content using the platform's flagging tool were given an option that read: "This is nudity or pornography," with "sexual arousal," "sexual acts," and "people soliciting sex" as possible choices.

This, too, is a particularly American conclusion. In the 1964 case *Jacobellis v. Ohio*, Supreme Court Justice Potter Stewart famously defined hardcore pornography by saying, "I know it when I see it." Less than a decade later, *Miller v. California* resulted in the development of a three-pronged legal framework to determine obscenity—known as the Miller test—based on what an "average person," applying "contemporary community standards," might find offensive. More than two decades later, *Sable Communications of California v. Federal Communications Commission*—a case that dealt with the legality of "dial-a-porn," an analogue precursor to the various "Tube" sites offering an array of pornography—clarified that sexual expression that is indecent but not obscene is protected by the First Amendment.

The Miller test may have worked in 1970s America, but who is the "average person" for a global platform like Facebook? The company has always insisted that nudity is restricted because "some people in our community may be sensitive to this type of content," but those community members are never defined—and if they were, would they represent the average?

We may never know, but one thing is clear: Facebook must bend to the will of those with power. And, as scholar Ben Wagner posits, those who hold the power over internet governance are a small elite crew of government and corporate actors.[36] The result is what Wagner calls "the global default" of permissible speech, defined by a narrow set of actors and replicated by less powerful ones, that has become the status quo online. "This definition of common boundaries of speech on the Internet," writes Wagner, "represents this status quo."[37]

Ultimately, Facebook and its counterparts operate more like churches than courts; they are subject to influence by states and the wealthy, and all too content with disregarding the needs of their subjects in favor of those with power. When you peel back the façade of participatory governance, there is no case law, no record of decision making to allow for comparisons, and—until recently—no due process. Instead, there is a patchwork of dogma and oxymoronic canon that, when scaled, results in a unique cultural colonialism of myopic morality and deeply suspect values.

The dawning of the social media era presented an opportunity for modernity to push back against deeply rooted manufactured morality, but instead, staid tradition and fear won out, at least among the majority. And at the root of it? A deep-seated distaste for—or fear of—pornography.

7

The War on Sex

The internet is for porn! The internet is for porn! Why do you think the net was born? Porn! Porn! Porn!

—*Avenue Q*

Before broadband internet, it was not so easy for a young person to find pornography in the United States. As a teenager in the mid-1990s, I encountered porn just twice: once in an old *Playboy* found in my parents' basement and another time on a VHS tape while visiting a friend in college. "Nudie mags" were legal, but shameful enough to be hidden behind the counter at convenience stores, concealed in a paper bag. Videos were tucked away in the back rooms of video rental stores, accessible only to those eighteen years or older, and pay-per-view was a no-go for anyone who did not pay their own bills. Skeevy, twenty-four-hour sex shops on the side of the highway catered mainly to truckers—there was no high street chain stores like Good Vibrations in those days.

Though hard to find, pornography was legal in the United States then, but that was not the case everywhere. Around the world, from one country to the next, the laws governing the creation and distribution of pornography vary greatly. For instance, although porn has long been produced across Europe, its sale was tightly regulated or forbidden in several European countries, including Iceland, Bulgaria, and Ukraine. Across North Africa, the Middle East, and much of Asia, it was and is illegal to create and often unlawful—though not always impossible—to obtain and possess.

The internet changed all that. By the middle of the 1990s, pornographic images abounded on Usenet newsgroups and single-purpose websites, enabling anyone with a dial-up connection and a little bit of privacy to access them. Within just a few years, porn had become so ubiquitous online that the Broadway musical *Avenue Q* even dedicated an entire song to it, aptly titled "The Internet Is for Porn." The term "the great equalizer", once reserved to describe education, now rang true for the internet in the hands of porn consumers.

Not everyone appreciated this equalizing effect. In July 1995, the cover of *Time* magazine depicted a small child at a computer screen, eyes wide and mouth open, with the word "CYBERPORN" just under his chin in capital letters. Underneath the word, the headline read: "Exclusive: A new study shows how pervasive and wild it really is. Can we protect our kids—and free speech?" The feature story was based on a study by Martin Rimm, an undergraduate student at Carnegie Mellon, that had been published in the *Georgetown Law Journal*. Rimm's paper claimed that 80 percent of images on newsgroups at the time were pornographic in nature—an alarming figure, perhaps, had it been true.

The student had somehow managed to deceive a *Time* magazine journalist, who had called the study "exhaustive" and attributed it directly to Carnegie Mellon's research arm, but he was not able to fool the lawyers and experts with the greatest expertise about the internet. Once they were able to get their hands on Rimm's paper, they ripped it apart and found that Rimm had not surveyed newsgroups as a whole, but had rather looked only at files found on adult-oriented bulletin boards.[1]

The criticism, however, was little matter for two senators, Democrat Jim Exon of Nebraska and Republican Slade Gorton of Washington, who saw a crisis at hand. In June 1995, the two senators proposed an amendment to the Telecommunications Act that would later become the Communications Decency Act (CDA), extending existing indecency and anti-obscenity laws to the internet. The basis of their proposal? Rimm's study. On June 14, 1995, Exon opened an address to the Senate with a prayer written by the Senate chaplain, which began: "Almighty God, Lord of all life, we praise You for the advancements in computerized communications that we enjoy in our time. Sadly, however, there are those who are littering this information superhighway with obscene, indecent, and destructive pornography. Virtual but virtueless reality is projected in the most twisted, sick, misuse of sexuality."

Just one month later, Rimm was lambasted by critics and discredited by even the *New York Times*, which dismissed his paper for containing "sloppy writing, misleading analysis, ambiguous definitions and unsupported conclusions." But it was too late: the Exon-Gorton amendment passed, and on February 8, 1996, President Bill Clinton signed the CDA into law, imposing sanctions on anyone who knowingly "uses an interactive computer service to send to a specific person or persons under 18 years of age or ... uses any interactive computer service to display in a manner available to a person under 18 years of age, any comment, request, suggestion, proposal, image, or other communication that, in context, depicts or describes, in terms patently offensive as measured by contemporary community standards, sexual or excretory activities or organs."

Free speech advocates and civil liberties organizations were outraged and worked diligently to get the amendment overturned. The Electronic Frontier Foundation (EFF) sent a missive to its supporters claiming that the CDA "represents a grave threat to the very nature and existence of the Internet as we know it today." The American Civil Liberties Union (ACLU) argued that the censorship provisions of the CDA were unconstitutional because they would criminalize expression protected by the First Amendment, as well as because the terms "indecency" and "patently offensive" were unconstitutionally vague.

The EFF and ACLU were not wrong. What is more, the act did not stop the spread of online porn. Just a few months after Clinton signed it into law, Sex.com launched, selling expensive ads and pulling in millions of dollars just by existing. The site's success inspired others, and soon there were dozens of websites raking in cash by selling outlinks—tracked clicks that generate revenue for external

URLs—to porn sites. But "as the moguls of porn became the envy of the internet, the federal government conveniently got out of their way."[2] In a landmark 1997 ruling, the Supreme Court ruled that the CDA created an "unacceptably heavy burden on protected speech" that threatened to "torch a large segment of the Internet community." In the decision, Justice John Paul Stevens wrote that "the interest in encouraging freedom of expression in a democratic society outweighs any theoretical but unproven benefit of censorship."

From there, porn was free to spread online. Websites touting collections of video porn also began cropping up, available to anyone with a credit card. Later, as download speeds increased and peer-to-peer file sharing became a widespread phenomenon, explicit videos were traded across networks. For those for whom paying for porn was not an option—including, of course, minors—this was a profound shift.

By 2006, the global porn industry was worth $97 billion and the traditional porn industry was freaking out. "People are making movies in their houses and dragging and dropping them" onto free sites, complained the CEO of a payment processor for adult sites. "It's killing the marketplace."[3] Cam sites abounded, rentals and sales of pornography DVDs dropped 15–25 percent between 2006 and 2007, and pay-per-view revenue was on the decline, leaving the industry scrambling.[4]

Then, in the middle of the decade, three revolutionary technological developments created the conditions for anyone to create and share videos: the smartphone, video-sharing platforms, and fast internet speeds enabled millions of people to capture, distribute, and consume video—and porn—online. And with that, the video-sharing revolution was underway. YouTube was followed shortly by Facebook, and later Instagram, Twitter, and Vine, while xHamster, Pornhub, and RedTube rode YouPorn's coattails. Despite the prevalence of tube and premium sites, as well as indie porn platforms, porn quickly found its way into the margins of other spaces, including blogging and social media platforms. Some videos were willingly traded and shared, while others—as well as outlinks to porn sites—were more akin to spam.

Although a handful of platforms made the choice to allow porn, others—most notably Facebook and YouTube—chose to ban sexually explicit content from the outset. These companies launched at a time when porn was flooding all corners of the internet, and the market demanded something different. They therefore had good reason to set themselves apart from competitors like MySpace, which, as danah boyd observes, had come to be perceived as being "filled with risky behavior."[5] Journalist Adrian Chen, who was among the first to cover content moderation practices, speculated to me that "Facebook succeeded because it was seen as so clean and safe for young people" in comparison to MySpace. But although they may have launched with anti-porn policies, neither platform was prepared to deal with the moderation of porn en masse. These companies quickly sought solutions to ensure that their platforms were not inundated with pornography, lest they become undesirable to advertisers. Thus began the race to rid the social web of porn.

In 2009, Facebook was employing just around 150 content moderators, who worked primarily from Palo Alto, making around $50,000 per year (consider that salary in light of the already-skyrocketing Bay Area rents at the time). Although the moderators' focus was broad, covering an array of topics, a *Newsweek* article from that year called failed to appreciate the workers' broad responsibilities, calling them "porn cops", but also conceded that they were key to the company's growth.[6] Simon Axten, a twenty-six-year-old Facebook employee profiled in the article, was quoted in the *New York Times* just four months later as saying that Facebook had tried outsourcing content moderation, but "had not done so widely."[7]

As it turns out, battling porn was not so easy for social media companies and, within a few short years, most had begun outsourcing content moderation to firms in the Philippines and other countries where labor was cheap. But no matter how much they invested in content moderation, purveyors of porn found their way in. In the summer of 2010, a site vulnerability allowed pranksters to inject YouTube with scripts that redirected viewers to porn. According to one article, Justin Bieber videos, beloved by tweens and teens, were hit particularly hard.[8] The vulnerability was fixed within days, but just over a year later, hackers gained access to Sesame Street's channel and replaced all of the videos with hardcore porn.[9] Around the same time, Facebook was flooded with graphic imagery, both sexual and violent. Users logged in expecting to see baby or party photos and were instead inundated with images of dead dogs and penises. The company was entirely unprepared. In a piece for the now-defunct blog *AllFacebook*, Jackie Cohen commented: "The fact that these photos spread for as long as 48 hours unchecked [shows] how much Facebook relies on individual users to flag inappropriate content: people were commenting on the images' novelty more than clicking on any 'report' links."[10]

No site was immune. Flickr—owned at the time by Yahoo!—was facing angry advertisers who did not want their ads turning up next to sexually explicit photos, Wikipedia's co-founder was blogging about the site's "porn problem," and *Mashable* was publishing opinion pieces arguing for Twitter to lay down the ban hammer.[11]

In the end, most platforms tightened up their processes in an effort to appease the angry public. The amount of porn on major platforms decreased, but so too did plenty of other things, such as adult nudity, LGBTQ content, and sexual health information. As it turns out, the best way to get rid of undesirable content is to cast a wide net … no matter if a few dolphins get caught up in it.

Of course, finding porn on social media sites is not hard if you're looking for it. It's on YouTube, emanates from Facebook Live casts, and can even be located on LinkedIn. Social media platforms do their best to find and erase it, but attempting to do that is an endless game of Whac-A-Mole. The damage from these attempts, which all too often employ broad filtering techniques, is not to porn but to those whose art, identity, or livelihood depends on what platforms determine to be "adult" content.

Bardot Smith calls herself a "corporate finance escapee." Petite and exuding intellect, she looks the part, but for the past ten years she's been involved in a different industry: the precarious world of sex work. She is also, alongside a growing community of sex workers, actively challenging Silicon Valley's status quo through research and activism. I first encountered her work in the form of an essay she wrote for the critical Silicon Valley publication *Model View Culture* in

2014. In it, she argued that "the increasing presence of women's skill and success represents a challenge to tech culture" and that "women's success and agency are in direct conflict with an industry culture that caters to the priorities—and egos—of males."[12] Her words resonated and stuck with me.

I hadn't put two and two together and realized she was the author of that piece until we met nearly five years later on the sidelines of a tech conference in Spain where, over salads and wine, she led a conversation about the struggle sex workers were facing to survive in the face of rampant censorship online. Because I have thought about this issue for nearly a decade, it is a rare that a new insight blows me away, but I left that lunch feeling humbled and determined. Despite years of research into how social media companies censor the human body, I had not fully understood how these restrictions were affecting an entire industry and the people who work in it.

Just a few months before I met Smith, the window of permissibility for sex and sexuality online had narrowed considerably with the passing of SESTA-FOSTA or, in shorthand, FOSTA. The law, a combination package of US Senate bill SESTA (Stop Enabling Sex Traffickers Act) and House bill FOSTA (Fight Online Sex Trafficking Act). Ostensibly designed to fight sex trafficking on the internet, the effects of FOSTA's broad provisions were immediately felt across a variety of online communities.

Serving as the impetus for FOSTA was law enforcement's frustration at their perceived inability to hold platforms—most notably Backpage, a classifieds website—legally liable for illegal content posted by their users. In 2016, following the dismissal of a lawsuit by a judge explicitly citing Section 230—the law that enables companies to host speech without risk of liability—a Senate investigation into Backpage was launched and a flurry of public advocacy to shut it down ensued. Key to the story is that Backpage, in response to backlash, decided to shut down its adult section rather than put in the time and resources required to constantly moderate its classified ads. That is not a choice that a platform should have to make but, as the post-FOSTA internet has demonstrated, when faced with such options, it's the choice platforms *will* make.

Almost immediately after the passing of FOSTA, the blogging site Tumblr, which had long served as a home for a range of sexual content, announced that it would be banning all sexual imagery. In the announcement, then CEO Jeff D'Onofrio wrote: "We've realized that in order to continue to fulfill our promise and place in culture, especially as it evolves, we must change."[13]

But whose culture, exactly? For many years, and as Facebook's dominance grew, Tumblr remained a place where sexual minorities gathered and—thanks to the platform's policy on allowing pseudonyms—felt safe in doing so. As Courtney Demone told me over Skype, "Tumblr was such a huge thing for my personal life ... They had such a wonderful community, allowing people to explore and share stuff they couldn't in everyday life. Tumblr having a lax policy was really helpful for that."

Kali Sudhra, an activist, sex worker, and educator who works to give voice to sex and porn workers of color, sees Tumblr's decision as a direct consequence of FOSTA. The law, she says, is "outraging because we know that the best way to stop trafficking is to work *with* sex workers, not criminalize them." Tumblr's ban on adult content created a space where there is "no place for sex workers, women, trans folk, queer folk to express themselves ..."

At a time when attitudes toward sex work, transgender individuals, and other sexual minorities are by and large changing for the better, it is perhaps ironic that Silicon Valley's CEOs are so rapidly closing off the spaces where such communities have long gathered. Or maybe it's not right to describe it in ironic terms—after all, the disregard for these spaces has been accompanied by an agenda of rapid growth in San Francisco that has all but closed down the city's legendary queer spaces so that Silicon Valley's highly paid workers can drink $7 cups of coffee and dine at the latest hip restaurants.

While the effects of FOSTA have been felt across a spectrum of communities, no single group has been more heavily impacted than sex workers, for whom social media had in many ways made their jobs safer. This includes sex workers engaged in perfectly legal professions such as pornography or exotic dance, as well as those working in countries and jurisdictions where prostitution is legal.

Sex workers have reported that Instagram has removed their accounts and images, even when they contain no explicit content. They've documented instances of Facebook discussion groups being shut down for featuring sex work–related conversations. LinkedIn prohibits the listing of sex work in one's profile, thus de-legitimizing it as work (regardless of jurisdiction). Payment processors from PayPal to Square regularly shut down accounts of sex workers, and nearly every online advertising tool bans sexual content.[14]

While takedowns can be tracked by the user in most cases, Twitter and Instagram engage in a more subtle—and therefore nefarious—practice widely referred to as "shadowbanning," whereby a hashtag or keyword is suppressed from search—either temporarily or per-manently—preventing users from finding content on a given subject unless they know what they're looking for. Twitter has explicitly denied engaging in shadowbanning, but sex workers—as well as a number of other activists I've spoken with—offer evidence to the contrary.[15]

Smith, who owns the URL "jackisanazi.com" (referring to Twitter CEO Jack Dorsey), has been particularly vocal about Twitter's methods. In a piece arguing that shadowbans deny sex workers income and a sense of community, Smith is quoted as saying: "I have multiple tweets a day that will garner hundreds of likes and then I will post a picture that will get two. That isn't how the internet works, typically pictures get way more engagement than straight text."

Danielle Blunt, whom I met at that same fateful lunch, concurs. A queer-identified sex worker with a master's in public health, Blunt is the co-founder of Hacking//Hustling, a platform created by and for sex workers after the passing of FOSTA with the idea of "flipping the script and centering sex workers as producers of knowledge and expertise."[16] Over the past few years, Blunt has given a number of talks about the impact of FOSTA at conferences and other events. "There have been conferences where I'm organizing around sex work," she told me, "and the first result [when people search my name] is that of a fake account, an impersonator. You can't find my profile." Twitter also hides certain keywords from users' replies, deeming them "offensive" and requiring multiple clicks to reach them. Among the words deemed offensive? "Vagina."

Like Twitter, Instagram employs subtle enforcement mechanisms in its adjudication of sexual content. In April 2019, the company announced: "We have begun reducing the spread of posts that are inappropriate but do not go against Instagram's Community Guidelines."[17] The policy is reminiscent of the Supreme Court's delineation between obscenity and indecency or the United Kingdom's attempts to define and regulate non-illegal "harmful content." Instagram admits to blocking such content from its Explore page or in hashtag searches. One recent example was the hashtag #poledancing, used more by exercise enthusiasts than exotic dancers. Blunt, who's spent time observing the phenomenon, notes that she's seen Instagram ban hashtags like #femdom and even #women—while #maledom remains available.

For some, a shadowban is a mere annoyance, but for many sex workers, it can be severely alienating. "How am I supposed to make money, how am I supposed to organize, and how am I supposed to build community?" Blunt explained to me. "A lot of sex workers work in isolation, a lot of queer folks live in isolation."

But shadowbans are also only the tip of the iceberg for sex workers. Smith argues that Silicon Valley deems these workers to be engaged in sexual activity regardless of what they are actually doing. "The policies automatically sexualize you," she argues. She recalls an instance where a friend sent a Whole Foods gift card to her private email address, but the card was sent back to her friend with a note suggesting that fraud might have occurred. "I had to go to Amazon and ask about the status of the card," she recalls, "and they asked, 'Is this really a gift?' implying that there's no way a friend would just send me grocery money. Is her sending me money an 'adult' transaction, or is it just because I'm a porn star that it becomes 'adult'? What they're essentially trying to do is make it so there's no easy and direct way for [us] to send and receive money."

Sex workers, more than any other community I've spoken with, are acutely aware of how content moderation systems can be gamed. For more than a decade, I've observed the ways in which individuals, groups, bots, and state actors have found ways to silence other people by using reporting or flagging tools. For example, Vietnamese democracy activists have experienced being reported to Facebook for being underage, thus prompting requests for ID that they are reluctant to share.[18] But several sex workers that I spoke to stressed that a combination of toxic misogyny, the proximity of their work to criminal activity, and their online prominence make them easy targets.

"A big problem for content moderation is the ability of trolls to game it, and the companies don't do anything to stop it," says Blunt. Indeed, many companies deny that their systems can even *be* gamed. In a 2016 email to an Iranian activist on which I was copied, Facebook's current head of global policy management, Monika Bickert, states: "We work hard to make sure that our policies and procedures are responsive to the needs of our community, and are not gamed by malicious actors, including spammers, hackers, or those who seek to silence political dissent."

These are hard problems, and I have no doubt that Facebook and other platforms have considered them; yet at the same time I continue to see examples of content takedowns where malicious reporting is clearly at play. Imagine the following scenario: A sex worker sets up a new Facebook account using her legal name to connect with friends she met at an event. She's protective of her online identities but, throwing caution to the wind, posts a profile photo to the new account that's recognizable. Someone—a troll, a jilted client, or former lover, it doesn't matter—finds the account and decides to fuck with her. Using Facebook's flagging tool, he reports her for using a fake name or being under the age of thirteen, thus triggering the company to ask for her legal identification. She now has to submit her ID to keep her account, but she has no reason to trust Facebook with that information; she's been burned before. And so once again, she finds herself de-platformed.

This scenario is not far-fetched: I regularly receive e-mails from people in similar circumstances, who cautiously posted a recognizable image of themselves only to be reported to a platform for "violating" some rule or another. Although sex workers are often the target of such malicious reporting, it happens, more often than one might think, to people from varying walks of life.

Online censorship translates to real-world harm

The effect of this censorship is insidious. For the person who experiences this degree of censorship, whose life or livelihood depends on connection, the most likely outcome is self-censorship. Like the musician changing her lyrics to satisfy recording industry standards or the filmmaker cutting a sex scene to receive a lower movie rating, the platform user undoubtedly must self-censor in order to prevent himself from running afoul of the rules.

"We know what keeps people healthy, and taking away people's ability to earn income or their access to community or their ability to advocate and mobilize for themselves has deadly consequences," says Blunt. "These platforms are killing people—that's what happens when freedom of speech is eliminated. Being de-platformed from social media has chilled my speech ... They have built such powerful tools that my compliance to their terms of service is more important to me than saying exactly what I want to say."

Censoring sexuality to such an extraordinary degree is guaranteed to have a long-term impact on society. By forbidding any potentially sexual content, tech companies are furthering the sexual ideals proliferated by mainstream pornography sites—ideals that most feminists have long considered harmful. And, in particular, by banning positive and realistic depictions of women's bodies, many of which are created and shared *by women*, Silicon Valley companies are ensuring that the status quo—that is, the limited representation of body types outside a narrow norm and the harm to body image that such standards cause—will remain.

When Cindy Gallop, creator of the site MakeLoveNotPorn, found that one of her posts had been removed from Facebook, she responded with an impassioned warning:

When female sextech founders and the gender-equal, diverse, inclusive, non-#metoo, non-#timesup lens that we bring to bear, is not only not supported by Facebook and other social platforms, but actively obstructed and impeded with the aim of driving us out of business … you'd be right to predict an extremely negative downward trajectory for YOUR CHILDREN, and humanity.[19]

Erika Lust agrees. The Swedish erotic film director is known for making porn that contains artistic angles, feminist points of view, and ethnic- and gender-diverse actors. In her writing and public speaking, Lust has called for better sexual education and for extensive changes to porn—which she considers "the most important discourse on gender and sexuality."[20] Like Gallop, Lust has experienced censorship on several platforms, including Vimeo and YouTube.

"When pages that promote female pleasure are hidden, we understand that our pleasure is invalid," she wrote to me in an email. "When drawings of vaginas are removed, we learn that we should be ashamed of our bodies. When female nipples are censored but male nipples are not, we know that we must police our own bodies to ensure we do not arouse men … The bodies, sexualities and desires that are allowed online, translates itself into the bodies, sexualities and desires that are accepted in society."

Indeed, the same hypersexualized imagery of young celebrities and influencers abound on these platforms, as they do on American television. The now-infamous photo of Kim Kardashian's ample behind was permitted to remain on major platforms, as was a photo of Justin Bieber clad only in tight briefs. Meanwhile, less explicit images and information intended to empower historically marginalized communities are regularly deemed inappropriate.

For example, Twitter and Facebook—both of which happily hosted Kim Kardashian's nude bottom—removed the word "vagina" from an advertisement marketing a book about female anatomy, written by prominent gynecologist Dr. Jen Gunter.[21] Similarly, journalist Sarah Lacy found that she was unable to advertise her book, entitled *A Uterus Is a Feature*, on Facebook.[22] Plus-sized women have had their Instagram accounts removed for posting selfies in bikinis—something that skinny women do all the time without reprisal.[23] Both platforms have also blocked advertisements for information about teen pregnancy, proper bra fitting, and gynecologist visits.[24]

This puritanism seems to disproportionately affect queer, and particularly trans, users, as Sudhra and others point out. One clear example involves a YouTube channel, called Watts the Safeword, that seeks to provide "kink-friendly sexual education." One of the channel's creators, Amp, told me that the thumbnails he and his team had carefully selected to represent their videos were not showing up in search results. After several days of correspondence with YouTube, they were told that the custom thumbnails were "considered inappropriate for viewers."

Amp said that he's seen instances where queer content was demonetized, demoted, or removed while nearly identical heterosexual content was left untouched. Another YouTube user, Chase Ross, reported that merely including "trans" in a video's title was enough to trigger demonetization. And still others have reported seeing anti-LGBTQ ads show up on their content.[25]

With so many examples readily available, it's hard to imagine that the companies' policy teams are unaware of the problem. Instead, it seems likely that they simply don't see queer users as important—at least not as important as the conservative US users whose loud protests are rewarded with significant attention. Or, as Sudhra surmised to me, perhaps it's something worse: "Puritan values. Blatant transphobia, whorephobia, racism, ableism."

What we might lose

At a time when millennials and their younger counterparts are redefining sex, sexuality, and gender norms and claiming public space for marginalized identities, Silicon Valley's values seem remarkably regressive. If these platforms are the new terrain for long-standing debates about the content and character of public discourse, what does it say about our society that they have the tolerance of a nineteenth-century priest? Moreover, what effect will it have on future generations? What does it mean that we're encouraged to spend every waking hour on these platforms but can't be ourselves on them? Furthermore, in requiring creators to stay within the lines or risk self-censorship, are we creating an archive of sexuality for the future that hardly resembles our current—and far more permissive—reality?

I cannot help but think about what was lost when the Nazis seized power, decimating the freedoms that had flourished in the Weimar Republic. In that unique and brief period of history, Berlin was a hotspot of queer activity, from nightclubs to political organizing. There were numerous queer publications, including *The Third Sex*, most likely the world's first transgender magazine. Sex work was mostly legal. And, of course, there was the Institut für Sexualwissenschaft, a sexology institute that advocated for LGBT rights, among other things.

Perhaps the Weimar Republic comes to mind because, one hundred years later, my home city of Berlin is once again flourishing in its sexual freedoms while also facing the threat of right-wing populism. Or perhaps it's because, while these companies cannot and should not be directly compared to the Nazis, they wield the same prudish and authoritarian tendencies when it comes to sexual freedom. And I fear that, without intervention, we will see the erasure of our living history in quite the same way our ancestors did a century ago.

These are important concerns that affect society as a whole, and they deserve a more prominent place in the public discourse. But, as I seek to illustrate, it is the most vulnerable members of society who suffer the most from bad policy. Unsurprisingly, the most marginalized members of society are rarely invited to the table to lend their views as policy is being created—and when they do speak out after the fact, they're often ignored. "Think about social media as the real world," says Sudhra, who says that the people that face the most discrimination are "trans folk, Black and Indigenous people of color, sex workers and people living with disabilities."

Those who make the rules—whether lawmakers or corporate executives—rarely engage in social media use to the same degree as the communities Sudhra mentions, because they don't have to. The ruling class has money, and access to the New York *Times* opinion page—they do not need to rely on Twitter to get their voices heard. To them, social media is not real life, and their online acquaintances aren't members of their communities.

But for some, access to online platforms can mean everything. "I can pretty confidently say that I do not think I would've transitioned if it weren't for Tumblr," Courtney Demone told me, and she is not the only one. Countless queer friends have, over the years, told me that online platforms, and the connections made through them, are what helped them understand their identities. It is true for me, too. If I had not had access to online bulletin boards from a young age, I too might not have learned the terms that helped me find my own sexual identity until I was in college.

I believe that those at the top know how much online platforms can mean to people like Demone and me. I believe that they have spent at least some time thinking about the consequences of restricting certain types of vital speech. So what conclusion can I possibly arrive at other than that they have simply put profit before people?

Fighting back

The opposition to FOSTA from sex workers and other vulnerable communities was clear from the outset. While major celebrities like Amy Schumer lent their voices in favor of the bill, sex workers were using their online platforms to call on their followers to take action against it. In March of 2018, adult performer Lorelei Lee pleaded with her followers to oppose the bill, writing on Instagram:

> This bill claims to target human trafficking, but does so by creating new penalties for online platforms that are overwhelmingly used by consensual, adult sex workers to screen clients, to share "bad date lists," to work indoors, and to otherwise communicate with each other about ways to stay alive. Data shows that access to these online platforms decreases violence against sex workers, but I don't need data to know that my friends are safer with the ability to screen clients, to share information, and to work indoors.[26]

Rights groups quickly joined in resisting the bill. In a lawsuit brought forth by a group made up of two human rights organizations, an individual advocate for sex workers, a non-sexual certified massage therapist, and the Internet Archive (with the Electronic Frontier Foundation serving as co-counsel), the plaintiffs challenged the law as an unconstitutional violation of the First and Fifth Amendments. In an amicus brief supporting the plaintiffs, the Center for Democracy & Technology argued:

> Without limits on liability for hosting user speech, [intermediaries] are likely to react by significantly limiting what their users can say, including a potentially wide range of lawful speech, from discussions on dating forums about consensual adult sex, to resources for promoting safety among sex workers. Indeed ... that has already started to happen, with platforms restricting access to information that promotes public health and safety, political discourse, and economic growth.[27]

In other words, in an effort to enforce a vague and overly broad law, Silicon Valley's already-prudish policymakers have chosen to err on the side of extreme caution, restricting a range of legitimate expression—the proverbial dolphin in the tuna net. Of course, lawyers will be lawyers, and some might argue that platforms can hardly be blamed for attempts to enforce the law. But that argument might hold more weight if these companies were not already exporting paternalistic American cultural values to the world.

In late 2019 as the presidential race began to heat up in the United States, a handful of Democrats put out a proposal to study the law's impact on sex workers online. (All but one of the legislators, Elizabeth Warren, had opposed the bill from the beginning.) The bill instructed the Department of Health and Human Services to conduct a national study on the legislation's harmful effects. At the time of writing, the bill had been referred to the House Subcommittee on Health. Although its passing would certainly be a step in the right direction, many experts I spoke to believe that it is too late, that the changes inspired by FOSTA will stick even if the study is able to demonstrate concrete harm. Without the force of law, they say, companies simply have no incentive to restore the ability to share adult content. And, as a result of the unique legal framework that exists in the United States, the law cannot force a private actor to host any specific type of speech.

As such, without change emerging from within the companies, we are stuck, stagnant.

Never too late

The re-mystification of sex, the human body and, in particular, the female form is a destructive social phenomenon, but it isn't too late for these platforms to change course. For instance, given that Facebook employs image-recognition technology widely to identify everything from pornography to "terrorist" content, why not turn that technology over to the users and allow them to select what they want to exclude from their feeds? Users with snake phobias could exclude snakes, those who aren't fond of babies could preclude such images from their Facebook experience without alerting the new parents, and those of us whose ideas about the human body are more egalitarian and progressive than Mark Zuckerberg's could opt in to allow women's breasts into our feeds.

Platforms like Instagram could block certain "borderline" content only for young users, rather than suppressing it for everyone. They could also allow users to moderate their own content, either on an individual or community basis. "I would think that making trigger and content warnings would be a great way to give the viewer the option to see the content or to pass on it," Sudhra posits. Tumblr (which is under new ownership once again) could, and ought to, reverse its wholesale ban on adult content. Every platform could do with a lot more transparency about how it moderates content.

Of course, if major platforms refuse to listen to their users, another option is on the table: we can build new spaces, spaces that genuinely promote freedom of expression and not a sanitized, prude-approved version of it.

"I think an ideal platform would be one that is built and organized by BIPOC [Black, Indigenous, people of color], trans folk, and sex workers," says Sudhra. "I think there should be a platform for freedom of expression, not just sexual freedom but to be able to talk about politics and our experiences." Sudhra's version of free expression is not without limits either, but the ones she would like to see applied stand in stark contrast to the status quo: "anything involving minors, self-harm, physical violence."

Sudhra's point gets at the subjectivity of defining what is "harmful"—and, viewed in light of most Silicon Valley platforms' actual policies, it becomes clearer that their version of "harm" lines up almost precisely with historical American definitions of the same. That is why Facebook allows gun shops to advertise on their platform, but a book about vaginas is barred from doing so. It is why Donald Trump can call for the violent invasion of another country on Twitter with no consequence, but breasts are hidden behind an interstitial.

The proponents of these policies are perhaps too deeply embedded in their own regressive worldview to see the breadth of the harm they are perpetrating. That is why it is imperative to claim space so people of color, queer and trans individuals, women, people with disabilities, and all other manner of marginalized individuals can have a seat at the table.

8

From Humans to Machines

The A.I. tools are a blunt instrument. They can easily function at scale in a way that humans cannot, but with the terrible downside of being overly broad in yielding hits, unable to make fine or nuanced decisions beyond what they have been expressly programmed for.

—Sarah T. Roberts

In a few short years, automation has crept into nearly every aspect of our online lives. It determines what we see when we open our Twitter feeds. It is used to serve us ads for products that might be of interest to us. It is in use every time we search for something on Google, it keeps spam out of our inboxes and, increasingly, it is being deployed to enforce the content policies set by platforms.

Automation's basic predecessor—what I'll refer to as "technology-assisted content moderation"—has been around since well before Mark Zuckerberg even dreamed of Facebook. Basic filtering software intended for use in the home or by libraries and other public access points was popularized in the 1990s following the development of the Children's Internet Protection Act (CIPA) in the United States. Numerous governments have long used some type of filtering—first IP blocking and DNS filtering, then moving to more sophisticated methods—to prevent their citizens from accessing certain information online. And the widespread adoption of email three decades ago gave rise to a variety of filtering techniques to counter spam.

These forms of technology-assisted content moderation were

strikingly rudimentary and resulted in much of the same kind of overbroad moderation that we see today. To understand the root of the problem, we must travel back in time to rural England in the mid-1990s.

Before it entered the lexicon of technologists and free speech enthusiasts, the town of Scunthorpe, in North Lincolnshire, wasn't known for much beyond steel manufacturing. But in 1996, Scunthorpe became internationally known for an interesting problem: sandwiched in between "S" and "horpe" lies a profanity unspeakable in the United States—so much so that comedian George Carlin famously included the word in his famous 1972 monologue "Seven Words You Can Never Say on Television."

Though British standards differ considerably, that hardly mattered to the Web portal AOL, which included the word in a list of banned terms. The result? Scunthorpians seeking to register accounts with the online service provider were unable to do so, as their town was not recognized as valid. According to an article in the Scunthorpe *Evening Telegraph*, the company chalked up the situation to an "internal software problem" and, as a stopgap, temporarily renamed the town to "Sconthorpe" for its users.[1] One might imagine that this humorous incident served as a lesson for AOL's developers, but sure enough, the problem soon arose again, this time for a user whose last name, Kuntz, triggered the same filter.[2]

Of course, were the issue limited to AOL, we might be able to toss it into the annals of history as a funny problem from another era. In fact, the Scunthorpe dilemma has never been solved. Over the years, dozens of entities from the British House of Commons to Google have employed technology that's led to this sort of collateral damage. There was the time that the town of Whakatāne, New Zealand, censored its own name from its free wireless internet because the software's phonetic analysis correctly identified the Māori pronunciation of the word (where "wh" takes the "f" sound).[3] The time when a gourmet fungus enthusiast was prevented from registering the URL "shitakemushrooms.com."[4] The Winnipeg-based publication the *Beaver* had to change its name after eighty-nine years after the magazine repeatedly fell victim to basic spam filters that registered its title as a banned slang term.[5] And London's Horniman Museum's own spam filters blocked it from receiving any email because the filters perceived "Horniman" as akin to "horny man."[6]

These stories provoke laughter, in part because they were more or less harmless. In each, a resolution or workaround was found, and the "victim" of the filtering got some free press out of it. But that isn't always the case; sometimes, lazy filtering can cause serious harms to those caught up in its reach. Take, for instance, the high-achievers who cannot get a foot in the door because they graduated cum laude, or the individuals whose given name—such as Natalie Weiner—prevents them from signing up for basic web services.[7] To engineers, these are edge cases, but for some of the people whom they affect, they can amount to discrimination.

This remains a complex problem because it requires the filtering technology to be able to understand the context of a given sentence. That is, the *Beaver* is a perfectly acceptable name for a publication, but "beaver" typed alongside other terms will surely bring up pornographic content. For all the advances we've made in the development of automated technologies, today's machine learning algorithms still struggle with the basics of nuance.

Analysing sentiment

For as long as they have existed, online comment sections have been a cesspool of harassment, profanity, and spam. As a writer, I've always avoided reading the comments and I'm not the only one—"Don't read the comments" has become a sort of mantra among the women writers I know. Therefore, some of my friends were at first pleased to see that Jigsaw—formerly Google Ideas, and still a department of Alphabet—had developed a tool to downrank or filter "toxic" comments.

The tool, called Perspective API, uses machine learning to try to determine the intent or tone of a segment of text. In its initial iteration, it ranked the text on a toxicity scale of 0 to 100, based on the text's similarity to comments ranked previously by humans. Those individuals had been asked to rate online comments on a scale from "very toxic" to "very healthy," with the "toxic" label applied to aa "rude, disrespectful, or unreasonable comment that is likely to make you leave a discussion." A demonstration currently available on the Perspective API website shows that comments beginning with "I think" or "I believe" tend to rank as less toxic, while more direct language and text that contains profanities tend to rank higher.[8]

It didn't take long for critics—myself included—to start pointing out Perspective's flaws. The artist and machine learning researcher Caroline Sinders observed that the API was rating tone rather than toxicity, and criticized its developers for using too narrow a dataset. "This is a data set of agitation and anger, and perhaps, not really toxicity," she wrote in 2017, not long after the product's alpha launch.[9]

My own criticism that year echoed Sinders'. I surmised that because Perspective was trained on text from actual comments, its interpretation was limited—"because 'fuck you', an inherently negative sentiment, is more common in online comment sections than the inherently positive 'fuck yeah.'"[10] I conducted my own tests and found that while the phrase "fuck off" registered at 100 percent toxic, sentences like "women are not as smart as men" and "genocide is good" ranked very low on the toxicity scale.[11] Similarly, a more recent Brazilian study found that the language used by drag queens ranked higher on the toxicity scale than that used by white supremacists, in part because it contained slang terms and terms once considered derogatory but since reclaimed by the LGBTQ community.[12]

Just as with filtering, the problems with Perspective API is a human problem—that is, these technologies are only as good as the information that humans give them. But unlike simple filters, machine learning algorithms learn from data inputs and build a model of the world based on that data. Artificial intelligence (AI) therefore reflects the worldview of its creators. It can be biased or discriminatory, and it can acquire harmful cultural associations that can hurt real people.

Scholars such as Kate Crawford and Virginia Dignum have demonstrated how automated technologies used in a growing number of areas in our lives, from law enforcement to self-driving cars, have the potential to cause significant harm. Yet AI-based consumer products, marketed for everything from emotion detection to face-matching, continue to proliferate unregulated.

Across Silicon Valley, AI continues to be seen largely as a force for good, despite ample evidence to the contrary. Intermediary platforms employ AI pervasively, but their use of it remains highly opaque, despite repeated calls from civil society for more transparency. We know that it's used to deliver search results for us that—as Safiya Umoja Noble demonstrates in her 2018 book *Algorithms of Oppression* through examples such as the sexualized search results that emerge when an individual searches terms like "black girls"—often comes at the expense of minority groups.

We know that our Twitter timelines, Facebook feeds, and YouTube queues are populated with content that an algorithm decided we might enjoy, based on data we ourselves provided. But what we know least about is how, behind the scenes, AI is increasingly being put to use to enforce platform policies, thus assisting or replacing human content moderators.

The human in the loop

"Machine learning" is a sloppy catchall term for a number of mathematical regressions used to extrapolate trends and derive meaning from given data sets. Algorithms are, however, only approximations of the world as we know it. For humans, who have a different understanding from machines of the quantified world, this means that algorithms are fallible, especially when their results have real-world consequences.

Machine learning is fundamentally made possible by surveillance capitalism. Reporter Rolfe Winkler explains that while "theories underlying AI date back decades, …. machine learning for commercial use became possible only with the amassing of huge data sets used to train computers to think on their own … and the parallel development of faster semiconductors."[13] These data sets, derived from what users share on platforms, are transformed into behavioral data for analysis and, ultimately, profit.

Scholar Shoshanna Zuboff depicts the phenomenon as a quest by corporations to predict, and control, our behavior. The output of unpaid users, she wrote in a 2014 essay, is "asserted as 'exhaust'— waste without value—that [is] expropriated without resistance," thus allowing corporations to extract what they wish and utilize it for their own gains. Under surveillance capitalism, argues Zuboff, "populations are not to be employed and served. Instead, they are to be harvested for behavioral data."[14]

Although it is the data accumulated from what users share—our intimate imagery, our cries for action, our passionate political arguments—that enables surveillance capitalism in the first place, that data is only useful to companies when it can be turned into profit. While to the user, a given post might constitute a lifeline, to the company it has little meaning beyond the money it might generate.

While machine learning technologies are being applied to numerous sectors, over the past few years, Silicon Valley has increasingly found them useful for content moderation. Now, the quest by companies to institute machine learning technologies throughout not only their social platforms but their entire digital infrastructure has become a virtual arms race with no end in sight.

The pioneers of this competition have large swaths of social data at their disposal, gleaned from more than a decade of operations and purchased with their massive war chests. The data used to test and train machines comes directly from users—that is, from the personal photograph collections, profile data, and even text posts shared by individuals over time, as well as offline data pertaining to our IRL (in real life) identities such as information purchased from third-party data brokers.

Today, that amalgamated data is being used for some of the most taxing and contentious labor on the planet: regulating what is acceptable expression on the largest platforms in the world. It informs what our timelines and content feeds look like, helping companies to determine popular content well as informing content moderation processes to keep certain content *off* the platforms ... increasingly before it's even published.

It is important to note that not all machine-assisted or automated filtering involves machine learning. For example, Twitter appears to use rudimentary filtering technology to remove potentially offensive replies from users' feeds, falling victim to the "Scunthorpe effect".

Still, machine learning is increasingly being used, with varying success, to moderate visual content.

As the Open Technology Institute, a program of the think tank New America, has observed, "The accuracy of a given tool in detecting and removing content online is highly dependent on the type of content it is trained to tackle." That is to say, engineers and developers have succeeded in training tools so they focus on certain types of easily classifiable content—such as child sexual abuse imagery, copyrighted content, and nudity. "This," the Institute observes, "is because these categories of content have large corpora with which tools can be trained and clear parameters around what falls in these categories."[15]

Think of the process of machine learning like this: When a young person is learning to read, they learn distinct attributes of each letter. Over time, it becomes easier to distinguish an *n* from a *m* or a *b* from a *d*. Similarly, researchers use "training data" to teach a neural network the parameters of images that engineers want to "find"; a robust "training data" library composed of many different versions of the same type of image creates the contours of the image-classification algorithm. Because companies already have a repository of content that human moderators have removed, they can use those images to train machines to quasi-replicate the task. However, because the human body comes in many forms, an algorithm may classify a type of permitted content (for example, a male nipple) in the category of banned content (for example, a female nipple). When the former is conflated with the latter, it's called a "false positive" (and conversely, if a system classifies a banned image as an acceptable image, it's called a "false negative").

Because such systems are proprietary, there is barely any opportunity to audit the neural networks that the platforms use. And while transparency reporting may depict classification errors made by moderators—human or machine—companies rarely publish their actual error rates. Because machines will allow or deny a piece of content on the basis of a confidence threshold that a given set of pixel gradients is in fact a female breast—and not say, a bald head—the potential for bias is great.

The birth of a new technology

Of course, in order to train a tool to identify materials within a given category, humans must first create a database of that content. In 2008, computer science professor Dr. Hany Farid was tasked with building a tool that could detect child sexual abuse imagery, and thus relieve human moderators of the demoralizing task. In this case, a database with that content had already been compiled by law enforcement; in the United States, it was held by the National Center for Missing and Exploited Children.

"There was concern about how you could build technology that would efficiently and accurately remove content without catching in its net innocent material," Farid said in a 2017 interview.[16] But, weighing the costs of over-moderation against the harms of child sexual abuse imagery, his team pressed on, and a new technology was born.

PhotoDNA, as it is called, extracts a distinct signature from the images on which it is trained. That signature is stable for the life of the image, even if that image is modified. It is "very similar to our human DNA," as Farid tells it. "It's incredibly accurate because we don't try to solve that very hard problem of asking a computer to distinguish in reality between child porn and not—that's still the job of a human that is really, in my opinion, uniquely qualified to do that. But then once it's done, we let the technology loose and can be very effective in filtering this content online."

"Human in the loop" is a commonly used term for a model requiring human interaction. In the context of automated technologies used for content moderation, this typically means one of two things: human involvement in the process of database creation, as Farid describes; or human oversight—auditing—of automated processes. He says: "The breakthrough we had in 2008–2009 was to develop a technology that did not actually take the human out of the loop; it actually left the human in the loop to make that very hard determination about what qualifies as child pornography and what does not, and then it would let the technology loose looking for that content that had been previously determined to be very clearly, unambiguously child pornography, and that's why it's actually been so successful in the worldwide deployment."[17]

When it comes to child sexual abuse imagery, society is largely comfortable with the potential of over-moderation. The negative impact of accidentally removing a video or image of a young-looking adult engaged in sexual activity is outweighed by the importance of ensuring that non-consensual, abusive images of children engaged in such activities are eradicated from the internet.

But when it comes to other types of content, the calculation may be different. As legal scholar Evelyn Douek once succinctly tweeted: "We need to get better at talking about what kinds of errors we prefer and want to accept. Content moderation at scale means errors are inevitable."[18]

Context is everything

If errors are inevitable, then it is imperative that we analyze these errors to understand the weight of the harm they cause.

In 2017, Facebook removed a photo posted by a prominent journalist from the United Arab Emirates of Hezbollah leader Hassan Nasrallah with a rainbow Pride flag overlaying it—a satirical statement commenting on the group's popularity among a certain segment of the left despite its lack of support for LGBTQ rights. We do not know whether removing the photo was a human or automated decision, but were it the latter, it's easy to understand how a machine trained to detect and remove images of the man could fail to grasp the nuance.

This example might seem silly to some readers, but consider this: By tackling "terrorist content" with a blunt instrument, are we disempowering the voices that could rise up to fight back against it? Are we enabling the silencing of people who dare to criticize a group that could very easily kill them?

And are we okay with the erasure of history? As documented in chapter 5, it is automation that has led to the mass removal of video evidence of war crimes in Syria, Libya, and elsewhere. It is certainly easy to understand how an automated tool trained to identify and remove graphic violence could fail to understand the historical significance of a given video—and much harder to solve the problem without a willingness to dedicate serious resources to it, which companies have demonstrated time and time again that they lack.

But if it is difficult to create training technology that recognizes classifiable visual content, imagine the complexity of doing so for text-based content. We have already seen how complicated it is to simply separate "cunt" from "Scunthorpe" or differentiate "fuck you" from "fuck yeah"—and yet Silicon Valley continues to insist that it can build technology to identify concepts that humans have struggled for decades or longer to define.

In early 2020, Facebook announced that AI "proactively detects 88.8 percent of the hate speech" the company removes, up from 80.2 percent the previous quarter—an improvement the company attributes to the development of "a deeper semantic understanding of language, so our systems detect more subtle and complex meanings," and the broadening of "how our tools understand content, so that our systems look at the image, text, comments, and other elements holistically."[19] Although Facebook acknowledges that its systems "will never be perfect" and that "context and subtle distinctions of language are key," evidence suggests that the problems related to its AI are much bigger than the company is willing to admit.

The Open Technology Institute describes the challenge thus: "In the case of content such as extremist content and hate speech, there are a range of nuanced variations in speech related to different groups and regions, and the context of this content can be critical in understanding whether or not it should be removed. As a result, developing comprehensive datasets for these categories of content is challenging, and developing and operationalizing a tool that can be reliably applied across different groups, regions, and sub-types of speech is also extremely difficult. In addition, the definition of what types of speech fall under these categories is much less clear." The Institute concludes that "these tools are limited in that they are unable to comprehend the nuances and contextual variations present in human speech."[20]

Dave Willner seems to agree. On one of our several phone calls, he echoed an idea that nearly every expert has acknowledged: automation works well for classifiable content, but for most other things it is a poor substitute for human moderation. He explained that a machine provided with an image of, say, Kim Kardashian's naked behind cannot say, "This is a famous photo of a person who is nude.' The context isn't in the photo in any way. You have to know other facts, you have to know history ... those problems are really hard, much harder than the descriptive problems." The same, he says, goes for detecting names. "There's no reason a particular word is or isn't a name—you have to know that people use it as a name, which is just this out-of-context fact. If you ask moderators to know those rules, you're going to be disappointed at scale—there are too many names, and too many photos, and people just aren't reliable in large groups."

That is why mononymous Indonesians—those who are known by a single name—have complained of having to make up real-sounding second names in order to register for certain platforms. It is why Native Americans, whose names are often descriptive in nature, have been systematically booted from Facebook, and why a Japanese woman with the surname of "Yoda" was told by the company that her moniker was a fake.[21] Facebook's executives speak often of the platform being a global community, but those whose names do not fit within an Anglocentric idea of what is a name are subject to punitive measures that are not experienced by other users.

Cultural complexities

Several years ago, Google Photos rolled out auto-labeling of user photo libraries. An algorithm would "scan" each image and classify it according to its attributes; however, the company ran into controversy when its automated system labeled Black people as "apes."[22] Around the same time, researchers demonstrated how Google Images search results displayed gender-based bias when returning results for both "doctor" (the search returned mostly images of men) and "nurses" (the search was populated primarily by images of women health care workers).[23]

These examples show two of the many unintended consequences that can and do arise from a reliance on automated content detection.

First, algorithms must be "trained" to complete a task that—even to young children—is as "simple" as differentiating a human from a non-human. Second, despite new techniques like unsupervised learning, automated systems in many ways suffer from the "garbage-in, garbage-out" data problem. Societal inequalities (like gender over-representation in particular professions) can therefore be reflected in the form of biased system output.

At scale, thanks to content moderation's reliance on technology, societal biases are dramatically manifested. Engineers may not be aware of the bias that their automated systems have developed due to skewed training libraries, and without dedicated teams to search out and eliminate bias, the inferences made by neural networks may not be apparent until they have caused harm. This problem has been exacerbated by the lack of diversity on Silicon Valley's engineering teams, where frontline engineers may never experience the algorithmic idiosyncrasies that deprive users of dignity.

Training data libraries that do not reflect the diversity of global user bases can create normative attributes for certain types of image classifications. A Black person is seen to have more in common with a primate than a white person; or, a photo of a body with large breasts is assumed to belong to a woman. When action-based moderation systems are built on this same logic, a user's physical appearance must essentially "pass" for "acceptable" or face algorithmic false-positive consequences (female body + nipple = *delete*). Similarly, when algorithms are designed to carry out tasks under a binary logic (male nipple = *ignore*; female nipple = *delete*), systems don't have the ability to understand nuances of self-identity.

Although many companies now have globally robust user bases, that has not always been the case. Because early adopters of these platforms came primarily from high-bandwidth countries—North America, Europe, and Asia—the data that companies have collected over the past decade is asymmetric, and reason dictates that the data ingested by machine learning systems create results that are not truly representational of the world at large. Unfortunately, because algorithms are proprietary and secretive, we can't see inside to know how the data is being used—or to what degree it's skewed.

When it comes to text, the problem is again fraught with even more complexities. As we have seen, machines have trouble differentiating between "fuck you" (inherently negative in sentiment) and "fuck yeah" (nearly always positive). That differentiation becomes even more difficult when the word in question is of foreign origin: not only must a company's engineering team consider the sentiment in the word's use, but it must also consider *all possible sentiments*, in *all cultural contexts*.

While there are advancements in natural language processing technology to identify sentiment, the meaning of language is still entangled in the mouth of the speaker and the ear of the listener. This is a phenomenon with which artful translators are deeply familiar, of course, as they must convey the meaning intended in the original language using words and phrases with which their new audience is culturally familiar.

But when it comes to content moderation, the problem is clear: companies simply do not put the same amount of resources into non-major languages as they do into English, Spanish, French, and a handful of others (sometimes leading, as we saw in Myanmar, to dire consequences). In some cases, they entirely lack support for certain languages—such as Luganda, which is the most widely spoken language of Uganda with more than 8 million speakers.[24] This, of course, has an impact on both the effectiveness of human and automated content moderation—if there's next to no one with expertise in a given language, it's no surprise that content will be wrongfully deleted (or wrongfully ignored).

One stark example of the difficulties presented by applying automation to a foreign language with insufficient resources arose in Myanmar with the Burmese word *kalar*. Though the etymology of the word remains disputed by scholars, it is traditionally used to refer to people of East Indian origin, or as an adjective meaning "Indian."[25] As Burmese journalist Thant Sin notes, "In recent years, the rise of radical nationalist movements has given the word an extremely derogatory connotation. 'Kalar' is used by ultra-nationalists and religious fundamentalists to attack Muslims in Myanmar especially the Rohingya minority in the northwest part of the country."[26]

As such, Facebook decided to systematically ban the word from use. The company acknowledges that this and related issues pose a "hard question." In a thoughtful Facebook blog post authored by public policy vice president Richard Allan in 2017, he noted, "It's clear we're not perfect when it comes to enforcing our policy. Often there are close calls—and too often we get it wrong."[27] Allan continued: "Sometimes, there isn't a clear consensus—because the words themselves are ambiguous, the intent behind them is unknown or the context around them is unclear. Language also continues to evolve, and a word that was not a slur yesterday may become one today."

As Sin wrote that same year, "'Kalar' may be commonly associated with racism today, but the word on its own does not necessarily constitute hate speech. Context matters—many people have reported that posts in which they discussed the use of the term, or expressed concern about its usage, were censored as well." He continued: "Moreover, there are several Burmese words with completely different meanings that contain the same string of characters as 'kalar'. For instance, chair in Burmese is also written 'kalar htaing', which contains the same characters, as well as other words such as 'kalar pae' (split pea), 'kalar oat' (camel) or 'kalarkaar' (curtain)."[28]

Just like Perspective API and Bing Search before it, Facebook fell into the insoluble trap of trying to ban a word that has both caused great harm and exists in perfectly banal (or positive) usage. Although the company has not been transparent about its use of automation with respect to such terms, it is reasonable to assume that it is not reliant on humans to review every use of a single word.

It really does come down to deciding what kinds of errors we are willing to accept. Does the importance of banning a word like *kalar* that has been weaponized against the Rohingya outweigh the need to be able to discuss camels, curtains, and split pea soup? Is it so important that we be allowed to exclaim "fuck yeah!"? And can we trust machines to differentiate between discussions of breasts, breast cancer, and chicken breasts?

Again, Facebook has openly recognized that its systems will result in collateral damage. In his post, Allan wrote:

In Russia and Ukraine, we faced a similar issue around the use of slang words the two groups have long used to describe each other. Ukrainians call Russians "moskal," literally "Muscovites," and Russians call Ukrainians "khokhol," literally "topknot." After conflict started in the region in 2014, people in both countries started to report the words used by the other side as hate speech. We did an internal review and concluded that they were right. We began taking both terms down, a decision that was initially unpopular on both sides because it seemed restrictive, but in the context of the conflict felt important to us.[29]

Facebook is right about one thing: these are indeed hard questions with no correct answers. But they are questions that we as a society must debate, rather than leaving their outcomes to corporations.

Move fast and break things

The complexities of automation—and the ability of users to understand how it is being used to moderate their speech—is exacerbated by the fact that the algorithms used by companies are, in nearly every case, proprietary. As such, neither the public nor regulatory officials have the right to inspect training data or how algorithms are being implemented.

On top of that, Silicon Valley companies have historically been extraordinarily secretive about the degree to which they are using automation to moderate given categories of expression. Although many observers and scholars have suspected the use of automated technologies for this purpose for nearly a decade, the major platforms have only been forthcoming about their use for the past three to four years—coinciding with increased public and governmental pressure to eradicate online extremism.

One early example of external pressure leading to the implementation of automation, says Anna (the former Facebook operations staffer) was the 2015 Paris attack at the Bataclan theater. "The morning after the Bataclan attack in France," she recalled, "the French government asked Facebook to take down all the pictures of victims, which was a lot of work. I got [to work], and I saw not just the French team but every single person who speaks French in all of community operations. We got engineers to help us build automations, and all sorts of resources mobilized around this specific thing when, on a regular basis, we would have all similar problems in other markets—say, an explosion in the Urdu market or the Arabic-speaking market—and we never once got this kind of resources."

Not long after the attack, companies began to open up slightly about their use of automated tools. Google announced in 2017 that it would use machine learning to detect extremist content. Two months after the announcement, the company stated that 75 percent of videos removed under its definition of "violent extremism" were taken down "before receiving a single flag."[30] Facebook followed suit shortly thereafter, announcing that, according to the *New York Times*, "artificial intelligence will largely be used in conjunction with human moderators who review content on a case-by-case basis." But, the company's head of global policy management Monika Bickert told the *Times*, "developers hope its use will be expanded over time."[31]

Similarly, Twitter boasted in 2018 of the removal of 1.2 million terrorist accounts during a two-year period that were "flagged by [the company's] internal, proprietary tools"—while 74 percent of those accounts "were suspended before their first tweet."[32] Not stated, however, are the criteria the company used to define "terrorism" or identify the accounts—and the arrival of the aforementioned GIFCT (Global Internet Forum to Counter Terrorism) in 2017 has done little to provide greater transparency.

Without that transparency, researchers are left guessing. Dia Kayyali has been documenting the removal of content from Syria, along with colleagues at Syrian Archive, for several years. "It appears to us that machine learning algorithms are detecting content specifically based on region and language, not only what's actually in the video," they said. "So there's been a large range of content actually removed. Of course, I focus on human rights content, so that includes videos of protest, videos of chemical weapons attacked, videos filmed by perpetrators of human rights abuses—for example, a video filmed by ISIS showing them killing people."

Attempts by civil society organizations and academics to push companies toward more transparency have been with great resistance. Most often, companies claim that their tools are "protected as trade secrets in order to maintain their competitive edge in the market," or that sharing them might allow bad actors to "[learn] enough to game their systems."[33] Some researchers are less concerned about the proprietary issues as they are of the challenges of interpreting what they suspect is unwieldy data. They contend that opening the black box to research would "yield a large volume of incomprehensible data that is a combination of inputs and outputs and that would require significant data analysis in order to extract insights," and that although processing such data is not inherently impossible, it "would not generally provide any transparency around how the actual decision-making occurred, as well as how a company is ensuring tools are being used fairly."[34]

One way that companies could—and reportedly do—mitigate the harms perpetrated by technological decision making is to guarantee human oversight. "Automatic detection produces too many false positives; in light of this, some platforms and third parties are pairing automatic detection with editorial oversight," writes scholar Tarleton Gillespie.[35]

These layers of complexity suggest that when it comes to automated tools for content moderation, Silicon Valley has put the cart before the horse. Rather than unleashing a set of opaque, proprietary technologies on a sensitive set of subjects, companies might have worked with external (or internal) experts to ensure that fairness, transparency, and clarity prevailed. Instead, they chose to move fast and break things.

During one of our conversations, Nicole Wong, the early Google policy "decider," shared her concerns about the direction that companies are now taking. When I asked her about the use of algorithms to distinguish terrorism online, she said: "We [shouldn't] do that by algorithms; there's no algorithm that's ever going to be able to do that in a consistent and principled way."

Wong says she "didn't sleep a lot during those seven years" that she was at Google, but she nevertheless felt at the time that moderation was possible at scale, "if you had enough triage—people really well trained at the front line and escalating the right things, which is what we were trying to do. You could actually have human review." But today, she says, "that gets hard at the scale that these platforms are trying to do and in the variety of countries [in which they operate]."

A failed proposition?

There are, and have always been, thoughtful people at each company who have considered the pitfalls of applying automation to something that humans still struggle to get right. I spoke with a number of them in the course of my research. And yet, they are themselves in many ways just cogs in a much larger machine. Their concerns may get heard, but rarely seem to result in change.

Ultimately, business interests come first. Companies are rightly under increasing pressure to provide their human content moderators—wage laborers—with better pay, benefits, and mental health support, to mitigate the harms of what is a grueling, sometimes heartbreaking job. They are simultaneously under pressure, of course, to make more and more money, and while the upfront costs of building technology can be steep, automation in the long run costs far less than paying content moderators a livable wage.

But, as the next billion people come online, the impossibility of moderating content at scale will only grow. Although it feels inevitable that companies will continue to turn to automation to solve this paradox, there is a rising tide of opposition from researchers, activists, and governments with which companies must reckon.

Much of the prominent opposition thus far has been aimed at uses of automation that have far more dire consequences than the moderation of online speech—such as predictive policing and criminal sentencing—but the underlying problems are nevertheless similar. The Center for Democracy & Technology has called proprietary algorithms "barriers to social justice"; the rapidly growing AI Now Institute has a collection of works documenting the problems inherent to artificial intelligence; and the Institute of Electrical and Electronics Engineers, the largest technical professional organization in the world, is working on a standard for algorithmic bias considerations.[36]

This is a problem that will not go away. Algorithms are simply incapable of encapsulating human experience, regardless of what Silicon Valley would have us believe. And once companies have taken humans out of the loop and relinquished the reins to machines, there is no telling the sort of cultural norms they will eventually propagate in the future.

9

The Virality of Hate

They have rules, but enforcement is completely random.
—Roger McNamee

In 2009, when Mark Zuckerberg was just twenty-five and Facebook two decades younger than that, the company faced its first hate speech controversy. The topic? Holocaust denial.

After news emerged that Facebook was knowingly playing host to several groups dedicated to denying the atrocities committed against Jews during World War II, a storm of criticism erupted on blogs and in the media. The firestorm culminated in an open letter from Brian Cuban, the brother of billionaire Mark Cuban, calling on Facebook to be transparent "on the specifics of how [the company] went about arriving at [its] controversial decision" to not remove the groups.[1] Addressing Zuckerberg directly, Cuban wrote:

Were you involved? Do you offer any input in these types of discussions? How does Facebook define "internal debate"? How many people were involved? What was their expertise to discuss this issue? Did they bring their personal beliefs to the table? What safeguards were employed to ensure objectivity in a decision that is innately subjective? Were attorneys consulted that have experience in such matters or was it general counsel? Do you agree that something can be legal but still constitute hate speech? Was the final decision yours? Did the buck stop with you?

Cuban was asking important questions at a time when most saw social media as a thing to be enjoyed, or utilized for career progress. His concern that the company may have been less than diligent in creating its community standards was not unfounded. As a result of his letter, Facebook did shut down a handful of Holocaust denial groups, but most were left in place. Barry Schnitt, who served as Facebook's director for corporate communications and public policy for four crucial years of the company's growth (2008–2012), stated at the time:

> We have spent considerable time internally discussing the issues of Holocaust denial and have come to the conclusion that the mere statement of denying the Holocaust is not a violation of our terms …
>
> Many of us at Facebook have direct personal connection to the Holocaust, through parents who were forced to flee Europe or relatives who could not escape. We believe in Facebook's mission that giving people tools to make the world more open is a better way to combat ignorance or deception than censorship, though we recognize that others, including those at the company, disagree.[2]

In those early days, Facebook's position with respect to Holocaust denial was mainly consistent with their broader handling of hate speech on the platform. But the largely hands-off approach taken by Facebook as well as other companies would soon be challenged as the emergence of the Islamic State was immediately followed in quick succession by the rise of harassment and right-wing propaganda online.

An amorphous concept

Although policymakers around the world have tried to argue otherwise, defining "hate speech" is a next-to-impossible task, one that transcends even the "I know it when I see it" nonsense applied to obscenity. Many have endeavored, and many have failed, but that hasn't stopped Silicon Valley from trying.

Around the world, hate speech is an amorphous concept most often defined by state actors with national (or nationalist) interests at heart, able to be weaponized against critics or used in the pursuit of justice.

International human rights frameworks are intended to provide clarity, but to some, offer contradiction instead. Article 7 of the Universal Declaration of Human Rights (UDHR) a "all are equal before the law and are entitled without any discrimination to equal protection," including "any discrimination in violation of the Declaration itself, and against any incitement to such discrimination." Article 19 doesn't address hate speech directly, but guarantees that everyone has the right to "seek, receive and impart information and ideas through any media and regardless of frontiers."

In 1960, at a time when the horrors of the Holocaust were still fresh in most of the world's collective memory (and yet antisemitism was still alive and well), and the messy process of decolonization was coming to an end in much of Asia and Africa, the United Nations General Assembly adopted a resolution condemning "all manifestations and practices of racial, religious and national hatred" as violations of the UN Charter, and the UDHR and called upon states to "take all necessary measures to prevent all manifestations of racial, religious and national hatred."

The International Covenant on Civil and Political Rights (ICCPR), a multilateral treaty adopted by the UN General Assembly in 1966, commits its signatories to respect the civil and political rights of individuals, which includes the right to life; freedom of speech, religion, and assembly; and the right to due process and a fair trial, among other things. There are, at the time of this publication, 173 state parties to the Covenant, as well as 6 signatories without ratification. Some states ratified the treaty with stated reservations, and its enforceability varies from country to country.

The United States—which did not ratify the ICCPR until 1992, after the fall of Eastern Communism—is among those with significant reservations. Most pertinently, the US does not allow any of the articles of the ICCPR to restrict the right of free speech and association, which functionally means that the Constitution, which does not allow for restrictions on hate speech, trumps any provisions of the treaty that do.

The ICCPR was followed by a draft resolution from the UN's Economic and Social Council on "manifestations of racial prejudice and national and religious intolerance," calling on governments to educate the public against intolerance and to rescind discriminatory laws. A number of newly independent African nations—including the Central African Republic, Dahomey (now Benin), Cote d'Ivoire, Mali, and Mauritania—pushed for an international convention addressing racial and religious intolerance, but in the end, split opinions among the various nations resulted in two separate resolutions, one calling for a declaration and draft convention addressing racial discrimination and another addressing religious intolerance.

On that basis was created the International Convention on the Elimination of All Forms of Racial Discrimination (ICERD). The ICERD, adopted by the UN General Assembly in December 1965 and entered into force in 1969, seeks to address racial discrimination at all levels of society, from ensuring equality before the law to guaranteeing the right of access to all public services and spaces. Article 4 in particular addresses the matter of speech, by criminalizing incitement to racial discrimination.

Article 4 has never been without controversy. During debates about the article, there were two drafts: one originated with the United States and the other with the Soviet Union and Poland. The US took the more conservative approach, proposing that only incitement "resulting in or likely to result in violence" be prohibited, while the other party sought to "prohibit and disband racist, fascist and any other organization practicing or inciting racial discrimination." The final text, which was the result of a compromise proposed by the Nordic countries, reads:

States Parties condemn all propaganda and all organizations which are based on ideas or theories of superiority of one race or group of persons of one colour or ethnic origin, or which attempt to justify or promote racial hatred and discrimination in any form, and undertake to adopt immediate and positive measures designed to eradicate all incitement to, or acts of, such discrimination and, to this end, with due regard to the principles embodied in the Universal Declaration of Human Rights and the rights expressly set forth in article 5 of this Convention, inter alia:

(a) Shall declare an offence punishable by law all dissemination of ideas based on racial superiority or hatred, incitement to racial discrimination, as well as all acts of violence or incitement to such acts against any race or group of persons of another colour or ethnic origin, and also the provision of any assistance to racist activities, including the financing thereof;

(b) Shall declare illegal and prohibit organizations, and also organized and all other propaganda activities, which promote and incite racial discrimination, and shall recognize participation in such organizations or activities as an offence punishable by law;

(c) Shall not permit public authorities or public institutions, national or local, to promote or incite racial discrimination.[3]

As with any declarative statement, the ICERD is a document trapped in time, of an era where, for many, racial justice seemed paramount. At the same time, it was heavily formed by the hands of states that didn't hesitate at the thought of limiting freedom of expression. While the heart of many of its supporters was in the right place, others saw the push from the Soviets as a cynical ploy from a nation that had, under Nikita Khrushchev, only begun to consider the rights of its own minorities. The Soviet position is perhaps more understandable when placed into context: The USSR had brutally quashed rebellions in its satellite blocs throughout the previous decade, leading to anti-Russian sentiment in a number of nations. In any case, the ICERD, with sixty-eight signatories spanning every continent, was established at the end of the decade as the preeminent global document addressing hateful speech.

The United States is a signatory to the ICERD, but with a number of reservations. One in particular addresses Articles 4 and 7, specifically by rejecting any obligation under the Convention to restrict the rights of individual freedom of speech, expression, and association, in alignment with the US Constitution. Another relevant reservation addresses Article 22 of the ICERD, which defers disputes between states to the International Court of Justice; the United States asserts that any such referrals require its consent first.

In 1969, the same year in which the ICERD was adopted, *Brandenburg v. Ohio* reached the US Supreme Court.[4] The infamous case hinged on the question of whether a white supremacist and Ku Klux Klan (KKK) leader, Clarence Brandenburg, had the right to advocate violence against minorities. Beyond his eponymous legal case, Brandenburg the man is largely forgotten. Despite his grandiose speeches in which he (not unlike his alt-right successors today) bemoaned the fate of the "White Caucasian race" at the hands of the government, he is an unsympathetic figure rightly left to the annals of history. Yet his case lives on.

After making a speech at a KKK rally advocating violence, Brandenburg was charged under Ohio's Criminal Syndicalism Act. The act, a relic of the first "red scare" that swept the United States in 1919 after the Russian Revolution, prohibited individuals from advocating for "crime, sabotage, violence, or unlawful methods of terrorism as a means of accomplishing industrial or political reform" and "voluntarily assembl[ing] with any society, group, or assemblage of persons formed to teach or advocate the doctrines of criminal syndicalism."[5]

Brandenburg was convicted, fined $1,000, and sentenced to imprisonment for one to ten years, but he saw the Criminal Syndicalism Act as unconstitutional and challenged it in the intermediate appellate court of Ohio, which affirmed his conviction without opinion. The state's Supreme Court also dismissed his appeal, and so fatefully he took his challenge to the US Supreme Court. In the end, the Supreme Court found that Ohio had violated Brandenburg's constitutional right to freedom of speech.

Although other restrictions on expression, most notably those placed on "obscene" content and foreign terrorism, have grown over time in the United States, hate speech remains untouchable by law. It is this set of norms that set the scene for how the policymakers at US social media companies would create the platforms' early rule sets for hateful speech.

Hate speech in the digital era

In September 2005, the Danish newspaper *Politiken* published a story that detailed the difficulty children's book author Kåre Bluitgen was facing finding a publisher for his book on the life of the prophet Mohammed. Bluitgen's book was not intended to be offensive; it followed a long line of books by the author that presented worldly topics to children along with illustrations. But because of the Islamic prohibition on depictions of the prophet, Bluitgen had encountered difficulty finding an illustrator for his book, a fact that center-right broadsheet *Jyllands-Posten* decided to capitalize on. The paper's culture editor wrote to members of the country's illustrator union, asking them to submit their own depictions of the prophet as a bit of an experiment. Of the union's forty-two members, nine submitted drawings, as did three newspaper employees. Two of the cartoons didn't directly depict the prophet. All were published.

The global reaction was explosive: ambassadors from various Muslim nations demanded to meet with the Danish prime minister, who in turn refused the meetings and urged them to air their grievances in court. A boycott of Danish products swept the Middle East. Saudi Arabia recalled its ambassador, while protesters hit the streets of Cairo, Benghazi, Lagos, Beirut, and a number of other cities. Muslim journalists were arrested for publishing the cartoons in Jordan, Algeria, and Yemen, while those who republished the cartoons in Europe and elsewhere faced death threats.

The publication of and ensuing fallout from the cartoons occurred at a time of particularly strained relations between Muslims and the West. Just four years after 9/11 and only two after the United States' invasion of Iraq, the decision by *Jyllands-Posten* to publish the cartoons appeared to many as an unnecessary provocation, and by others as a challenge to a growing climate of fear and self-censorship. As the *Washington Post* put it aptly at the time, "On one side is a defense of freedom of expression, on the other an unforgivable insult to a sacred figure."[6]

Jyllands-Posten eventually issued a tepid apology for offending Muslims, while defending its right under Danish law to publish the drawings. Finally, in January 2006, the prime minister of Denmark stated on television and in a press statement that he would never have depicted a prophet in an offensive way, but insisted the government could not apologize for one of the country's newspapers. He further stated in no uncertain terms that freedom of speech was absolute, but that "we are all responsible for administering freedom of speech in such a manner that we do not incite hatred and do not cause fragmentation of the Danish community."[7]

At least one journalist, Ehsan Ahrari of the *Asia Times*, pointed out the double standards of European countries in defending the freedom of expression to publish something so offensive to Muslims while enforcing censorship (such as Holocaust denial) in other instances. "To Muslims, the West appears stubbornly against compromising on the freedom of expression, and they see hypocrisy in this because this freedom is not as absolute as it is pretended to be in some quarters," he wrote in a syndicated column.[8] Ahrari additionally noted the impact of Western imperialism on Muslim countries and how it has quashed citizens' hopes for true democracy and freedom: "The rot of authoritarianism, nepotism and corruption has been so entrenched that people cannot realistically aspire to be free, prosperous or see prospects of technological advance."

The UN Commission on Human Rights Special Rapporteur on "contemporary forms of racism, racial discrimination, xenophobia and related intolerance"—a position that emerged from the Commission on Human Rights in 1993—diagnosed the cartoon controversy as stemming from the increase in the conflation of Islam with terrorism; the "worldwide crisis of identity" in adapting to multiculturalism; and, with an eye toward combating racism and discrimination, the inadequacy of international human rights instruments.[9] In effect, the cartoons were a form of "punching down."

The debate over whether the cartoons constitute hate speech perfectly illustrates the difficulty of clearly defining it. In this instance, as in most, answering that question requires context: the publication of the cartoons would likely not have provoked such an intense reaction had it occurred in the 1970s, or even five years before. There would have been anger, perhaps even protests or death threats, but overall, cooler heads might have prevailed. The complexity of hate speech is that the extent of its impact is entirely contingent on the station of the person or group it's directed at, as well as on the person or group that voices it.

But the conflict did not occur in the 1970s; it occurred at a time when many around the world were beginning to find their voices online. The world before social media was different, as only certain voices were able to rise to the top, creating a skewed perception of what is globally tolerable. But when nearly everyone has equal access to the same platforms, the simple fact that not everyone thinks alike—and certainly not everyone shares the same values as those in the United States—becomes strikingly clear.

Nevertheless, in 2006, American opinions were still the loudest and most dominant online, and corporate policymakers certainly gave them more credence—with seeming disregard for who, exactly, was weighing in. Michelle Malkin, a right-wing provocateur whose odiousness seems quaint in light of what was to come, was among the loudest voices speaking out in support of *Jyllands-Posten*. In response to the situation, she created a musical montage showing victims of Muslim terrorist attacks and uploaded it to YouTube, only to find herself banned from the platform.[10]

Malkin was arguably among the first notable individuals to be banned by a major platform under its hate speech policies, and one of the first non-expert commentators to reflect on the inconsistencies of content moderation. In 2017, she remarked upon her situation, writing that eleven years after the *Jyllands-Posten* incident, "the selective censors at Google-YouTube still can't competently distinguish terrorist hate speech from political free speech."[11]

On that point, she is not wrong, but like most ideologically motivated commentators, Malkin believes that people on the right end of the political spectrum are being uniquely persecuted while those on the left—as well as those promoting Islamist rhetoric—are left alone. In fact, this could not be farther from the truth: The majority of online platforms have poured money and resources into tackling Islamist extremism while taking a scattered, inconsistent approach to other forms of hate speech, an approach that is made even worse when the perpetrator of such speech is a world leader.

One story in particular stands out to me: In 2015, before he was elected to the presidency, Donald Trump used social media to call for a "total and complete shutdown" of US borders to Muslims, reportedly sparking internal strife at both Twitter and Facebook. Mainstream US media framed the debate inside Facebook as one between executives and Muslim employees who, according to reports, were "upset that the platform would make an exception" for Trump's hateful speech. According to the reporting, the post "triggered a review by Facebook's community operations team, with hundreds of employees in several offices worldwide."[12] Other reports framed the story as one of Muslim employees trying to "censor" Trump.[13]

What stands out for me in this story is the seeming fact that Mark Zuckerberg and co. only pay attention to internal resistance when it reaches critical mass, which it only seems to do when the cause is American. I am aware of a number of attempts Facebook employees have made over the years to raise concerns about the handling of, for example, wrongful takedowns of Palestinian content or inattention to the growing problem of harassment … all of which were dismissed.

Another thing stands out from the story, the discovery for which I can thank former members of Facebook's Dublin-based operations team who were present in 2015 for the Trump "shutdown" call and the review that followed it. They plainly debunked the reporting for me, saying that there was "no internal Facebook group" where opposition was organized, and that discussion primarily occurred in a community operations group for the Arabic-language content team—a team whose job it was, in part, to engage on such topics.

The team, I was told, tried to explain the global impact of allowing exceptions for the sake of US politics while systematically censoring political content from elsewhere. Some of the team were Muslim, my sources informed me, but some of the loudest members were from other religious groups or were not religious at all.

Inside the United States, the failure of this scattershot approach has been apparent not only when it comes to Trump, but with respect to right-wing ideologues, from British poseur Milo Yiannopoulos to fascist politician Paul Nehlen and conspiracy theorists like Alex Jones, all of whom held onto various social media accounts for quite some time despite what looked to be clear violations of the rules. While companies like Facebook and Twitter have boasted of their ability to remove large swaths of "terrorist content" and have made strides in tackling serial harassment, their approach to populist and right-wing hate is deeply connected to the country's politics du jour, and has repercussions not just in the United States but around the world.

The rise of 4chan politics

Since the early days of Twitter, bots and trolls—terms colloquially and sometimes interchangeably used to describe both automated and human accounts that engage in what companies euphemistically call "inauthentic activity"—have plagued the platform. Though I'm certain that earlier examples exist, my first recollection of this phenomenon is from 2011 when, in response to the growing number of tweets condemning the Syrian government's crackdown on protesters, a bevy of bots sprang up, "flooding [the #Syria hashtag] with [a] predetermined set of tweets– every few minutes–about varied topics such as photography, old Syrian sport scores, links to Syrian comedy shows, pro-regime news, and threats against a long list of tweeps who expressed their support of the protests."[14]

By the following year, as the Syrian civil war escalated, a group of online hacktivists got involved, defacing Syrian government websites and engaging in other attacks in support of the Syrian opposition. That group, Anonymous, had emerged from 4chan not long after the site's creation in 2003 as a meme and a name under which to conduct online pranks. Over time, Anonymous morphed into a decentralized, global hacktivist movement.

Although the decentralized nature of Anonymous render it difficult to define, Gabriella Coleman, an anthropologist who has studied Anonymous extensively, writes: "To be sure, Anonymous is not a singularity, but is comprised of multiple, loosely organised nodes with various regional networks in existence. No one group or individual can control the name and iconography, much less claim legal ownership over them, and as such their next steps are difficult to predict. Although many individual participants therein do resist institutionalisation or even defining their norms ... there are logics at play and stable places for interaction."[15]

Anonymous's first major foray into the broader world took place in 2008 and targeted the Church of Scientology. Hacktivists launched distributed denial of service attacks, or "ops," against the church's website and sent "black faxes" designed to use up printer ink to their offices. On 4chan boards and other channels, those claiming to be members of Anonymous coordinated actions that soon spilled offline. On February 10, 2008, thousands of individuals donning Guy Fawkes masks turned out on the streets of major cities all over the world to protest in front of Church of Scientology facilities.

It was that protest that introduced me to Anonymous. Strolling down Boston's Beacon Street that day, I'd stumbled upon it by chance. The Boston protest only attracted a few dozen people, most of whom appeared to be young men, but the Guy Fawkes masks and my own dislike of Scientology prompted me to search for information about the protest after arriving home that day.

Over the next few years, Anonymous would engage in increasingly elaborate and risky ops against governments including those of Tunisia, China, and Israel, but it was their support of WikiLeaks that drew the most attention and in 2012, the movement was named to TIME Magazine's list of the world's 100 most influential people. The magazine's reader poll—which, unlike the official list, ranks its contenders—placed Anonymous at the top of the list.

Indeed, at the time, Anonymous was popularly viewed to be in the pursuit of justice, targeting abusive governments and corporations and acting in support of perceived underdogs. But an amorphous collective can only stand in unity for so long, and eventually the movement would spawn a variety of others, each with its own aims and moral code. The success of Anonymous, combined with the growing popularity of 4chan (and the flourishing racism on its boards), created conditions for other movements to employ the same tactics ... but in the service of very different goals.

In 2014, the hashtag #EndFathersDay emerged, seemingly out of nowhere, playing host to tweets like "#EndFathersDay because I'm tired of all these white women stealing our good black mens."

The hashtag quickly became fodder for conservative pundits, one of whom mocked it as "drivel" "from the feminist outrage machine."[16]

Shafiqah Hudson, a Black American Twitter user who uses the handle @sassycrass, saw that tweet and, suspicious of its origins, began to dig through the hashtag. According to *Slate* journalist Rachelle Hampton, Hudson asked if anyone on her timeline "had any idea what was up. No one she knew could verify that the women behind these accounts actually existed" and further exploration demonstrated that the accounts utilizing the hashtag did not follow any popular Black feminist accounts. "No one who knew or liked a black feminist was fooled," she told *Slate*.[17] Meanwhile, some of the troll accounts began harassing other users.

Hudson created a hashtag, #YourSlipIsShowing, to flag the fake accounts that she and other Black feminists suspected of being part of a trolling operation. As Hampton describes, "your slip is showing" is a phrase "rooted in the particular Southern black dialect of the South Florida community where Hudson grew up" and refers to something that should be hidden but is instead on full display.[18] Other Black feminists, including I'Nasah Crockett (@so_treu), began digging into the origins of the #EndFathersDay hashtag and discovered that it stemmed from a post on 4chan. Hampton describes the "op" as "part of a crusade by men's rights activists, pickup artists, and miscellaneous misogynists hoping to capitalize on previously existing rifts in the online feminist movement related to race and class."[19]

A number of prominent Black feminists began documenting the accounts and flagging them using Twitter's reporting mechanisms but, Hampton writes, "Hudson and Crockett felt that Twitter basically did nothing." The company suspended a few of the troll accounts, but otherwise, the women were left to their own devices to fight back against the harassment.

Not even a year later, another trolling campaign spawned by 4chan would utilize similar tactics to target women who had criticized the gaming industry, eventually morphing into a broader movement that targeted women in other sectors of tech as well. Attempts to fight back against the campaign, dubbed "GamerGate", were sometimes met with threats of physical violence. Women who were targeted by the campaign tried flagging tweets to Twitter, but often to little avail. At its peak, the hashtag was used hundreds of thousands of times per day, with most tweets in support of the campaign. It would be difficult to overstate the breadth of the campaign: In my own work, I hardly remember any other major topics from 2015. GamerGate affected dozens of women I know; it sucked up all the air in the room and came back for more.

One insidious legacy of GamerGate is the co-optation and appropriation of "free speech"—a term that has always come with limitations—by misogynists and far-right status seekers, who have used it as cover for their hate-filled ideologies, often arguing against or circumventing platform policies. Another is how it how its "success" demonstrated the ease with which mass harassment campaigns—also called "brigading"—can be coordinated on secondary platforms and conducted on Twitter. As writer John Biggs put it aptly in a foundational piece about the rise of so-called 4chan politics, "The folks spreading outrage on the Internet – the outraged Facebookers, the alt-right, the vociferous VCs who don't know when to shut up – are hacking the system. Hackers aren't what they look like in the movies and they aren't 400 pound men in their basements. They are people who have been given a megaphone and prefer to burp and curse and shout into it rather than help. They are the ones who yell "Jump" to the man on the bridge because of his implied weakness." The tools provided by social media, writes Biggs, "are powerful and important and to hijack them is to hijack a mode of discourse."[20]

I never wrote about GamerGate until years later but at the time, I believed that companies should never moderate speech. But while I still strongly believe that corporations should not be the arbiters of speech, I no longer believe that they should never step up to the role that they have been given. As scholar Mary Anne Franks writes, "The cumulative effect of misogynist online abuse is the silencing of women."[21] In the years since GamerGate, a number of women have walked away from social media. Others have locked their accounts. Still others—myself included—self-censor, avoid certain topics, approach the internet with trepidation.

From this phenomenon have also emerged technical tools for dealing with harassment, most of which have come not from the companies, but from external actors. One in particular is blocklists—that is, tools that allow users to collaborate and create lists of individuals that they wish to block. There are a variety of such tools, and they are an important part of a user's arsenal, but they cannot be the only solution.

As stated in previous chapters, when it comes to speech, there will always be tradeoffs and decisions must be based on a holistic understanding of who is harmed—by censorship or inaction. When it comes to harassment, we must consider the harm that comes from threats, from incitement, from brigading—but we must always be careful in how we define those threats, and who we allow to define them.

There is no doubt in my mind that GamerGate was a precursor to the populist online movements, including the alt-right and the QAnon conspiracy-turned-cult, that came after; movements that—at the time of this writing—are growing and splintering like fractals. Its deep, societal impact is beyond the scope of this book, but has been captured by writers such as Zoe Quinn, who experienced it firsthand, and Caroline Sinders, who has documented the history of online harassment.

These legacies should have prepared Silicon Valley for what was to come. Engineering hours could have focused on the development of tools and architectural changes that would lessen the blow of harassment and make it easier for users to block or filter trolls. Companies could have made a real effort to bring in anti-harassment experts to their teams full-time. Instead, it seems, they listened to the media that largely downplayed GamerGate's real-world harms, and as such, were unprepared for what came next.

The rise of the right

Not long after the citizens of the United States elected Donald Trump to the highest office, I read an article suggesting that previously divided white supremacist groups in the United States were beginning to find common ground. The book, an excerpt from Vegas Tenold's 2018 book *Everything You Love Will Burn: Inside the Rebirth of White Nationalism in America*, suggested that many of these groups were thriving thanks to the contributions of media-savvy young people—that is, people of my own generation—like Matthew Heimbach and Richard Spencer.[22]

The article was chilling, and raised new questions for me. How could Americans my age, raised on a healthy diet of diverse television characters and taught at school to respect differences, revert to an odious ideology that had, in the past century, resulted in the cruel deaths of millions? How could young Americans possibly turn toward a belief system that their grandparents had killed people to eradicate?

The answer still confounds me, but the article was correct: during the past decade, white supremacists across America put aside their (minor) differences and, often taking on a more palatable image than the white robes and cross-burnings of the KKK of yore, found common ground with the anti-immigration and anti-Muslim right, as well as with a whole bevy of other disaffected (and disenfranchised) white youth.

In August of 2017, a motley crew of protesters representing all the filthy flavors of white supremacy took to the streets in Charlottesville, Virginia, carrying cheap tiki torches and weapons and chanting racist slogans. The two-day rally, presciently dubbed "Unite the Right," ended with the murder of Heather Heyer, a counter-protester, with a car driven by a young white man who had previously espoused neo-Nazi ideals.

As scholar Joan Donovan explains, "platforms knew very concretely the role that their technology had played in organizing that hateful event" but failed to acknowledge it or enact meaningful change. Donovan argued in an interview with *NPR* that platforms have a responsibility to enforce rules consistently. "Ultimately, these corporations have to think about, well, what is the content moderation strategy? But also how do they enforce it across all of the platforms consistently so that you don't get this blowback effect?"[23]

This book is not about the rise of white supremacy in the United States and will therefore not seek to address the broader factors that led to this point. Rather, I posit that just as social media allowed for disparate communities across the Middle East and North Africa to come together, find common ground, and ultimately change the face of the region, so too has it allowed for white supremacists to do precisely the same.

"Social media empowers previously marginal people," Dave Willner stated in our final interview, "and some of those previously marginal people are trans teenagers and some are neo-Nazis. The empowerment sense is the same, and some of it we think is good and some of it we think is not good. The coming together of people with rare problems or views is agnostic." Indeed. Therefore, in the absence of regulations on hate speech, it is left to companies to decide what is good and what is intolerable.

Within days of the hate rally, there was an outpouring of reporting and opinion pieces about the role social media had played in its organization—and what to do about it. While some argued for the rethinking of the First Amendment, others observed how people were using social media to identify those who had participated in the protests.[24] Still others criticized the companies for not doing enough, arguing that both the rules and the tools to eradicate white supremacy from social platforms were already in place.[25]

Indeed, by 2017, Facebook, Twitter, and YouTube all had published policies prohibiting most forms of hate speech—policies that were rarely interpreted or applied consistently. For example, while content blatantly advocating Nazism would almost certainly be removed if reported, anti-Muslim speech—regardless of how repugnant the actual words—might not be. Speech denying the existence or validity of transgender or other queer people was largely permitted as "opinion" by most platforms, as was Holocaust denial. As always, speech against some of the most vulnerable groups was simply not taken seriously, despite its greater propensity for harm.

The events of Charlottesville served as an inflection point for Silicon Valley, which had up until that point dismissed the public's growing concerns about hate speech flourishing on social media platforms. Suddenly, amid growing political, public, and advertiser pressure, major tech companies started retooling their systems.

Airbnb, which had issued a policy the year prior asking all users to sign a non-discrimination agreement, doubled down, banning known Nazis and members of the alt-right from its platform. CEO Brian

Chesky told the media: "Violence, racism and hatred demonstrated by neo-Nazis, the alt-right, and white supremacists should have no place in this world."[26] Google and GoDaddy booted Nazi rag the *Daily Stormer* from using their services, and Cloudflare, which had notoriously had a policy of providing services to anyone (sometimes being accused of illegally hosting terrorist groups), followed suit.

Major social media platforms emphasized their existing policies to the media, but began to take more action against high-profile racist, Nazi, and alt-right sympathizers for engaging in hate speech. Some mainstream media sites suggested that "the choice to intervene represents a significant philosophical shift in policy"[27]—while in actuality, the shift was neither significant nor philosophical in nature, but a somewhat belated response to calls for action, driven by consumer and advertiser pressure.

Here, it is worth pausing to note the sheer disingenuousness of the major companies implying that they had always applied their prohibitions on hate speech consistently. As reporting from the time demonstrates, the removal of *actual, self-described Nazi accounts* came, in many instances, only after significant external pressure.[28] Meanwhile, right-wing conspiracy theorists like Alex Jones continued to promote dangerous misinformation across multiple platforms at the same time that queer and trans people were being de-platformed left and right for fighting back against harassment or using reclaimed terms like "dyke" and "tranny" to refer to themselves.[29] The picture that remains is one of companies watching, and waiting, for the public sentiment around any given controversy to gain enough momentum that they had to respond accordingly.

Nothing more aptly evidenced the conundrum that companies face—that they are damned if they do and damned if they don't. They face at times extraordinary amounts of pressure to *do something*, where "something" is all too often defined as censoring or de-platforming—a strategy that can mitigate harm in the short term, but does not aim to solve any problems in the long run.

At the same time, it is imperative that we remember that these are corporations and their primary goals are to make profits and satisfy their shareholders. If public opinion seems largely against white supremacy and hate, then taking down hate leaders makes financial sense. But if—as it has certainly seemed for some time—public opinion favors white supremacist ideas, then ensuring that they remain online is profitable.

Of course, as this volume has demonstrated, the values of those making and enforcing the rules also play a role in who is allowed to participate in the online conversation. While accusations that Twitter CEO Jack Dorsey is a Nazi are surely exaggerations, it is not a stretch to say that white supremacy is alive and well in certain segments of Silicon Valley. From Oculus founder Palmer Luckey, a Trump donor who reportedly ran a "shitposting" account on Reddit, to Facebook board member Peter Thiel, known for attending white nationalist–friendly events and undermining free expression, to Clearview AI CEO Hoan Ton-That, perhaps Silicon Valley's most notable alt-right supporter, the field is rife with white supremacist sympathizers.[30]

The consequences of de-platforming vulnerable communities while allowing prominent right-wing figures to retain their platforms remain fuzzy for many in the United States, where it's still the case that a diverse press is free to report with minimal (though growing) state interference and a majority of citizens can access the internet. But elsewhere, such as the southeast Asian country of Myanmar (formerly Burma), the ramifications are much clearer.

As the United States was grappling with the rise of the right, halfway around the world a country was in the grips of a nascent genocide.

Myanmar is a former British colony that fell under oppressive military rule in 1962 that ended only in 2011. Just a few years prior, small groups of demonstrators had begun to brave the streets for the first time in a decade, protesting rising consumer prices. Embedded in the country's collective psyche were memories of a 1988 uprising, brutally repressed by the regime, and to which thousands of civilian deaths were attributable. The February 2007 demonstrations initially faced a military crackdown, but that only served to strengthen the protesters' resolve: by September of that year, thousands of monks marched in the streets across several cities and towns, earning the protests the title of "Saffron Revolution" in homage to the deep maroon of the monks' robes.

As tens, even hundreds of thousands joined the movement, the military junta responded with force. Troops barricaded Shwedagon Pagoda in the city of Yangon, firing tear canisters at those gathered there, while prominent supporters of the protests were arrested. Soldiers fired at students, and on September 28, seeking to dampen communications and global awareness of the events, the government cut off internet access—making Myanmar only the second country to do so, after the island nation of Maldives three years prior.[31]

A technical report on the shutdown from the OpenNet Initiative (the project that studied government internet filtering, which I later worked on) at the time stated that "what makes the Burmese junta stand out ... is its apparent goal of also preventing information from reaching a wider international audience."[32]

Internet penetration in Myanmar in 2007 hovered at around .02 percent of the total population, meaning that there were only around ten thousand internet users (compare that with Tunisia's 4 million users in 2011, representing 38 percent of the population at the time). And yet, the Myanmar military junta's control over the media was perhaps even stronger than Tunisian president Ben Ali's, with the state owning and controlling all television, radio, and newspapers and heavily censoring the country's handful of private publications.

Just like Tunisia, however, internet service providers heavily restricted access to information and communications technologies, and the government employed Western-made tools for surveillance and censorship. OpenNet Initiative researchers Nart Villeneuve and Masashi Crete-Nishihata later aptly observed that "severing national Internet connectivity in reaction to sensitive political events is an extreme example of *just-in-time-blocking*—a phenomenon in which access to information is denied exactly at times when the information may have the greatest potential impact, such as elections, protests, or anniversaries of social unrest."[33]

Though sporadic violence continued throughout the country, the events of 2007 led to a constitutional referendum the next year that put Myanmar on a path toward democratic reforms. Peaceful yet contested elections were held in 2010, and in 2011, the military junta was dissolved.

When online hate leads to genocide

In 2014, I traveled to Myanmar as a guest of the East-West Center, an institution founded by the US Congress in 1960 with the goal of promoting better relations and understanding among the people of the United States, Asia, and the Pacific. I went to speak at a conference alongside luminaries including Burmese Nobel peace laureate Aung San Suu Kyi.

At that time, I was only marginally aware of the plight of Rohingya, the predominantly Muslim and mostly stateless ethnic group that has resided in the Myanmar state of Rakhine for generations. The majority-Buddhist government refuses to recognize them as citizens, viewing them as illegal migrants from Bangladesh. Qatari broadcaster Al Jazeera English (for which I wrote at the time) had been reporting consistently on the emerging conflict between the Rohingya and Rakhine's Buddhist majority since 2012. Violence broke out between the groups after the gang rape and murder of twenty-five-year-old Buddhist seamstress Ma Thida Htwe.[34]

Although a group of Muslim suspects were detained, crowds of Buddhists demanded that they be handed over to the mob, and leaflets containing inflammatory anti-Muslim rhetoric began to be distributed. Over the next two years as the violence escalated, organizations including Human Rights Watch, Open Society Foundations, Reporters Without Borders, and the International Crisis Group issued urgent reports, but Western media remained largely silent, despite the fact that Myanmar was now open to international journalists.[35]

As part of my trip to the country, I was invited to join a tour, organized by the East-West Center, of local religious communities in Yangon. We visited St. Joseph's Catholic Church; a Hindu temple where a prayer to Lord Shiva was received with the offering of a red dot to the forehead; and one of the city's oldest mosques. Our final stop was Payathonzu Buddhist Temple and Monastery where, in a slightly darkened room away from the punishing March heat, we sat on the floor and got to speak with a Buddhist monk.

I cannot recall the details of the conversation, but I remember feeling uneasy when the subject of the Rohingya came up, and I recall the monk's dismissiveness toward concerns raised by members of our group of what appeared to be a budding genocide.

The next day, at the conference, I sat on a panel with Nay Phone Latt, a well-known blogger, former political prisoner, and executive director of the Myanmar ICT for Development Organization, where we discussed the "cyber challenges" facing the country. Although most others I'd spoken to were optimistic about the country opening up, Latt—who was sentenced in 2008 to twenty years in prison and released after the fall of the junta—expressed concern: "We have some extent of freedom [here], but we are not so safe."[36]

Ethan Zuckerman keynoted the event and blogged about it afterward. "Virtually every conversation I had about the internet in Myanmar centered on hate speech," he wrote, but added, "People really don't want to talk about the Rohingya."[37] In his speech, Zuckerman spoke of the promises of the internet as a tool for mobilization as well as the difficulty of being heard amid the noise. He also talked about censorship, placing it in historical context. Finally, using an example from Kenya's disputed 2007 elections, he warned: "Censorship is the wrong way to deal with hate speech."[38]

Given the context at the time, he was not wrong: Myanmar had just emerged from decades of heavy censorship and was still experiencing limits to press freedom. Any calls for censorship by necessity would be directed at the government—the same government that held the keys to the internet and the press, and was a majority-Buddhist body. Though hate speech was flourishing, calling on the government to counter it with censorship would have undoubtedly caused collateral damage.

One afternoon, Ethan and I took a ferry across the river to Dala Township and explored the villages as our skin burned from the scorching sun. As we wandered, we discussed some of our observations of Yangon. We noted the excellent food and kind people, the colonial architecture falling to urban decay, and the surprising prevalence of

Facebook URLs and logos throughout Yangon——on billboards, the backs of trucks, and even the menus of modest restaurants.

Burmese gained widespread access to the mostly mobile internet at an odd time, just as the blogging era was coming to a close, to be replaced by centralized, simple-to-use social media. As such, there was no need for businesses to spend money on building websites when they could simply set up a Facebook page in a few minutes flat.

Later that year, Facebook, along with the Opera browser, capitalized on its popularity in the country by striking a deal with telecom provider Telenor, giving the company's customers free access to Wikipedia and Facebook Zero.[39] Facebook Zero is a special initiative launched by the company in 2010 that offers a stripped-down, text-only, cost-free version of the platform——using a practice known as zero rating——to emerging markets to address the issue of data caps. The initiative was followed by Facebook's Internet.org——also known as Free Basics and later rebranded as Facebook Discover——which became available in Myanmar in 2016.

Myanmar's mobile penetration grew rapidly between 2012 and 2017, and consequently, the number of Facebook users soared. This in turn led to the oft-repeated trope that in Myanmar, "Facebook is the Internet and the Internet is Facebook."[40] My colleague Gennie Gebhart calls the trope a "willful misunderstanding" that "played into more convenient storylines."

While not entirely accurate, there is some truth to the cliché. As one Mozilla analyst reported in 2017, "Zero rating is not serving as an on-ramp to the internet."[41] In other words, Burmese internet users were being served Facebook ... and not much else. "Facebook is not introducing people to the open internet where you can learn, create and build things," said Global Voices' advocacy director Ellery Biddle that same year. "It's building this little web that turns the user into a mostly passive consumer of mostly western corporate content. That's digital colonialism."[42]

As internet use gained ground in Myanmar, so too did violence against the Rohingya minority. Four months after I visited the country, a Muslim teashop owner was falsely accused of raping a Buddhist employee. The incident was reported by a blogger and quickly spread to Facebook where, according to reports, the story exploded.

Among those who had shared the post was an ultra-nationalist monk named Ashin Wirathu, who is based in Mandalay but has followers throughout the country. "He's sort of like an equivalent to Steve Bannon or Gavin McInnes," Dia Kayyali told me much later. "The language that he uses sounds just like white supremacist language and Hindu supremacist language."

The incident sparked riots in Mandalay. The government, which had no direct line to Facebook at the time, was at a loss. A senior official who had previously been a high-ranking figure in the military junta called Chris Tun, the head of operations for the local branch of the accounting firm Deloitte, to see if he could help. Tun tried to get the attention of Facebook officials, but was unsuccessful. The office of the president, out of diplomatic options, temporarily blocked access to Facebook in Mandalay.[43]

Though Facebook had sought rapid growth in Myanmar, it had not done its due diligence when entering the country, had not—it seems—attempted to understand the fragile political situation, the burgeoning genocide, and set up necessary structures to protect users there. Their strategy appears to have been purely capitalistic. The platform's community standards were not made available in Burmese until mid-2015, and according to reports, there were just *two* Burmese-speaking content moderators for the country's several million Facebook users.

Researchers warned Facebook of the growing strife as early as 2013, but their calls fell on deaf ears. Australian journalist Aela Callan met with one of the company's most senior officials, Elliot Schrage, who referred her to Internet.org and to two officials who liaised with civil society groups. "He didn't connect me to anyone inside Facebook who could deal with the actual problem," she later told Reuters.[44]

Over the course of the next four years, sporadic reports emerged of how Facebook users were fanning the flames of violence. Inside the platform's insular echo chamber, with no outsiders watching and minimal capacity for content moderation, anti-Muslim speech was flourishing. "After every IS or IS-inspired terrorist attack in Paris,

London and elsewhere, the hate speech in Myanmar increased."[45]

During that time, Facebook finally posted a Burmese translation of its community standards, localized its reporting tools, and added a small number of Burmese-speaking content moderators, but their approach to the growing problem was "decidedly ad-hoc," especially for "a multi-billion-dollar tech giant that controls so much of popular discourse in the country and across the world."[46]

For instance, one counter-speech initiative included virtual Facebook stickers "to empower people in Myanmar to share positive messages online," while another provided "locally illustrated false news tips." The company additionally conducted educational workshops with local partners on their policies and tools "so that they can use this information in outreach to communities around the country."[47] But with anti-Rohingya sentiment continuing to thrive on Burmese celebrity and government pages, none of Facebook's attempts at counter-action were sufficient.

A military crackdown in August 2017 sent more than seven hundred thousand Rohingya fleeing across the border to Bangladesh, prompting a UN investigation. Zeid Ra'ad Al Hussein, the UN high commissioner of human rights at the time, called the military's offensive a "textbook example of ethnic cleansing," while the chairman of the UN Independent International Fact-Finding Mission on Myanmar, Marzuki Darusman, stated that social media had played a "determining role" in Myanmar.[48] Another investigator, Yanghee Lee, commented specifically on Facebook, saying: "We know that the ultra-nationalist Buddhists have their own Facebooks and are really inciting a lot of violence and a lot of hatred against the Rohingya or other ethnic minorities."[49]

In response Facebook said that there was "no place for hate speech" on its platform, but Mark Zuckerberg was nevertheless called to testify before the US Senate.[50] Vermont senator Patrick Leahy pressed the executive about the company's inaction, citing a post in which a death threat against a Muslim journalist was found not to violate the platform's rules. "Hate speech is very language-specific," Zuckerberg testified. "It's hard to do it without people who speak the local language, and we need to ramp up our effort there dramatically."[51] He added that Facebook was hiring dozens more Burmese speakers to moderate hate speech in the country.

When pressed on the issue by journalist Ezra Klein, Zuckerberg was glib, saying, "The Myanmar issues have, I think, gotten a lot of focus inside the company," and "I think now people are appropriately focused on some of the risks and downsides as well. And I think we were too slow in investing enough in that. It's not like we did nothing."[52]

In turn, a group of civil society organizations from Myanmar that had been working with company to tackle hate speech penned a letter to the Facebook CEO, writing: "We were surprised to hear you use this case to praise the effectiveness of your 'systems' in the context of Myanmar. From where we stand, this case exemplifies the very opposite of effective moderation: it reveals an over-reliance on third parties, a lack of a proper mechanism for emergency escalation, a reticence to engage local stakeholders around systemic solutions and a lack of transparency."[53]

On August 15, 2018, Reuters published a blockbuster investigation into how Facebook's inaction had helped fuel the ongoing genocide, alleging that as of June of that year, the company was still only contracting a scant sixty Burmese-speaking content moderators at an Accenture office in Kuala Lumpur, Malaysia, with three full-time Burmese speakers on staff in its Dublin office.[54] By then, Facebook had just over 20 million users in Myanmar.

The report included a sampling of posts found on the platform that month that wouldn't be out of place in Nazi Germany. "These non-human kalar dogs, the Bengalis, are killing and destroying our land, our water and our ethnic people," wrote one user. "We need to destroy their race."[55]

On the same day the report was released, Facebook published an update in which it admitted: "The ethnic violence in Myanmar is horrific and we have been too slow to prevent misinformation and hate on Facebook." The company announced updates to its policies on credible violence, and wrote that it was working with a network of independent organizations to identify such posts. Facebook explained further: "This new policy will be global, but we are initially focusing our work on countries where false news has had life or death consequences. These include Sri Lanka, India, Cameroon, and the Central African Republic as well as Myanmar."[56]

The following day, the *Guardian* published a piece entitled "Facebook's Failure in Myanmar Is the Work of a Blundering Toddler," in which journalist Olivia Solon reported attending a Facebook phone briefing the night before the release of the Reuters report. Solon called the press briefing "an ass-covering exercise" and remarked: "Civil society groups have been underwhelmed by [Facebook's] results so far."[57]

"This is definitely a situation where Facebook's decisions cost lives, and they can't say that they weren't warned," says Kayyali, stating concern for similar events underway in India, also fueled by incitement on Facebook.

Less than two weeks later, news broke that Facebook had banned twenty individuals and organizations in Myanmar, including Senior General Min Aung Hlaing, commander in chief of the armed forces, and the military's Myawady television network. Citing evidence from the April UN report that "many of these individuals and organizations committed or enabled serious human rights abuses in the country," a Facebook statement read: "We want to prevent them from using our service to further inflame ethnic and religious tensions."[58] The following month, some of the very same generals turned up on Russian network VKontakte, while one of them posted to Facebook urging his followers to move there, writing: "Forsake dictator Facebook. Move to VK, a place more appropriate for patriots [nationalists]."[59] The post received more than five thousand likes.

While some in Myanmar reportedly lauded the decision as a timely and necessary intervention by Facebook, others questioned whether banning the generals, including the military commander in chief, was in fact censorship. "Hopefully, Facebook's ban on the Myanmar military won't overshadow who is really being silenced—critical voices and independent media," wrote two commentators in the country.[60]

Of course, the story doesn't end there. What happened on Facebook in Myanmar likely served as the impetus for the creation of Facebook's new External Oversight Board, an independent body of experts tasked with adjudicating controversial decisions made by the company's moderators that as of this writing has yet to launch but which has already faced ample criticism: for being too American, for including a former Israeli government censor, and for lacking any sort of real teeth.

It also sparked the creation of the Next Billions Network, a new coalition of young activists from the so-called global South that seeks to mitigate the harms that major technology platforms have caused throughout much of the world—harms like incitement against India's Muslim population and Turkey's Kurds, and fears of election violence in Togo and the Democratic Republic of Congo.[61]

But, just as Twitter failed to respond to the serious threats made on its platform during GamerGate, Facebook's inaction when faced with reports of a burgeoning genocide raises countless questions about the company's supposed, and dueling, commitments to free expression and combating hate.

In essence, these companies have crafted policy after policy for expedience rather than sustainability. They respond to edge cases in countries halfway around the world because, in their myopic world-view, those are the "easier" cases to solve. But, as my partner, tech ethicist Mathana has said, as they cast out their extemporaneous quick-fixes into a world they hardly know, the "solutions" to problems of their own making create ripple effects of negative externalities. Prohibitions become ammunition to those who seek to use these platforms to harm.

The COVID-19 pandemic has limited companies' resources in a very real way, but it hasn't stopped violent sentiments from prolifer-ating across platforms. In Myanmar and India, the United States and Britain, hate continues to spread, largely unchecked, and often driven by government figures and other "inauthentic" actors seeking to drive division. And yet, deciding what to do about that speech remains a deeply complicated question with no easy answers.

In light of this complexity, it is notable that rather than handling the problem with the delicacy it requires, most companies have instead turned to the blunt instruments of automation, which are simultane-ously insufficient in capturing all of the nuances of hateful speech and overly broad in doing so, frequently resulting in collateral censorship.

At the time of the ICERD's creation, in 1969, the idea behind such treaties was to protect people from states. But in the age of the platform, we can see two different streams emerging: One, in which governments of countries like Germany seek to protect people from platforms through regulation, and another in which platforms find themselves in the position of having to protect people from government. This is evidenced by Twitter's June 2020 decision to label certain tweets from the president of the United States as misleading, or in Facebook's measures to restrict posts from Burmese generals.

These actions are understandable, and to a degree feel timely and necessary ... and yet, we should be deeply troubled by the very idea that such power lies in the hands of an unelected, unqualified CEO of a U.S. corporation. What does it mean for the future of democracy that ensuring the fairness of an election, or stopping a genocide in its tracks, is ultimately up to Mark Zuckerberg or Jack Dorsey? It is ultimately quite absurd to expect the corporations that have enabled these scenarios to solve them.

I have been looking for an answer to the problem of hateful speech for more than a decade and the truth is, I still don't have one. I used to believe that it was best left out in the open, that that sunlight was the best disinfectant, and counter speech a primary tool for fighting back against it. I did—and still do—worry that by censoring hate speech in primary fora, we drive it underground and allow it to fester and that those who engage in it are artful dodgers, capable of easily finding ways to circumvent whatever prohibitions they find themselves facing.

Were it not for platforms, I would still hold these views. But the trouble with platforms is not that they allow anyone to say whatever they wish, but that their very architecture is designed to monetize and capitalize on whatever is elevated to popularity, be it Kim Kardashian or calls for genocide. This fact more than any other explains why major social media companies are so often behind the curve when it comes to acting on incitement and harassment.

In this environment, we must consider not the question of freedom of speech, but freedom of reach. Hate speech is far less of an issue when the person spewing it has just a few listeners. But on today's social media platforms, anyone can become an "influencer", and recommendation algorithms all but guarantee that controversial content will float to the top. Now, it's just a few small steps from being the guy holding the sandwich board scrawled with end-times proclamations to holding a megaphone with the power to reach millions—especially if a figure like Donald Trump happens to spot your tweet.

Now, it must be said that the people inside these companies who are entrusted with making the architectural and policy decisions that deal with these difficult questions are—despite my criticism—smart, savvy individuals who have thought long and hard about these issues. Many of those that I've spoken with acknowledge that these are hard problems with no easy solutions, and with that I agree. But many of them have also acknowledged that the companies for which they work have been slow to act—we can see this evidenced by the resignations, protest actions, and criticism of former employees, particularly in the years following the 2016 US election. Still, we mustn't forget that while these individuals can be viewed as complicit, they are still the workers; they are not the ones who hold the power to change the tide.

Of all the companies criticized throughout this book, Facebook is perhaps the most powerful, and the least responsive to criticism. In 2020 alone, stories have emerged of Facebook's highest-ranking policy staffer in India intervening to keep incitement by the country's ruling BJP party online; of board member Peter Thiel dining with white nationalists; and of the prior role played by Facebook's External Oversight Board Member Emi Palmor in censoring Palestinians' speech. In each of these cases, the response from Facebook executives has been weak at best. The line where the state ends and Facebook's rule begins is increasingly murky.

Addressing the hate that plagues our societies is an urgent imperative, but it must not be viewed as merely a symptom of social media. Platforms have enabled and amplified its spread, and we must address its role, but so too must we address it at the root—in homes and in classrooms, and in the halls of power. Censorship may be able to prevent some of the worst atrocities from happening, but it will never solve the underlying problem.

10

The Future is Ours to Write

The master's tools will never dismantle the master's house.

—Audre Lorde

On March 11, 2020, I walked five kilometers to pick up my freshly repaired bicycle and stopped into a few shops to find hand sanitizer—a futile effort, for the news of the novel coronavirus had hit Berliners that week, leading them to stockpile soaps and cleaning agents and toilet paper. I went home, made some phone calls and some lists, and settled in. Within just a few days, it felt as if the world had changed completely.

Before the big tech companies had made any announcements, we keen observers knew that they would be relieving the content moderators of their duties and sending them home. Although it was an understandable decision—it is unreasonable to expect a human being to do that kind of work from home, without support and the assurance of privacy—and one made with great care (the laborers still received full pay), it is a decision that is already showing signs of lasting impact on how our speech is regulated and policed in the quasi-public sphere.

As the spread of COVID-19 morphed into a global pandemic, content moderators were sequestered to their homes in Manila, Dublin, Berlin, Austin, and elsewhere, and automated tools were implemented in their stead. Although some companies—namely YouTube and Twitter—readily acknowledged the shortcomings and risks of automation and added key backstops to mitigate harms,

Facebook rather notably focused its attention on combating misinformation and "removing harmful content," saying little about how the company would respond to wrongful takedowns.[1]

The effects of the pandemic on companies has also made remedy for wrongful decisions even more elusive. Most platforms have been transparent about their inability to respond to appeals; Facebook, for instance, offers users the option to register their disagreement with a given decision. While it is understandable that companies are operating with limited resources during this time, the increased use of automation in content moderation—largely a pre-pandemic development—coupled with constant pressure to remove more content, has resulted in even more content being wrongfully removed, and most often without any opportunity for users to seek remedy.

On May 25, 2020, the evening before Memorial Day in the United States, forty-six-year-old George Floyd entered a shop to purchase cigarettes. The shopkeeper, believing that Floyd had used a counterfeit bill to pay for the item, confronted him to return the cigarettes but, unsuccessful, called the police, who arrived shortly thereafter and handcuffed Floyd, removing him from his vehicle. He sat calmly on the sidewalk until another set of officers arrived and formally arrested him, moving him to their car. When he protested, stating he couldn't breathe, officer Derek Chauvin kneeled on Floyd's neck, pinning him to the ground while he cried for help no fewer than sixteen times. Although bystanders repeatedly tried to intervene, Chauvin—who had racked up eighteen official complaints in his nineteen years on the force—continued to press his knee into Floyd's neck, a smug look on his face, until Floyd was unconscious. He died an hour later at the hospital.

Demonstrations honoring Floyd and protesting police violence began in Minneapolis almost immediately, spreading in less than a week to all fifty states. On June 6, the demonstrations went global, the streets of hundreds of cities filling with protesters who turned out to demonstrate their solidarity and, in more cases than not, to fight back against local injustices. By that day, the call was clear: Defund the police.

June 6 marks the day in 2020 that the world turned out in solidarity, but it is also the date of another, deeply connected event: the brutal police killing of Khaled Saeed, halfway around the world and ten years ago to the day. Police brutality and repression in Egypt and the United States are inextricably linked, through global networks of power and capitalism and more directly through military aid and training, but also through the similar ways in which the powerful seek to quash dissent—which includes platform censorship.

While we, the people, are waking up to the parallels of injustice that tie us together, it is apparent from the past few months that most Silicon Valley companies are doing no such thing. Between March and May, as they focused their efforts on COVID-19, there were numerous examples of hashtags being suppressed, sex workers being de-platformed, and activists being censored. The move toward near-full automation, coupled with more scrutiny to take down harmful content, has made accurate moderation even harder, the result of which is more collateral censorship than ever before. As Kate Klonick wrote when her Twitter account was suspended for a joke involving the word "kill": "Right now, the public-relations cost for Twitter of keeping up an account that might be spreading violent propaganda is very high—and the downside to the company of suspending the average user is very low."[2]

Despite having minimal resources to moderate content, companies still found the time to institute new and harmful rules that have had an outsized impact on many users who, stuck at home, have come to rely on online platforms far more than ever before. We have traded the water cooler for Slack channels, the classroom for Zoom, the conference for YouTube. Our children attend class online, we organize mutual aid through Google groups, and raise funds for health care and rent on sites like GoFundMe, which we advertise on Twitter.

It seeks to reason, then, that in our current zeitgeist, decisions about what we are allowed to express should be given *more* human attention and more care, not handed to the whims of unaccountable actors and algorithms.

* * *

Over the past decade and often through pocket-sized screens, we have borne witness to an unprecedented state of perpetual protest, a series of movements throughout the world that are seemingly independent and yet also deeply interconnected. It is impossible to pinpoint their precise beginnings. Some might say it was the second Palestinian intifada, others might point to the 1999 WTO demonstrations in Seattle. To the broader public, that question is not so important. What *is* important are the ties that bind these varied movements: the quest for justice, the recognition and preservation of hidden histories, and the desire for true equality worldwide.

In 2017, Zeynep Tufekci observed that "digital technologies [are] profoundly altering the relationship between movement capacities and their signals."[3] This is undoubtedly true, whether evidenced by protesters in Beirut sending their love to the streets of Brooklyn, or Egyptians and Tunisians sharing tips and stories over the years, or the Movement for Black Lives in the United States taking on new dimensions in Europe, Africa, and beyond. As a consequence, we the people have begun to recognize an interminable fact: we are all interconnected.

But, just as Palestinians and Seattleites alike made clear at the turn of this century, so too are the centers of power interconnected. Globalization, often viewed solely through the lens of capitalism, has brought many of the world's governments together, consolidating power among global elites. But as right-wing fanaticism and white supremacy have found their way to the highest echelons, interconnected and globalized governance has taken on a new, even more dangerous shape.

The COVID-19 pandemic has demonstrated the failures of American (and of course many other) institutions. But it has also shown us something interesting: although Silicon Valley companies have for years only wrung their hands as calls for genocide, death threats, and misinformation have proliferated globally on their platforms, now, in the face of widespread disease and death in the United States, they suddenly found the will to moderate certain expression.

This is perhaps best evidenced in the near disappearance of a video known as "Plandemic." The twenty-six-minute video, released on May

4, 2020, promoted numerous false claims about the novel coronavirus, from the idea that hydroxychloroquine (a drug used to treat malaria and lupus, among other things) could be used to cure COVID-19 patients to the false claim that flu vaccines increase one's chances of contracting the new virus.

YouTube, Facebook, and Twitter have all but evaporated the video from existence, which some observers have taken as proof positive that the companies were capable of moderating harmful content all along. But, as the astute observer knows (and the previous chapters have demonstrated), companies *have been* disappearing certain forms of expression for the past decade, leaving nary a trace.

And yet, at the same time, as the far right gains power and influence in the United States (and of course, elsewhere), companies have taken only minimal steps to prevent the spread of incitement, often acting as if their hands are tied, their policy decisions often seemingly lining up with what the Trump administration might want.

The internet, and social media in particular, has boosted the signals of mainstream, centralized American media, whose interests lie first and foremost in US affairs—and not just US affairs, but the things that matter most to the country's elites, who are still overwhelmingly white. That is why, over the course of the Trump presidency, the broader US public has been surprised to learn what my peers and I have known for a long time: our expression is now mostly controlled by a concentrated few.

But dig a little deeper, and you will find the sex workers whose voices and livelihoods have been systematically stifled on social media platforms. Look beyond the mainstream, and you'll see the activists from Syria and Palestine and Egypt; Chile and Sudan and Hong Kong; Myanmar and Tunisia and well beyond who were silenced because the companies that promised to make the world more open and connected never really gave a damn about their stories—unless, of course, their stories aligned with the goals of American cultural and economic hegemony.

As I think back to the early days, a narrative begins to emerge: in the beginning, the core platforms—Google/YouTube, Twitter, and Facebook, at least—employed policy teams who approached their jobs with significant care, and even though they were prone to error as all humans are, they tried to make the platforms spaces where everyone, equally, could have a voice. There was Nicole Wong, the early deputy Google lawyer upon whom the decision to geographically block content at the behest of governments still weighs heavy. Also, Alex Macgillivray, during whose tenure Twitter resisted the US government's demands to hand over information about alleged WikiLeaks volunteers. And Alex Stamos, the canary in the coal mine who left Yahoo! for Facebook, only to resign from there as well in frustration after a few short years. The Facebook employee who reached out to me, a twenty-five-year-old blogger obsessed with documenting the company's mistakes, to make a connection that ultimately led me here. And the list, of course, goes on.

As important as these individuals' good choices were, that era did not last. For above them in the company hierarchies were other individuals whose obsession with power and money took precedence. Despite their proclamations to the contrary, I have never believed that Mark Zuckerberg or Sheryl Sandberg cared for anything but that, and although Jack Dorsey seems to have come around in due time, his want for power, or proximity to it, in some ways led us to where we are now, watching the United States collapse under a president who may never have been elected had Twitter made different decisions. Companies are people, or so the US saying goes, but their opinions and doings are shaped not by the masses of laborers who rake in the profits, but by a select few whose ideologies and susceptibility to political and shareholder pressure ultimately lead to the decisions they make.

This book has documented what I believe to be inflection points for Silicon Valley platforms over the past few decades, but has also sought to demonstrate the myriad attempts by activists and civil society organizations over the years to hold these platforms accountable. The Arab uprisings of 2010–11 (preceded, of course, by a long prelude that encompasses the first and second Palestinian intifadas, the Kefaya movement, and a decade of network-building among digitally savvy activists) caused key platform policymakers to recognize that their tools were about more than just sharing vacation photos, leading to shifts in policies dealing with graphic violence and the implementation of rapid response measures and collaborations with civil society organizations.

This period of hope and revolution was followed, almost immediately, by the civil war in Syria and rise of the Islamic State, both of which brought a bevy of propaganda, botnets, and questionable state actors to the online battlefield. I distinctly remember this era as being the point at which Facebook lost the plot, pouring resources into mergers, acquisitions, and AI instead of getting their policies right. Twitter, operating with far fewer resources, has struggled with harassment, incitement, and "inauthentic activity", but with a far smaller user base has often been able to be more agile and responsive to civil society demands.

YouTube, which perhaps bore the brunt of the media's ire, at first tried to make things right. Nicole Wong later called it "a moment where we needed the [help of the] human rights community [in order to] understand what we needed to see so that we wouldn't make mistakes," but YouTube later closed ranks, according to many activists who tried to reach the company as the situation in Syria escalated. The incidents from that period should have served as a lesson for company policymakers a few years later when the right-wing onslaught began, had their myopia, profit-mindedness, and deep-rooted US-centricity not blinded them to the glaring similarities between white supremacists and ISIS.

At the same time that I was observing these changes in speech policies across Silicon Valley, civil society opposition to platforms was growing. Activists, academics, and other public intellectuals comprising this distributed, global movement observed that "every digital application that can be used for surveillance and control will be used for surveillance and control,"[4] and that "entire nations and their industries are fully dependent on critical infrastructure, software, and hardware provided by a handful of companies based in a small group of countries."[5]

These interconnected groups and individuals, some of whom have been collaborating for more than a decade, have worked hard to bring about important changes over the years. They have successfully agitated for amendments to specific policies; documented changes,

content removals, and created important policy principles.[6] They spoke
at conferences around the world, and rolled their eyes as corporate
shills gave bland and contradictory speeches while government officials listened intently. They exposed the complexities and potential
impossibility of content moderation at scale, and the cheap (and
mostly "global South") labor it requires so that those of us in the
so-called global North can be shielded from some of the internet's
most undesirable expression. And, perhaps most importantly, they
realized that the advertising-based business model—as well as the
increasing monopolization of Google and Facebook—was at the
root of everything.

For Silicon Valley, racism has been very profitable. By contrast, the
things that concern me most—ensuring that history is not erased; that
women, queer and trans people, and sex workers don't face discrimination; that counter-terrorism measures are not counterproductive;
that attempts to counter hate and incitement are not seen and removed
as the very thing they seek to counter—are not profitable, and in fact
seem to be viewed by companies as too economically risky.

In the first few days of the 2020 mass protests across the United
States, I was struck by something that Bree Newsome Bass said on
Twitter. (Newsome Bass, a filmmaker, is perhaps best known for an
act of civil disobedience in which she climbed the flagpole of the South
Carolina state house and tore down the Confederate flag.) "Please
recognize that all the things the political establishment does to address
racism in the aftermath of mass protest are things they could've done
all along & chose not to," she implored.[7]

Silicon Valley's response to the pandemic—swift, reasonable,
measured—is a precise example of this idea, evidencing that all along,
tech companies *could have* taken steps to mitigate harms ... but chose
not to, instead focusing their attention on the things that governments
and other powerful entities wanted them to censor.

The fact is that when the potential harm to Americans is big enough,
these companies will act. When the harm to foreigners is big enough,
they will act only in the face of extraordinary pressure. And sometimes not even then.

*   *   *

So what does this mean for expression, and what can we do about it?

A decade ago, the policies and practices of content moderation were shaped by, if not absolutism, then a shared belief in free speech maximalism. This is substantiated by Google's 2008 refusal to remove al-Qaeda videos, Twitter's resistance to banning nudity, YouTube's exceptions for graphic violence, and so on. But as time marched on, and both the companies and their user bases grew bigger and less centralized, that zeitgeist gave way to another—what my dear friend and mentor Ethan Zuckerman would call a framework of public health, in which the potential harms of given expression are weighed against the harms of censorship, or the benefits of leaving speech online (what companies often call "newsworthiness").

This is, to me, only partially accurate. In the United States, Europe, and much of the English-speaking world, this framework has emerged from a confluence of factors: activist, advertiser, and shareholder pressure to censor hateful speech, racism, gun sales, and government demands to do the same, as well as to control sexual expression. Of course, the past few years have shifted this discourse toward the alleged censorship of conservative speech, but only because a few massive media conglomerates and right-wing politicians insist on repeating such nonsense ad nauseum.

Throughout the rest of the world, things look quite different. The harms of Islamist extremism, though certainly real, have been distorted by Western actors, leading to the conflation of Marxists, democracy activists, anarchists, and other resistors of oppression with groups like al-Qaeda and ISIS who seek first and foremost destruction and mayhem. This has led to the widespread suppression of not only those views, but anti-extremist counter-speech, satire, and—in the case of Syria—collective memory.

The ongoing suppression of adults engaged in consensual sex work, whether legal or not, is one of the most disturbing stories of our time that has gone largely unnoticed by the media. Though exacerbated by US legal developments (namely, SESTA/FOSTA), it long predates them, and is the result of both well-meaning-but-misguided anti-sex trafficking activism and the conservative predilections of payment processors, corporate executives, and politicians. Its impact was deeply detrimental to sex workers long before the pandemic, but now—as, like the rest of us, sex workers are mostly stuck at home in self-isolation—it has become a dire issue of labor rights, and one that sex workers are working to fight largely in solitude.

The battle between rightsholders and platforms, and rightsholders and those who infringe upon their intellectual property rights has long been framed by commentators as a binary struggle, one between the little-guy creator and a collection of far biggers, but is actually so much more complex (so much so that, the reader will observe, I have chosen to leave it to those far more expert than me to explain for fear of not doing the story justice). It is not David versus Goliath, but rather a complicated set of philosophical questions about who owns ideas, and who should have the power to determine that ownership. Its implications in the platform age are not much different from those of other forms of content moderation: more often than not, it is the already marginalized who get the short end of the stick.

Globally, the effect that platforms have in shaping our very identities must not be understated. Whether that process unfolds literally, through policies that enforce the use of one's "real name," or figuratively, by way of Silicon Valley "verification" schemes effectively elevating anyone experiencing fifteen minutes of fame into a "public figure" with accompanying rule exceptions, unaccountable corporations are dictating to us who matters and who is expendable. These aren't the only ways in which platforms shape identity and agency; they enable us to create space for important discussions, find kinfolk, and—as Courtney Demone so aptly pointed out in chapter 7— discover things about ourselves. Sometimes the people who come together are united around a worthy cause … and sometimes they're united in hatred and racism.

The battle to preserve some semblance of free expression on corporate platforms often feels like a losing one. And it is fraught with complexity: Ensuring that young trans individuals can be safely anonymous means that criminals can be too. The same private Facebook groups that enable activists to organize are also used by those whose only goals are to foment hate and disorder. As we have witnessed throughout the past decade, protecting the ability of individuals to express themselves freely often comes with terrible tradeoffs—tradeoffs that must be considered with every policy decision. Expression cannot be absolute, but those tradeoffs should not stop us from seeking to maximize it.

I have been studying online censorship for nearly fifteen years now, and content moderation in particular for a decade. During that time, I have witnessed numerous attempts to mitigate the harms that companies pose not merely to our ability to express ourselves, but to our very identity and agency as people.

In the early years of my work in this field, I observed as an elite crew of law professors and media experts, State Department officials, and corporate executives sought solutions that centered free expression issues that aligned, almost perfectly, with the goals of the US government. I attended meetings where I was the only (so-called) digital native in the room, and where the conversation about social media platforms lacked any real understanding of how people were actually using them. I was there for the creation of the Global Network Initiative, the multi-stakeholder body whose early interventions stopped companies from making some truly hideous mistakes, but whose reliance on funding from those very same companies ultimately prevented it from holding them to any real measures of accountability. But as much as these observations frustrated me, I was also welcomed to speak up, and when I did in those early days, most of the time people listened.

Then, in January 2011, when Tunisia and Egypt rose up, I was suddenly in high demand as someone with solid contacts on the ground and moderate Arabic skills. I took press calls and connected journalists by phone with activists in Cairo. I wrote about the ways in which people were using social media, and how companies were responding to it, and in short order found myself in rooms with people like Sheryl Sandberg. It was exhilarating, but it also felt a lot like whiplash. And then I got a call from the Electronic Frontier Foundation, and within a few months, found myself in the job that I've held ever since.

That job has taken me all over the world, to activist and law school conferences, global leftist gatherings, and the occasional meeting with a prime minister. I have had chances to influence policymakers, and hope that I used them wisely. But the thing that has meant the most to me is the opportunity that I have been given to connect with activists from a diverse set of communities all over the world, to learn from them directly, and—I believe—help by making sure those in power heard their voices too.

And in the end, it is a combination of all these experiences that have led me to the following four conclusions.

First, it is imperative that we understand and view content moderation as existing outside of and apart from extant systems of governance. At worst, content moderation is inherently broken and, at best, is an imperfect system retrofitted to societal structures that are already deeply flawed. The processes of content moderation were not built to scale, nor were the rules created by companies; rather, they were built over time like an onion being peeled in reverse, layers stacked upon layers, always reactive to external forces. To mitigate its harms, this system must be subject to a comprehensive, external audit of both rules and processes, policies and procedures.

Second, we need true and meaningful representation and inclusion. Far too much of the external debate over the past decade has been dominated by white Americans, falsely framed as a First Amendment issue, and focused on political speech above all else, to the detriment of other key issues of free expression. And within companies—different as each may be—the focus is all too often on whatever pet issue the US media or lawmakers have adopted in a given week. Rarely is there sustained focus, inside or out, toward the threats faced by the world's most marginalized people. And when attention is paid—as was the case with Myanmar and Facebook as well as GamerGate and Twitter—it is almost always too little, too late.

Much of the problem stems from who is, or isn't, part of the conversation. Among critics, people in academia, and grassroots advocates, a strong effort has been made to rectify historical wrongs, and people of color, queer and trans folks, and other minority voices are beginning to be centered. We have a long way to go, but I am proud of and impressed by the progress that has been made by members of my communities.

At the same time, companies have failed miserably in their meager attempts to bring the right people into the room. This is evidenced by their broader failures to "attract diversity," but is also exemplified by a few key behind-the-scenes stories. These stories, scattered throughout this book, speak to the need to ensure inclusion and representation at every level of policymaking, engineering, and content moderation. The utter lack of it at major tech companies means that certain issues go unsolved, while others are entirely unseen. If, for example, there is only one person on the team from Uganda, the chances of that country's issues being raised to the fore are low—but if there is no one from Uganda, those chances are next to nothing.

In making a case for a "digital non-aligned movement," Juan Ortiz Freuler writes, "Big tech has exclusive access to the tower from which the full tapestry of cobwebs created by these connections becomes fully visible. Big tech now has privileged access to the knowledge that emerges from our collective work on the web, and a privileged position through which to define what knowledge is produced, prioritized and consumed."[8]

Freueler agrees that the "solidarity at a planetary scale" is necessary, but "we cannot expect the rich nations of the North to lead the shift in how we organize our systems of knowledge creation" and that if the web is to "avoid fragmentation, it will be because the South steps up to the challenge."[9] In the spaces in which I operate, I have witnessed the power and ingenuity of my comrades in the global South and I too believe that those of us from the North must make more spaces for their ideas to come to the fore.

Of course, it's impossible for a company's staff to replicate the diversity of the general population, but that is not reason to simply dismiss these concerns. Alexander Macgillivray, the first general counsel at Twitter, readily admits that the company lacked real diversity in his days there, but expressed the importance of listening to users' concerns in changing policies. "There are worse things than tokenization—like ignorance" he told me.

The story also alludes to the need for a new generation of commentators and observers, activists and academics, which we have already begun to witness. "The same people who have been doing this for twenty years don't need to be the ones who keep speaking about it," says Macgillivray, who recently launched a professional association for trust and safety workers that he hopes will contribute to rectifying the problem.

"The entrance of state actors and malicious state-backed actors seriously changes the dynamic of what the threat looks like," says Nicole Wong. The championing of new voices both inside and outside companies provides fresh perspectives on an old problem, but also ensures that those analyzing the emerging threats truly understand their nature, and are not just taking the US government at their word.

The third conclusion I've made is: if governments are collaborating, so must we. When it comes to expression, one thing remains certain: no one will moderate the speech of governments or their officials. Sure, Twitter will fact-check Trump, and Facebook will boot members of foreign governments (and maybe someday even the president of the United States), but in the grand scheme of things, we might be watching the watchers, but no citizen has the power to silence them.

The Edward Snowden revelations back in 2013 demonstrated to a broad audience the ways in which governments around the world cooperate and collaborate to spy on their—and each other's—citizens, with the help of willing corporations. Of course, this type of collaboration was not news to attentive Arab activists, who had long been aware that the spyware used by their governments was sold to them by US manufacturers, nor was it a surprise to civil rights fighters in the United States, who for years had pointed out the militarization of their country's police, trained by none other than the human-rights-violating Israel Defense Forces.

The fact that our governments are scheming together means that we must too. Nothing—not police killings, not speech regulations, not content moderation—happens in a vacuum, making it all the more important that we listen and learn from one another, connect the dots, and build concrete tactics, and solutions, that address problems holistically. In every debate about what speech should be permitted and what should be censored, there will be tradeoffs—but those of us who care deeply about the future of humanity but differ on solutions must stop seeing one another as enemies and come together in common cause.

The final conclusion I've made is that we, the people, must decide what comes next. The events of the past decade have brought to the public fore a fairly widespread recognition that certain speech is beyond the pale, but in nearly every instance I have seen, regulatory and legislative proposals to restrict such speech take the wrong aim, punishing companies (and their workers) for errors, or for not moving fast enough, while failing to do *anything* to address the problems at the root.

I am an advocate for free expression not because I believe that all speech is equally important, or that all speech is good, but because I believe that power corrupts, and absolute power corrupts absolutely, which makes it nary impossible to trust an authority to censor effectively—particularly when that censor is a dilettante CEO. Furthermore, I am increasingly concerned that—particularly given the speed at which politics and media now operate—most censorship that is implemented by corporations will do more collateral harm than it will do good. I'm especially concerned when censorship—as is almost always the case—is uncoupled with solutions that get to the core of the problem at hand.

We as a society have to start asking serious questions and interrogating the decisions made over our heads, and we have to do this without resorting to binaries. Does the harm of misinformation warrant its censorship? What is the right balance between sexual freedom and the protection of children? Are we willing to risk the freedom of certain cultures for the morality of others? Does taking away the right to anonymity really make anyone safer? Are we comfortable with the loss of history for the sake of "counterterrorism"? And who should decide who is a terrorist, anyway?

While these are hard questions we will be grappling with for the foreseeable future, there are changes that companies should make immediately. They should be transparent about what they censor, provide users with ample notification, and ensure that every user has the right to appeal removals. The Santa Clara Principles on Transparency and Accountability in Content Moderation, endorsed by more than a hundred civil society organizations, set forth a baseline for doing so.[10] Companies should provide users with information about the data is fed to recommendation algorithms, obtain meaningful consent for any data that is used, and give users more options about what they see in their feeds. They should work to immediately include civil society in policymaking, transparently, and should conduct a full audit to evaluate the compatibility of existing policies with human rights standards and make changes wherever necessary.

Censorship is, as I hope this book makes clear, inherently political, and the more complex the rules, the more difficult they are to apply at scale. On top of that, as the past few months have demonstrated, the individual right to free expression is inherently in tension with public health and freedom from harm. These are not easy problems, and we must be wary of anyone who claims to have easy solutions.

I am among those who do not. I used to believe that platforms should not moderate speech; that they should take a hands-off approach, with very few exceptions. That was naïve. I still believe that Silicon Valley shouldn't be the arbiter of what we can say, but the simple fact is that we have entrusted these corporations to do just that and, as such, they must use wisely the responsibility that they have been given.

Ten years of documenting, arguing, writing, consulting, and participating in activism have led me to a range of bespoke conclusions to various problems inherent to content moderation. Although I am certain, for example, that the US government should not dictate to companies who is a terrorist, and that widespread bans on women's partial nudity are discriminatory and harmful to the feminist cause, I still struggle to find the right answer to what we should about suspected bots, or brigading, or how we should handle hateful speech that doesn't quite reach the level of incitement.

Several novel ideas and solutions have recently emerged from within companies, such as Facebook's newly announced External Oversight Board and Twitter's addition of an advisory notice on tweets from politicians that contain falsehoods. To some in my field, these are mere window dressing, while to others, they hold much potential. To me, however, they are too little, too late. I have lost faith, if I ever had any, in Silicon Valley to solve the problems that it created in the first place.

On a late summer evening not long after Berlin relaxed its COVID-19 restrictions for the first time, I was sitting in a park late one night with my partner and a close friend, talking about the state of the world. We were all feeling pessimistic about the state of our countries, the US and Britain. My partner lamented that there is unlikely to be a global reckoning about what we just experienced. We won't see governments coming together to plan for the next pandemic, at least not with leaders like Trump and Bolsonaro at the helm. As a society, my partner surmised, we will allow the same mistakes to happen again and again, as we have done before, for we humans have a short memory.

Indeed, we cannot expect our governments to admit where they went wrong. There won't be any apologies for telling us that masks weren't necessary, for focusing on the economy at the expense of human life, for allowing so many people to die needlessly. Just as we should not wait for our governments to recognize their shortcomings in response to the pandemic, we must not wait for companies to recognize their failures either. They will seek to shift the blame, as they have done so many times before.

But we will not forget, as long as we remember how to remember. Our reckoning will happen through open debate and closed meetings. It will happen online, of course, at least for now, but it will also eventually happen again in the hallways of conferences, in hushed conversations over candlelight in smoky bars, at general assemblies and town halls. And it will happen through writing, writing that we must remember to put on paper, for we cannot trust the internet to keep it safe.

Wael Abbas knows all too well what happens when we entrust our writings to a private corporation. Syrians have felt the pain of seeing their history erased by platforms, allowing their government's narrative to prevail, and seen the erasure of evidence that could have held their government accountable. Egyptian revolutionaries who fought so hard to keep memory alive know how words can be erased in an instant. And every blogger—nay, journalist—who forgot to pay their bills or fell victim to a DDoS attack knows the pain of losing their writings to the ether.

The harms of censorship are vast, but this is the one that pains me in the most visceral way: Its ability to obscure and erase our very history, preventing us from learning from our past mistakes and growing, progressing as a society.

This is not an abstract threat. In 2019, I had the pleasure of interviewing Renaissance scholar Ada Palmer for a project entitled *Speaking Freely*. I asked her if she had a "free speech hero" and in response, she told me a story about the eighteenth century French philosopher Denis Diderot that has stuck with me ever since.

Diderot, an atheist, co-edited the *L'Encyclopédie de Diderot et d'Alembert*, a radical enlightenment encyclopedia with the aims to "to change the way people think" and to include all of the world's knowledge. Eventually, the book was banned by Rome and as such, France was also meant to destroy it. But by that point, the *Encyclopédie* had become popular enough that despite it being officially forbidden, censors turned a blind eye.

As Palmer describes it, "It was a project to try to transform the world to where everybody had the power that only elites had before. And, as he also articulates it, it's insurance against a new dark age."[11] But, there are always tradeoffs, and in order to ensure that the *Encyclopédie* would outlive him, Diderot censored himself and hid his atheism— and his other works—leaving orders that they only be printed after the death of his daughter.

As such, one of his works—*Rameau's Nephew*—was lost for more than a hundred years until it turned up in a book stall along the River Seine in the late nineteenth century. The book, which Palmer calls one of the "most absolutely most amazing philosophical works [she's] ever read", sees Diderot "wrestle with the fact that by radically changing the education of the new generations, and encouraging them to dismantle current institutions and create better ones,"[12] ultimately realizing that this also means creating a future in which his generation's values become outdated and replaced by better ones.

This story is a reminder not only of what censorship—and self-censorship—can take from us, but also of the fact that we must not seek easy answers or remain staid in our views. In order to develop a better future, we must learn from the past, and recognize that the future is not yet written, that it doesn't have to be this way. There are countless moments throughout history where a seemingly minor decision or discovery led us on a new and different trajectory or, inversely, where the failure to act in the face of atrocity led to even greater suffering. Our willingness and ability to study, examine, and explore our mistakes and to imagine alternative futures is imperative.

The continued erosion of democracy, free expression, and human rights is not inevitable, but can only be stopped if we take immediate action. The future is ours to write.

Acknowledgements

This book is the culmination of more than a decade of work, and would not have been possible without the guidance, education, input, collaboration, love, and care of so many people who have worked with me, listened to my rants, gently guided me in the right direction, and helped me grow along the way. While any errors or oversights are mine alone, this book would not exist without you, and is as much yours as it is mine.

I am deeply grateful to my editor, Leo Hollis, who believed in my ideas and provided me with guidance—and a deep well of patience—as I worked through them these past few years. Special thanks to Adam Greenfield, who kept encouraging me to write a book and helped to make it happen by introducing me to Leo. Thank you to Brian Baughan, whose painstaking edits have made this a much better book than it would have been without them.

Numerous friends and colleagues read through various versions of this manuscript and provided invaluable feedback, including my colleagues Corynne McSherry, from whom I have learned so much over the years and nash sheard, whose insight into US political movements was invaluable. Thank you Łukasz Król—your sharp eyes and candid comments enabled me to get several points across more clearly. Kate Klonick, your sincere and honest input, as well as our many conversations and debates about the best way forward, have been a tremendous help in refining my ideas. Sarah Myers West, you are one of my favorite people to work with and your scholarship and feedback on early versions of this book were indispensable. Thank you to all of my wonderful readers—I owe you more than you will ever know.

So many people have shaped my views and helped me to grow as an activist and as a person over the years. First, my colleagues (both current and former) at the Electronic Frontier Foundation: it is your support and your knowledge that has enabled my scholarship on this subject. I owe special thanks to Cindy Cohn, Danny O'Brien, Lindsay Oliver, Eva Galperin, Gennie Gebhart, Katharine Trendacosta, Erica Portnoy, Kim Carlson, Soraya Okuda, Rainey Reitman, Cory Doctorow, David Greene, Jason Kelley, and Elliot Harmon, but I value and adore every single one of you and am proud to work with you every day. I also hold a special place in my heart, and a well of gratitude, for my former colleagues at the Berkman Klein Center for Internet & Society—particularly Rob Faris, who took a chance not only on hiring me, but supporting me through my early foray into this subject matter, and Jonathan Zittrain, from whom I've learned so much. Thank you also to all of my colleagues at Global Voices—including Solana Larsen, Amira Al Hussaini, Ivan Sigal, and Georgia Popplewell—and at IFEX, particularly Annie Game and Rachael Kay.

To all of the current and former Silicon Valley workers who generously shared their thoughts with me under the protection of anonymity, I am deeply grateful and acknowledge the risk you took in speaking with me. Over the years, a great number of employees of Silicon Valley companies have answered my questions, listened to my recommendations, and offered their assistance, and although I have chosen not to name them (so as not to put anyone at risk!), I am deeply grateful to each and every one of them.

I also want to give special acknowledgement to every person who spoke to me on the record for this book: Amine Derkahoui, Kacem El Ghazzali, Rasha Abdulla, Danielle Blunt, Abdelrahman Mansour, Hossam Hamalawy, Adrian Chen, Courtney Demone, Erika Lust, Azza El Masri, Bardot Smith, Alexander Macgillivray, Dave Willner, Nicole Wong, Kali Sudhra, Dia Kayyali, and Wael Eskandar—and to those who spoke to me anonymously. Thank you all so much for sharing your thoughts, your personal stories, and your time with me. This book would not exist with you!

Over the years, a handful of individuals have been absolutely essential to my understanding of platform governance. Rebecca MacKinnon, one of the first scholars to tackle this subject in writing, thank you so much for all of the support and encouragement you've given me. Zeynep Tufekci, danah boyd, and Sarah T. Roberts, it is your early scholarship that set me on a course that ultimately led to this book. There many other individuals whose insight and scholarship have challenged my own thinking over the years. To name just a few: Tarleton Gillespie, Jac sm Kee, David Kaye, Ron Deibert, Sami Ben Gharbia, Mary Anne Franks, Danielle Citron, Nic Suzor, Kate Klonick, Joan Donovan, Rasha Abdulla, Marc Lynch, Timothy Garton Ash, Gabriella Coleman, Rikke Frank Jørgensen, Liara Roux, Daphne Keller, Flavia Dzodan, Jennifer Grygiel, Jennifer Cobbe, Lisa Stampnitzsky, Soraya Chemaly, Jo Weldon, Evgeny Morozov, and Evelyn Douek.

I am so profoundly lucky to have friends, colleagues, collaborators, and comrades who over the years have taught me, listened to my fears and rants, encouraged me to write, plotted with me along the sidelines of conferences, collaborated with me, challenged my ideas, or simply held space for me. This list is undoubtedly incomplete but includes: Rima Sghaier, Abir Ghattas, Marwa Fatafta, Alex Feerst, Nic Suzor, Dalia Othman, Lorax Horne, Ellery Biddle, Afef Abrougui, Ásta Helgadóttir, Ben Wagner, Mohamed El Dahshan, Sarah Kay, Sarah Joseph, Nate Cardozo, Nada Akl, Blaine Cook, Nicholas Sera-Leyva, Mohamed El Gohary, Farah Wael, Reem El Masri, Katharina Mayer, Claudio Guarnieri, Yazan Badran, Mohamad Najem, Melissa Gira Grant, Geraldine de Bastion, Sandra Mamitzsch, Amr Gharbeia, Ahmad Gharbeia, Jeff Deutch, Hadi Al-Khatib, Oktavia Jonsdóttir, Ahmed Ghappour, Nasser Weddady, Nancy Goldstein, Sheera Frenkel, Wafaa Heikal, Smári McCarthy, Slim Amamou, Razan Ghazzawi, Ali Abdulemam, Manal Hassan, Ahmed Omran, Robert Guerra, Tarek Amr, Laila Shereen Sakr, Miriyam Aouragh, Hanna Kreitem, Jessica Dheere, Alex Stamos, Anas Qtiesh, Siva Vaidyanathan, Ulf Buermeyer, Wafa Ben Hassine, Andre Meister, Cynthia Wong, Sandy Ordoñez, Trinh Nguyen, Fiona Krakenbürger, Sarah Aoun, Kate Coyer, Gülsin Harman, Trevor Timm, Mathew Ingram, Amie Stepanovich, Asher Wolf, Ahmet Alphan Sabancı,

Rob Isaac, Duck, Nat Dudley, Henrik Chulu, Eleanor Saitta, Alison Macrina, Svea Windwehr, Kade Crockford, Karen Reilly, William Youmans, Frederike Kaltheuner, Matt Cornell, Nathalie Maréchal, Lina Attalah, Mahsa Alimardani, Karen Melchior, Sunny Singh, Musa Okwonga, Evan Greer, Caroline Sinders, Sara Yasin, Philip di Salvo, Walter Holst, Tin Geber, Joanna Bronowicka, Thomas Lohninger, Dragana Kaurin, Olivia Solon, Leila Nachawati Rego, Chris Soghoian, Emma Llansó, Renata Avila, Kate Crawford, Maya Ganesh, Barbara Dockalova, Mallory Knodel, Courtney Radsch, Ramzi Jaber, Birgitta Jónsdóttir, Lina Srivastava, Claudio Agosti, and Addie Wagenknecht, as well as the tremendous number of friends on social media who calmed me when I was stressed, helped me remember events I'd for-gotten, brainstormed chapter titles with me, and cheered me along. Thank you all from the bottom of my heart.

There are a few friends whose support and care, particularly during the process of writing this book, that warrants special acknowledge-ment. Dia Kayyali, my favorite accomplice and dear friend, thank you for always checking in on me and for being a rock. I have learned so much from you, and it is always such a pleasure when we get the chance to collaborate. Bryony and Robin Cooper, I am indebted to you for allowing me to write in your beautiful home (with your beautiful cat!), and for never failing to cheer me up when I'm down. Arikia Millikan, your writing and editing advice and belief in me has been indispensable. Tanya Karsou, thank you for lending me your space to write and your dog to snuggle, and for always being willing to lend an ear. Sonja Teofilović, you are a brilliant scholar in your own right, and I thank you for always being there through thick and thin. Tara Tarakiyee, I am always grateful for your willingness to tell me when I'm wrong, and when I'm on to something. Ethan Zuckerman, whom I consider a mentor—thank you for all of the opportunities and guidance over nearly fifteen years and for always being there to lend an ear. Ramy Raoof, thank you for always being able to see me, and sometimes see through me. Markus Beckedahl, I wouldn't have found my home, Berlin, or my place in the spotlight were it not for your invitation—thank you for being one of my biggest supporters. Alaa Abd El Fattah, I don't know if you will ever know the influence you've had one me; I miss you, and our conversations, dearly. Audrey Penven, Aaron Musalzski, Maxi-Sophie Labes, Lily Guncheva, Jeremy Williams, Amanda Rino, Nica Storey, Elio Qoshi and Shakeeb Al-Jabri—I don't know if I would have survived the pandemic without you. And finally, Carrie Portrie, Katherine Maher, and Angel Reynoso, you have all played key roles in my life and growth and I am grateful for all the love and support you've shown me over many years.

Of course, I owe everything I have to my parents, who raised me in so much love. To my father, Terry York, who passed away in 2011, I miss you terribly and think about you every day. I wish you could be here to see how far I've come, but I know that you would be proud. And to my mother, Sandie York: Your unconditional love lifts me up. You are the strongest person I know, and your capacity for honesty without judgement is something I try to aspire to every day.

Finally, this book would simply not have been possible without the support of my partner, Mathana, who has been there for every step of the way, providing me with emotional support, healthy meals, bold ideas, important critiques, a constant soundtrack, and so much encouragement throughout this process. Mathana, you are a brilliant philosopher and scholar, and your belief in my ideas—as well as the love, care, and humor you show me every day—is a driving force in my life. You are my rock, and I can't wait to see what you do next. Full speed ahead.

Notes

Prologue

1 Joshua Adams (@JournoJoshua), Twitter, January 13, 2019, https://twitter.com/JournoJoshua/status/1084439719008788480.
2 Karen Reilly (@akareilly), Twitter, January 13, 2019, https://twitter.com/akareilly/status/1084452673175330817.
3 Richard Barbrook and Andy Cameron, "The Californian Ideology," *Imaginary Futures*, accessed June 1, 2020, http://www.imaginaryfutures.net/2007/04/17/the-californian-ideology-2/.
4 Barbrook and Cameron, "The Californian Ideology."
5 Aaron Sankin, "Composting Toilets, or 'Pooplets', Move One Step Closer To San Francisco Sidewalks," *HuffPost*, December 8, 2011, https://www.huffpost.com/entry/composting-toilets-pooplet-report_n_1137963.

Introduction

1 That blog, which unfortunately no longer exists, was called *The Morocco Report*.
2 Ursula Lindsey, "Morocco suppresses poll despite favorable results for king," *Christian Science Monitor*, August 9, 2009, https://www.csmonitor.com/World/Middle-East/2009/0805/p06s07-wome.html.

Chapter 1: The New Gatekeepers

1 Julie E. Cohen, "Law for the Platform Economy," *UC Davis Law Review*, 51, no. 133 (2017): 72.
2 John Perry Barlow, "A Declaration of the Independence of Cyberspace," February 8, 1996, reprinted by the Electronic Frontier Foundation, January 20, 2016, https://www.eff.org/cyberspace-independence.

3 Bruce Sterling, "A Short History of the Internet, 1993, available at http://sodacity.net/system/files/Bruce_Sterling_A_Short_History_of_the_Internet.pdf, 3.

4 Sterling, "A Short History of the Internet."

5 Though they are used interchangeably throughout this book and convey similar concepts, "freedom of speech" is a more traditionally American term, while "freedom of expression" is typically preferred throughout the world, and conveys a broader meaning that more clearly includes imagery and physical expression.

6 Women, of course, were excluded from participation, which is why I haven't referred to Athens as a democracy.

7 Nicolas P. Suzor, *Lawless: The Secret Rules That Govern Our Digital Lives* (Cambridge University Press, 2019), 90.

8 Suzor, *Lawless*, 45.

9 Rebecca Tushnet, "Power without Responsibility: Intermediaries and the First Amendment," *George Washington Law Review* 76, no. 4 (2008): 31.

10 Kate Klonick, "The New Governors: The People, Rules, and Processes Governing Online Speech," *Harvard Law Review* 131 (2017): 73.

11 Jack M. Balkin, "Free Speech in the Algorithmic Society: Big Data, Private Governance, and New School Speech Regulation," *SSRN Electronic Journal*, 2017, https://doi.org/10.2139/ssrn.3038939.

12 Balkin, "Free Speech in the Algorithmic Society."

13 Marsh v. Alabama, 326 U.S. 501 (1946)

14 The White House, "Remarks by the President at a Facebook Town Hall," April 20, 2011, https://obamawhitehouse.archives.gov/the-press-office/2011/04/20/remarks-president-facebook-town-hall.

15 Klonick, "The New Governors."

16 Nadia Colburn, "In Facebook's Founding, A Hint Of The Privacy Issues To Come," WBUR, April 3, 2018, https://www.wbur.org/cognoscenti/2018/04/13/facebook-privacy-scandal-nadia-colburn.

17 Jillian C. York, "Policing Content in the Quasi-Public Sphere," OpenNet Initiative, accessed May 11, 2019, https://opennet.net/policing-content-quasi-public-sphere.

18 Kate Crawford and Tarleton Gillespie, "What Is a Flag for? Social Media Reporting Tools and the Vocabulary of Complaint," *New Media & Society*, 2016, https://journals.sagepub.com/doi/abs/10.1177/1461444814543163.

19 In one such instance, Cindy McCain—wife of late senator John McCain—wrongly reported an interracial family to authorities on suspicion of trafficking; she later apologized for "distracting" from the importance of "If You See Something, Say Something."

20 Typically, though not universally, content is judged against *all* of a platform's rules, not just the one it was reported for allegedly violating.

21 Sarah T. Roberts, *Behind the Screen: Content Moderation in the Shadows of Social Media* (Yale University Press, 2019).

22 Casey Newton, "Three Facebook Moderators Break Their NDAs to Expose a Company in Crisis," *Verge*, June 19, 2019, https://www.theverge.com/2019/6/19/18681845/facebook-moderator-interviews-video-trauma-ptsd-cognizant-tampa; Munsif Vengattil and Paresh Dave, "Some Facebook Content Reviewers in India Complain of Low Pay, High Pressure," Reuters, February 28, 2019, https://in.reuters.com/article/facebook-content-india-idINKCN1QH15E.

23 Adrian Chen, "Inside Facebook's Outsourced Anti-Porn and Gore Brigade, Where Camel Toes Are More Offensive Than Crushed Heads," *Gawker*, February 16, 2012, http://gawker.com/5885714/inside-facebooks-outsourced-anti-porn-and-gore-brigade-where-camel-toes-are-more-offensive-than-crushed-heads.

24 Casey Newton, "The Secret Lives of Facebook Moderators in America," *Verge*, February 25, 2019, https://www.theverge.com/2019/2/25/18229714/cognizant-facebook-content-moderator-interviews-trauma-working-conditions-arizona.

25 Alex also asked that I not identify their gender. Some names have been changed at the request of the individual. In those cases, I have noted with an asterisk.

26 Evelyn Douek, "Verified Accountability: Self-Regulation of Content Moderation as an Answer to the Special Problems of Speech Regulation," Hoover Institution, Aegis Series Paper, no. 1903 (2019).

27 Jonathan Zittrain and John Palfrey, "Reluctant Gatekeepers: Corporate Ethics on a Filtered Internet," in *Access Denied*, eds. Ronald Deibert et al. (MIT Press, 2008).

28 Marvin Ammori, "The 'New' New York Times: Free Speech Lawyering in the Age of Google and Twitter," *Harvard Law Review*, June 20, 2014, https://harvardlawreview.org/2014/06/the-new-new-york-times-free-speech-lawyering-in-the-age-of-google-and-twitter.

29 Catherine Buni and Soraya Chemaly, "The Secret Rules of the Internet," *Verge*, April 13, 2016, https://www.theverge.com/2016/4/13/11387934/internet-moderator-history-youtube-facebook-reddit-censorship-free-speech.

30 Jeffrey Rosen, *The Deciders: The Future of Privacy and Free Speech in the Age of Facebook and Google*, 80 FORDHAM L. REV. 1525 (2012), https://ir.lawnet.fordham.edu/flr/vol80/iss4/1.

31 "2017-12-07 All Things in Moderation - Day 2 Plenary 2 - Bowden and LaPlante, CCM Workers," YouTube, December 12, 2017, https://www.youtube.com/watch?v=PxLk7btG1Is.

32 Rebecca MacKinnon, *Consent of the Networked: The Worldwide Struggle for Internet Freedom* (Basic Books, 2012), 154.

41 MacKinnon, 156.

Chapter 2: Offline Repression Is Replicated Online

1   Linda Herrera, *Revolution in the Age of Social Media* (Verso, 2014), 31.

2   YouTube, Community Guidelines, 2007, https://web.archive.org/web/20070817230343/http://www.youtube.com:80/t/community_guidelines

3   Jonathan Zittrain and John Palfrey, "Internet Filtering: The Politics and Mechanisms of Control," in *Access Denied*, eds. Ronald Deibert et al. (The MIT Press, 2008).

4   "Vive La Liberté!," *The Economist*, November 23, 2000, https://www.economist.com/node/434168/print?Story_ID=434168.

5   "US Rebukes Yahoo over China Case," BBC News," November 6, 2007, http://news.bbc.co.uk/2/hi/technology/7081458.stm.

6   Rebecca MacKinnon, "America's Online Censors," *Nation*, February 24, 2006, https://www.thenation.com/article/archive/americas-online-censors.

7   Evelyn Douek, "The Rise of Content Cartels," Knight First Amendment Institute, February 11, 2020, https://knightcolumbia.org/content/the-rise-of-content-cartels.

8   Sarah Labowitz and Michael Posner, "NYU Center for Business and Human Rights resigns its membership in the Global Network Initiative," NYU Stern Center for Business and Human Rights Blog, February 1, 2016, https://bhr.stern.nyu.edu/blogs/cbhr-letter-of-resignation-gni.

9   Jeffrey Rosen, "Google's Gatekeepers," *New York Times Magazine*, November 28, 2008, https://www.nytimes.com/2008/11/30/magazine/30google-t.html.

10 "Government Requests to Remove Content – Google Transparency Report," accessed February 12, 2020, https://transparencyreport.google.com/government-removals/overview?hl=en&removal_requests=group_by:totals;period:Y2009H2&lu=removal_requests.

11 Eva Galperin, "What Does Twitter's Country-by-Country Takedown System Mean for Freedom of Expression?," Electronic Frontier Foundation, January 27, 2012, https://www.eff.org/deeplinks/2012/01/what-does-twitter%E2%80%99s-country-country-takedown-system-mean-freedom-expression.

12 "Pakistan: The Chilling Effects of Twitter's Country Witheld [*sic*] Content Tool," *Bolo Bhi* (blog), May 21, 2014, https://bolobhi.org/pakistan-the-chilling-effects-twitter-country-withheld-pakistan.

13 Claire Cain Miller, "Google Has No Plans to Rethink Video Status," *New York Times*, September 14, 2012, https://www.nytimes.com/2012/09/15/world/middleeast/google-wont-rethink-anti-islam-videos-status.html.

14 Kimber Streams, "YouTube Temporarily Censors Offensive Video in Egypt and Libya," *Verge*, September 13, 2012, https://www.theverge.com/2012/9/13/3328106/youtube-censorship-innocence-muslims-egypt-libya.

15 Jack M. Balkin, "Free Speech in the Algorithmic Society: Big Data, Private Governance, and New School Speech Regulation," *SSRN Electronic Journal*, 2017, https://doi.org/10.2139/ssrn.3038939.

16 "An Analysis of #BlackLivesMatter and Other Twitter Hashtags Related to Political or Social Issues," Pew Research Center, *Internet Technology* (blog), July 11, 2018, https://www.pewresearch.org/internet/2018/07/11/an-analysis-of-blacklivesmatter-and-other-twitter-hashtags-related-to-political-or-social-issues.

17 Bijan Stephen, "How Black Lives Matter Uses Social Media to Fight the Power," *Wired*, October 21, 2015, https://www.wired.com/2015/10/how-black-lives-matter-uses-social-media-to-fight-the-power.

18 Joseph Cox and Jason Koebler, "Facebook Decides Which Killings We're Allowed to See," *Vice*, July 7, 2016, https://www.vice.com/en_us/article/8q85jb/philando-castile-facebook-live.

19 "Text of Zuckerberg's Georgetown Speech," *Washington Post*, October 17, 2019, https://www.washingtonpost.com/technology/2019/10/17/zuckerberg-standing-voice-free-expression/.

20 Donie O'Sullivan, "Zuckerberg Said Facebook Helped Black Lives Matter. Activists Disagree and Are Bracing for 2020," CNN Business, October 24, 2019, https://www.cnn.com/2019/10/24/tech/black-lives-matter-facebook-2020/index.html.

21 "Facebook, Elections and Political Speech," *About Facebook* (blog), September 24, 2019, https://about.fb.com/news/2019/09/elections-and-political-speech.

22 "Facebook, Elections and Political Speech."

23 Douek, "The Rise of Content Cartels."

24 Miriyam Aouragh, *Palestine Online: Transnationalism, the Internet and the Construction of Identity* (Bloomsbury Academic, 2011).

25 "As Rockets Rain on Gaza, Facebook Does Nothing to Stop Hate Speech Against Palestinians," *Global Voices Advocacy* (blog), July 11, 2014, https://advox.globalvoices.org/2014/07/11/as-rockets-rain-on-gaza-facebook-does-nothing-to-stop-hate-speech-against-palestinians.

26 "As Rockets Rain on Gaza, Facebook Does Nothing."

27 Associated Press, "Facebook and Israel to Work to Monitor Posts That Incite Violence," *Guardian*, September 12, 2016, https://www.theguardian.com/technology/2016/sep/12/facebook-israel-monitor-posts-incite-violence-social-media.

28 "'Mothers of All Palestinians Should Also Be Killed,' Says Israeli Politician," Daily Sabah, July 14, 2014, https://www.dailysabah.com/mideast/2014/07/14/mothers-of-all-palestinians-should-also-be-killed-says-israeli-politician.

29 7amleh, "The Index of Racism and Incitement in Israeli Social Media 2018," *IFEX blog*, March 11, 2019, https://ifex.org/index-of-racism-and-incitement-in-israeli-social-media-2018/.]

30 Sophia Hyatt, "Facebook 'Blocks Accounts' of Palestinian Journalists," Al Jazeera, September 25, 2016, https://www.aljazeera.com/news/2016/09/facebook-blocks-accounts-palestinian-journalists-160925095126952.html.

31 Dob Lieber, "Facebook Restores Account of Ruling Palestinian Party," *Times of Israel*, March 3, 2017, https://www.timesofisrael.com/facebook-restores-account-of-ruling-palestinian-party-after.

32 "Facebook's Manual on Credible Threats of Violence," *Guardian*, May 21, 2017, https://www.theguardian.com/news/gallery/2017/may/21/facebooks-manual-on-credible-threats-of-violence.

33 Julia Angwin and Hannes Grassegger, "Facebook's Secret Censorship Rules Protect White Men from Hate Speech but Not Black Children," ProPublica, June 28, 2017, https://www.propublica.org/article/facebook-hate-speech-censorship-internal-documents-algorithms.

34 7amleh, "Palestinian Civil Society Organizations Issue a Statement of Alarm Over the Selection of Emi Palmor, Former General Director of the Israeli Ministry of Justice to Facebook's Oversight Board," May 14, 2020, https://7amleh.org/2020/05/14/palestinian-civil-society-organizations-issue-a-statement-of-alarm-over-the-selection-of-emi-palmor-former-general-director-of-the-israeli-ministry-of-justice-to-facebook-s-oversight-board.

35 My Pham, "Vietnam Says Facebook Commits to Preventing Offensive Content," Reuters, April 26, 2017, https://www.reuters.com/article/us-facebook-vietnam-idUSKBN17T0A0.

36 Angwin and Grassegger, "Facebook's Secret Censorship Rules."

37 Wael Eskandar, Twitter, August 14, 2018, https://twitter.com/weskandar/status/1029563198775676935; David Kaye (@davidakaye), Twitter, August 15, 2018, https://twitter.com/davidakaye/status/1029563506796847104.

38 Jillian C. York, "Companies Must Be Accountable to All Users: The Story of Egyptian Activist Wael Abbas," Electronic Frontier Foundation, February 13, 2018, https://www.eff.org/deeplinks/2018/02/insert-better-title-here.

39 Jillian C. York, "Egyptian Blogger and Activist Wael Abbas Detained," Electronic Frontier Foundation, May 25, 2018, https://www.eff.org/deeplinks/2018/05/egyptian-blogger-and-activist-wael-abbas-detained.

Chapter 3: Social Media Revolutionaries

1 Jadaliyya- ةيلدج and Jadaliyya, "Saeeds of Revolution: De-Mythologizing Khaled Saeed," Jadaliyya - ةيلدج, June 5, 2012, http://www.jadaliyya.com/Details/26148.

2 Jillian C. York, "On Facebook Deactivations," April 8, 2010, *Jillian C. York* (blog), https://jilliancyork.com/2010/04/08/on-facebook-deactivations.

3 York, "On Facebook Deactivations."

4 O'Brien now serves as EFF's director of strategy and has been instrumental

to many conversations with and about social media companies over the years, as well as to helping to advance my own work.

5 Rebecca MacKinnon, *Consent of the Networked: The Worldwide Struggle for Internet Freedom* (Basic Books, 2012).

6 Elliot Schrage to Rebecca MacKinnon and Danny O'Brien on November 26, 2010.

7 Jillian York, "Facebook: 'No Palestinian Pages,'" *Jillian C. York*, July 25, 2010, https://jilliancyork.com/2010/07/25/facebook-no-palestinian-pages.

8 Max Read, "Why Is Facebook Blocking the Word 'Palestinian' in Page Titles?," *Gawker*, July 26, 2010, http://gawker.com/5596192/why-is-facebook-blocking-the-word-palestinian-in-page-titles.

9 Jillian C. York, "When Social Networks Become Tools of Oppression," *Bloomberg*, June 7, 2011, https://www.bloomberg.com/opinion/articles/2011-06-07/when-social-networks-become-tools-of-oppression-jillian-c-york.

10 Jillian C. York, "Policing Content in the Quasi-Public Sphere," OpenNet Initiative, September 2010, https://opennet.net/policing-content-quasi-public-sphere.

11 Mohamed Zayani, *Networked Publics and Digital Contention: The Politics of Everyday Life in Tunisia* (Oxford University Press, 2015).

12 Amy Aisen Kallander, "From TUNeZINE to Nhar 3la 3mmar: A Reconsideration of the Role of Bloggers in Tunisia's Revolution," *Arab Media & Society*, January 27, 2013, https://www.arabmediasociety.com/from-tunezine-to-nhar-3la-3mmar-a-reconsideration-of-the-role-of-bloggers-in-tunisias-revolution.

13 Zayani, *Networked Publics and Digital Contention.*

14 A summary of this and other information about the Agence Tunisienne d'Internet and Tunisia's censorship regime can be found in a chapter I co-wrote with Katherine Maher: "Origins of the Tunisian Internet," in *State Power 2.0: Authoritarian Entrenchment and Political Engagement Worldwide*, Muzammil M. Hussain and Philip N. Howard, eds. (Routledge, 2013), https://www.book2look.com/book/KlcjYsZV2W.

15 Some Arabic speakers, particularly North Africans who may have French keyboards rather than Arabic ones, employ numbers to represent particular Arabic letters. The chat language is typically referred to as "Arabizi" or "3rabizi."

16 Global Voices is an international newsroom and blogging community co-founded in 2004 by Ethan Zuckerman and Rebecca MacKinnon while both were fellows at Harvard's Berkman Klein Center for Internet & Society, and was revolutionary in bringing international blogs and social media into mainstream media reporting.

17 "YouTube Bans Tunisian Site Nawaat from Uploading Videos," *Global Voices Advocacy* (blog), February 16, 2010, https://advox.globalvoices.

org/2010/02/16/youtube-bans-tunisian-site-nawaat-from-uploading-videos.

18   "Human Rights Implications of Content Moderation and Account Suspension by Companies," RConversation, May 14, 2010, https://rconversation.blogs.com/rconversation/2010/05/human-rights-implications.html.

19   Ethan Zuckerman: "Internet freedom: protect, then project," *My Heart is in Accra* (blog), March 22, 2010, http://www.ethanzuckerman.com/blog/2010/03/22/internet-freedom-protect-then-project/.

20   Kallander, "From TUNeZINE to Nhar 3la 3mmar."

21   Jillian York, "Anti-Censorship Movement in Tunisia: Creativity, Courage and Hope!," *Global Voices Advocacy* (blog), May 27, 2010, https://advox.globalvoices.org/2010/05/27/anti-censorship-movement-in-tunisia-creativity-courage-and-hope/.

22   Eva Galperin, "EFF Calls for Immediate Action to Defend Tunisian Activists against Government Cyberattacks," Electronic Frontier Foundation, January 11, 2011, https://www.eff.org/deeplinks/2011/01/eff-calls-immediate-action-defend-tunisian.

23   Alexis C. Madrigal, "The Inside Story of How Facebook Responded to Tunisian Hacks," *Atlantic*, January 24, 2011, https://www.theatlantic.com/technology/archive/2011/01/the-inside-story-of-how-facebook-responded-to-tunisian-hacks/70044/.

24   The HTTPS protocol encrypts any traffic or communications that are sent across it, making it immune to the keylogging strategy—that is, the attempt to capture the keystrokes of users—that was being employed by Tunisian internet service providers.

25   That massacre was confirmed by reporting. See Yasmine Ryan, "The Massacre behind the Revolution," Al Jazeera, February 16, 2011, https://www.aljazeera.com/indepth/features/2011/02/2011215123229922898.html.

26   Alex Nunns and Nadia Idle, eds., *Tweets from Tahrir: Egypt's Revolution As It Unfolded, in the Words of the People Who Made It* (OR Books, 2011).

27   Hossam el-Hamalawy, "Egypt's Revolution Has Been 10 Years in the Making," *Guardian*, March 2, 2011, editorialhttps://www.theguardian.com/commentisfree/2011/mar/02/egypt-revolution-mubarak-wall-of-fear.

28   Hossam el-Hamalawy, "Hundreds of Egyptian workers demonstrate for minimum wage," *Egypt Independent*, April 3, 2010, https://egyptindependent.com/hundreds-egyptian-workers-demonstrate-minimum-wage/.

29   Tom Isherwood, "A New Direction or More of the Same? Political Blogging in Egypt," *Arab Media & Society*, August 6, 2009, https://www.arabmediasociety.com/a-new-direction-or-more-of-the-same.

30   Summer Harlow, "It Was a 'Facebook Revolution': Exploring the Meme-like Spread of Narratives during the Egyptian Protests," *Revista de Comunicación* 12 (2013): 59–82.

31 "Crowds Swell As Protest Seeks a Leader," *Los Angeles* Times, February 9, 2011, https://www.latimes.com/archives/la-xpm-2011-feb-09-la-fg-egypt-google-20110209-story.html.

32 "Wael Ghonim's DreamTV Interview - Part 2," YouTube, February 9, 2011, https://www.youtube.com/watch?v=t57txvQszJI&t=84s.

33 Nunns and Idle, *Tweets from Tahrir.*

34 Jillian York, "Arab Swell: How Bloggers Built the Groundwork for a Revolution," *Makeshift*, no. 3 (Summer 2012).

35 Peter Beaumont, "Can Social Networking Overthrow a Government?," *Sydney Morning Herald*, February 25, 2011, https://www.smh.com.au/technology/can-social-networking-overthrow-a-government-20110225-1b7u6.html; Sam Graham-Felsen, "How Cyber-Pragmatism Brought Down Mubarak," *Nation*, February 11, 2011, https://www.thenation.com/article/how-cyber-pragmatism-brought-down-mubarak.

36 Malcolm Gladwell, "Does Egypt Need Twitter?," *New Yorker*, February 2, 2011, https://www.newyorker.com/news/news-desk/does-egypt-need-twitter.

37 Abdelrahman Mansour, "The Arab Spring Is Not Over Yet," *Foreign Policy*, March 8, 2019, https://foreignpolicy.com/2019/03/08/the-arab-spring-is-not-over-yet-sudan-egypt-algeria-bouteflika-sisi-bashir.

38 Adrian Chen, "Mark Zuckerberg Takes Credit for Populist Revolutions Now That Facebook's Gone Public," *Gawker*, February 2, 2012, http://gawker.com/5881657/facebook-takes-credit-for-populist-revolutions-now-that-its-gone-public.

Chapter 4: Profit over People

1 "Jordan's Protesters Are Young and Wary of Their Cause Being Hijacked," Arab News, June 4, 2018, https://www.arabnews.com/node/1314946/middle-east.

2 Abdelaziz Radi, "Protest Movements and Social Media: Morocco's February 20 Movement," *Africa Development / Afrique et Développement* 42, no. 2 (2017): 31–55.

3 Jennifer Preston, "Syria Restores Access to Facebook and YouTube," February 9, 2011," https://www.nytimes.com/2011/02/10/world/middleeast/10syria.html

4 "Syrians Call for Protests on Facebook, Twitter," CBS News, February 1, 2011, https://www.cbsnews.com/news/syrians-call-for-protests-on-facebook-twitter.

5 "President: Syria Immune to Unrest Seen in Egypt," CBS News, January 31, 2011, https://www.cbsnews.com/news/president-syria-immune-to-unrest-seen-in-egypt.

6 Lauren Williams, "Syria to Set Facebook Status to Unbanned in Gesture to People," *Guardian*, February 8, 2011, https://www.theguardian.com/

world/2011/feb/08/syria-facebook-unbanned-people.

7   Jillian York, "Unblocking Syria's Social Media," Al Jazeera, February 11, 2011, https://www.aljazeera.com/indepth/opinion/2011/02/2011212122 746819907.html.

8   Anas Qtiesh, "Syria: A Blogger Arrested, a Journalist Missing," *Global Voices Advocacy* (blog), March 23, 2011, https://advox.globalvoices. org/2011/03/23/syria-a-blogger-arrested-a-journalist-missing.

9   Adrian Blomfield, "Syria 'Tortures Activists to Access Their Facebook Pages,'" May 9, 2011, https://www.telegraph.co.uk/news/ worldnews/middleeast/syria/8503797/Syria-tortures-activists-to-access-their-Facebook-pages.html.

10 Jennifer Preston, "Seeking to Disrupt Protesters, Syria Cracks Down on Social Media," *New York Times*, May 22, 2011, https://www. nytimes.com/2011/05/23/world/middleeast/23facebook.html; Bob Chiarito, "'Chicago Girl' Leads Syrian Revolution from Des Plaines to Damascus," *Chicago Ambassador* (blog), February 28, 2015, https:// thechicagoambassador.wordpress.com/2015/02/28/chicago-girl-leads-syrian-revolution-from-des-plaines-to-damascus

11 "Number of Active Users at Facebook over the Years," Associated Press, October 23, 2012, https://finance.yahoo.com/news/number-active-users-facebook-over-years-214600186--finance.html.

12 Chris Taylor, "Twitter Has 100 Million Active Users," *Mashable*, September 8, 2011, https://mashable.com/2011/09/08/twitter-has-100-million-active-users/?europe=true.

13 "Facebook: Number of Employees 2009–2019 | FB," Macrotrends, https://www.macrotrends.net/stocks/charts/FB/facebook/number-of-employees.

14 Marc Herman, "An Activist Describes How Manning's Leaks Helped Topple a Dictator," *Pacific Standard*, August 28, 2013, https://psmag.com/ news/tunisian-activist-describes-mannings-leaks-helped-topple-dictator-65243.

15 Ewen MacAskill, "WikiLeaks Website Pulled by Amazon after US Political Pressure," *Guardian*, December 2, 2010, https://www.theguardian.com/ media/2010/dec/01/wikileaks-website-cables-servers-amazon.

16 "Why WikiLeaks Is Not Pentagon Papers 2.0," *Atlantic*, December 29, 2010, https://www.theatlantic.com/politics/archive/2010/12/why-wikileaks-is-not-pentagon-papers-2-0/342839.

17 John F. Burns and Ravi Somaiya, "WikiLeaks Founder Gets Support in Rebuking U.S. on Whistle-Blowers," *New York Times*, https://www. nytimes.com/2010/10/24/world/24london.html.

18 Alexia Tsotsis, "Twitter Informs Users of DOJ WikiLeaks Court Order, Didn't Have To," *TechCrunch* (blog), January 8, 2011, https://social. techcrunch.com/2011/01/07/twitter-informs-users-of-doj-wikileaks-court-order-didnt-have-to.

19 Ryan Singel, "Twitter's Response to WikiLeaks Subpoena Should Be the Industry Standard," *Wired*, January 10, 2011, https://www.wired.com/2011/01/twitter-2/.

20 Ramy Yaacoub (@RamyYaacoub), Twitter, December 19, 2011, https://twitter.com/RamyYaacoub/status/148764720143409153.

21 "Tweets Still Must Flow," Twitter (blog), January 26, 2012, https://blog.twitter.com/en_us/a/2012/tweets-still-must-flow.html.

22 Jillian C. York, "Twitter's Growing Pains," Al Jazeera, January 31, 2012, https://www.aljazeera.com/indepth/opinion/2012/01/201213091936736195.html.

23 "Why Facebook Buys Startups," YouTube, October 18, 2010, https://www.youtube.com/watch?v=OlBDyItD0Ak.

24 Alexia Tsotsis, "Facebook Scoops Up Face.Com For $55–60M to Bolster Its Facial Recognition Tech (Updated)," *TechCrunch* (blog), June 18, 2012, http://social.techcrunch.com/2012/06/18/facebook-scoops-up-face-com-for-100m-to-bolster-its-facial-recognition-tech.

25 Steve Tobak, "Did IPO Damage Facebook Brand?," CBS News, June 6, 2012, https://www.cbsnews.com/news/did-ipo-damage-facebook-brand; David Weidner, "Facebook IPO Facts, Fiction and Flops," *Wall Street Journal*, May 30, 2012, https://www.wsj.com/articles/SB10001424052702304821304577436873952633672.

26 Mark Zuckerberg, "(4) Founder's Letter, 2012," Facebook, February 1, 2017, https://www.facebook.com/notes/mark-zuckerberg/founders-letter/10154500412571634.

27 Jillian C. York, "Facebook: Now Open for Public Scrutiny," Al Jazeera, May 27, 2012, https://www.aljazeera.com/indepth/opinion/2012/05/201252782040308719.html.

28 "Facebook's 5 Core Values," Facebook, September 8, 2015, https://www.facebook.com/media/set/?set=a.1655178611435493.1073741828.1633466236940064&type=3.

29 Sam Howe Verhovek, "After 10 Years, the Trauma of Love Canal Continues," *New York Times*, August 5, 1988, https://www.nytimes.com/1988/08/05/nyregion/after-10-years-the-trauma-of-love-canal-continues.html.

30 "Sex, Social Mores, and Keyword Filtering: Microsoft Bing in the 'Arabian Countries,'" OpenNet Initiative, https://opennet.net/sex-social-mores-and-keyword-filtering-microsoft-bing-arabian-countries.

31 "The GNI Principles," *Global Network Initiative* (blog), https://globalnetworkinitiative.org/gni-principles.

32 "Insights to Go," Facebook IQ, https://www.facebook.com/iq/insights-to-go/tags/middle-east; Cyrille Fabre et al., "E-Commerce in MENA: Opportunity Beyond the Hype," Bain & Company, February 19, 2019, https://www.bain.com/insights/ecommerce-in-MENA-opportunity-beyond-the-hype.

33 "ITunes Yields to Petition from SMEX and Lebanese Band Al-Rahel

Al-Kabir," SMEX, May 21, 2018, https://smex.org/itunes-yields-to-petition-from-smex-and-lebanese-band-al-rahel-al-kabir.

34 "Alcohol Content," Twitter Business, https://business.twitter.com/en/help/ads-policies/restricted-content-policies/alcohol-content.html.

35 Nabila Rahhal, "Advertising Alcohol: The Business of Selling Responsibly," *Executive*, February 15, 2016, https://www.executive-magazine.com/hospitality-tourism/advertising-alcohol-the-business-of-selling-responsibly.

36 "Tripoli Alcohol Advertising Ban Draws Fire," *Daily Star* (Lebanon), August 11, 2014, https://www.dailystar.com.lb/News/Lebanon-News/2014/Aug-11/266821-tripoli-alcohol-advertising-ban-draws-fire.ashx.

37 AG Reporter, "Twitter Officially Launches Advertising Services in the Middle East," *Arabian Gazette*, January 28, 2013, https://arabiangazette.com/twitter-officially-launches-advertising-services-middle-east-20130128; Lorena Rios, "Drinking Alcohol Is Always an Open Secret in Egypt," *Vice*, August 19, 2016, https://www.vice.com/en_us/article/4xbbqj/drinking-alcohol-is-always-an-open-secret-in-egypt.

38 Greg Miller, "How the U.S. Maps the World's Most Disputed Territories," *Wired*, January 24, 2014, https://www.wired.com/2014/01/state-department-maps/.

39 Greg Bensinger, "Google Redraws the Borders on Maps Depending on Who's Looking," *Washington Post*, February 4, 2020, https://www.washingtonpost.com/technology/2020/02/14/google-maps-political-borders.

40 Colum Lynch, "Syrian Opposition Seeks to Wipe the Assad Name off the Map—via Google," *Washington Post*, February 14, 2020, https://www.washingtonpost.com/world/national-security/syrian-opposition-seeks-to-wipe-the-assad-name-off-the-map--via-google/2012/02/14/gIQAad5aER_story.html.

41 Mark Brown, "Nicaraguan Invasion? Blame Google Maps," *Wired*, November 8, 2010, https://www.wired.com/2010/11/google-maps-error-blamed-for-nicaraguan-invasion.

42 Steve Forrest, "Shezanne Cassim, Freed from UAE Prison, Returns to US," CNN, January 9, 2014, https://www.cnn.com/2014/01/09/world/meast/uae-freed-american/index.html.

43 Adam Schreck, "Facebook Opens Office in Dubai," *Christian Science Monitor*, May 30, 2012, https://www.csmonitor.com/Business/Latest-News-Wires/2012/0530/Facebook-opens-office-in-Dubai.

44 Vijaya Gadde, "Twitter Executive: Here's How We're Trying to Stop Abuse While Preserving Free Speech," *Washington Post*, April 16, 2015, https://www.washingtonpost.com/posteverything/wp/2015/04/16/twitter-executive-heres-how-were-trying-to-stop-abuse-while-preserving-free-speech.

45 Josh Halliday, "Lawyer and Champion of Free Speech Alex Macgillivray

to Leave Twitter," *Guardian*, August 30, 2013, https://www.theguardian.com/technology/2013/aug/30/twitter-alex-macgillivray-free-speech.

46 Theodore Schleifer, "Silicon Valley Is Awash in Chinese and Saudi Cash—and No One Is Paying Attention (except Trump)," Vox, May 1, 2019, https://www.vox.com/recode/2019/5/1/18511540/silicon-valley-foreign-money-china-saudi-arabia-cfius-firrma-geopolitics-venture-capital.

47 Thomas L. Friedman, "Saudi Arabia's Arab Spring, at Last," editorial, *New York Times*, November 23, 2017, https://www.nytimes.com/2017/11/23/opinion/saudi-prince-mbs-arab-spring.html.

48 "Impact of Office Locations on the Policies of Multinational Companies: The Cases of Facebook and Twitter," ImpACT International, September 19, 2019, https://impactpolicies.org/en/news/39/Impact-of-Office-Locations-on-the-Policies-of-Multinational-Companies-the-Cases-of-Facebook-and-Twitter.

49 Theodore Schleifer, "Silicon Valley Is Snubbing Saudi Arabia's Glitzy Conference a Year after the Khashoggi Killing," Vox, October 14, 2019, https://www.vox.com/recode/2019/10/14/20908630/saudi-arabia-silicon-valley-future-investment-initiative-conference-speakers.

50 Alex Kantrowitz, "How Saudi Arabia Infiltrated Twitter," BuzzFeed News, February 19, 2020, https://www.buzzfeednews.com/article/alexkantrowitz/how-saudi-arabia-infiltrated-twitter.

51 Elana Beiser, "China, Turkey, Saudi Arabia, Egypt Are World's Worst Jailers of Journalists," Committee to Protect Journalists, December 11, 2019, https://cpj.org/reports/2019/12/journalists-jailed-china-turkey-saudi-arabia-egypt.php.

52 Ruth Michaelson, "Threat of Jail Looms Over Even Mildest Critics under Egyptian Crackdown," *Guardian*, January 24, 2020, https://www.theguardian.com/world/2020/jan/24/threat-of-jail-shapes-egyptian-lives-nine-years-after-uprising.

53 Michael Safi, "Egypt Forces Guardian Journalist to Leave after Coronavirus Story," *Guardian*, March 26, 2020, https://www.theguardian.com/world/2020/mar/26/egypt-forces-guardian-journalist-leave-coronavirus-story-ruth-michaelson.

54 "'Leave, Sisi!': All You Need to Know about the Protests in Egypt," Al Jazeera, September 21, 2019, https://www.aljazeera.com/news/2019/09/sisi-protests-egypt-190921091738593.html.

55 Megha Rajagopalan, "Twitter 'Silenced' Dissenting Voices during Anti-Government Protests in Egypt," BuzzFeed News, October 25, 2019, https://www.buzzfeednews.com/article/meghara/twitter-egypt-protests-accounts-suspended.

56 Wael Eskandar, "How Twitter Is Gagging Arabic Users and Acting as Morality Police," openDemocracy, October 23, 2019, https://www.opendemocracy.net/en/north-africa-west-asia/how-twitter-gagging-arabic-users-and-acting-morality-police.

57 Simon Speakman Cordall, "Facebook deactivates accounts of Tunisian political bloggers and activists," *The Guardian*, June 4, 2020, https://www.theguardian.com/global-development/2020/jun/04/facebook-deactivates-accounts-of-tunisian-political-bloggers-and-activists.

58 Facebook, "May 2020 Coordinated Inauthentic Behavior Report," June 5, 2020, https://about.fb.com/news/2020/06/may-cib-report/

59 Marwa Fatafta, "Rights groups to Facebook on Tunisia's "disappeared" accounts: we're still waiting for answers," Access Now, June 23, 2020, https://www.accessnow.org/rights-groups-to-facebook-on-tunisias-disappeared-accounts-were-still-waiting-for-answers/.

60 Cordall, "Facebook deactivates accounts of Tunisian political bloggers and activists."

61 @Cartes, "Announcing the Twitter Trust & Safety Council," Twitter (blog), February 9, 2016, https://blog.twitter.com/en_us/a/2016/announcing-the-twitter-trust-safety-council.html.

62 Jacob Kornbluh, "Netanyahu Called Mark Zuckerberg to Voice Concerns over Facebook Suspension," Jewish Insider, February 12, 2020, https://jewishinsider.com/2020/02/netanyahu-called-mark-zuckerberg-to-voice-concerns-over-facebook-suspension.

63 My Pham, "Vietnam Says Facebook Commits to Preventing Offensive Content," Reuters, April 16, 2017, https://www.reuters.com/article/us-facebook-vietnam-idUSKBN17T0A0.

64 Saudi Arabia boasts high internet penetration and its citizens are major users of social media—according to the Saudi Ministry of Communications and Information Technology, more than 18 million Saudis use social media. https://www.mcit.gov.sa/en/media-center/news/89698

Chapter 5: Extremism Calls for Extreme Measures

1 Stephanie Busari, "Tweeting the Terror: How Social Media Reacted to Mumbai," CNN, http://edition.cnn.com/2008/WORLD/asiapcf/11/27/mumbai.twitter.

2 U.S. Senate Committee on Homeland Security and Governmental Affairs, "Lieberman Calls on Google to Take Down Terrorist Content," May 19, 2008, http://www.hsgac.senate.gov/media/majority-media/lieberman-calls-on-google-to-take-down-terrorist-content.

3 U.S. Senate Committee on Homeland Security and Governmental Affairs, "Lieberman Calls."

4 "Dialogue with Sen. Lieberman on Terrorism Videos," *Official YouTube Blog*, May 19, 2008, https://youtube.googleblog.com/2008/05/dialogue-with-sen-lieberman-on.html.

5 "No Exit: Human Rights Abuses Inside the MKO Camps: I. Summary," Human Rights Watch, https://www.hrw.org/legacy/backgrounder/mena/iran0505/1.htm#_Toc103593125.

6 Michael Rubin, "Monsters of the Left: The Mujahedin al-Khalq," Middle East Forum, January 13, 2006, https://www.meforum.org/888/monsters-of-the-left-the-mujahedin-al-khalq.

7 Glenn Greenwald, "Five Lessons from the De-Listing of MEK as a Terrorist Group," *Guardian*, September 23, 2012, https://www.theguardian.com/commentisfree/2012/sep/23/iran-usa.

8 Lisa Stampnitzky, *Disciplining Terror: How Experts Invented "Terrorism,"* (Cambridge University Press, 2013).

9 Jeffrey Gettleman, "Somalia's Rebels Embrace Twitter as a Weapon," *New York Times*, December 14, 2011, https://www.nytimes.com/2011/12/15/world/africa/somalias-rebels-embrace-twitter-as-a-weapon.html.

10 "YouTube Is Managing Graphic, Violent Videos from The Middle East with Community Help," *Business Insider*, June 4, 2013, https://web.archive.org/web/20130604053925/http://www.businessinsider.com/youtube-is-managing-graphic-violent-videos-from-the-middle-east-with-community-help-2011-5.

11 Liam Stack, "Video of Tortured Boy's Corpse Deepens Anger in Syria," *New York Times*, May 30, 2011, https://www.nytimes.com/2011/05/31/world/middleeast/31syria.html.

12 Ari Melber, "YouTube Reinstates Blocked Video of Child Allegedly Tortured in Syria," *Nation*, June 1, 2011, https://www.thenation.com/article/archive/youtube-reinstates-blocked-video-child-allegedly-tortured-syria/.

13 Melber, "YouTube Reinstates Blocked Video."

14 John F. Burns and Miguel Helft, "YouTube Withdraws Cleric's Videos," *New York Times*, November 3, 2010, https://www.nytimes.com/2010/11/04/world/04britain.html.

15 The National Center for Missing and Exploited Children maintains a database of child sexual exploitation/abuse imagery (the CSEI or CSAI, used interchangeably throughout the industry) with oversight from law enforcement authorities.

16 "Al-Shabab Showed Gruesome Social Media Savvy during Attack," CBS News, September 24, 2013, https://www.cbsnews.com/news/al-shabab-showed-gruesome-social-media-savvy-during-attack.

17 Adam Withnall, "Iraq Crisis: Isis Declares Its Territories a New Islamic State with 'Restoration of Caliphate' in Middle East," *Independent*, June 30, 2014, https://www.independent.co.uk/news/world/middle-east/isis-declares-new-islamic-state-in-middle-east-with-abu-bakr-al-baghdadi-as-emir-removing-iraq-and-9571374.html.

18 Roula Khalaf, "Selling Terror: How Isis Details Its Brutality," *Financial Times*, June 17, 2014, https://www.ft.com/content/69e70954-f639-11e3-a038-00144feabdc0.

19 Alice Speri, "ISIS Fighters and Their Friends Are Total Social Media Pros," *Vice*, June 17, 2014, https://www.vice.com/en_us/article/wjybjy/

isis-fighters-and-their-friends-are-total-social-media-pros; J. M. Berger, "The Sophisticated Social Media Strategy of ISIL," *Atlantic*, June 16, 2014, https://www.theatlantic.com/international/archive/2014/06/isis-iraq-twitter-social-media-strategy/372856.

20 Patrick Kingsley, "Who Is behind Isis's Terrifying Online Propaganda Operation?," *Guardian*, June 23, 2014, https://www.theguardian.com/world/2014/jun/23/who-behind-isis-propaganda-operation-iraq.

21 Paul Tassi, "ISIS Uses 'GTA 5' in New Teen Recruitment Video," *Forbes*, September 20, 2014, https://www.forbes.com/sites/insert-coin/2014/09/20/isis-uses-gta-5-in-new-teen-recruitment-video.

22 Rukmini Callimachi, "Before Killing James Foley, ISIS Demanded Ransom from U.S.," *New York Times*, August 20, 2014, https://www.nytimes.com/2014/08/21/world/middleeast/isis-pressed-for-ransom-before-killing-james-foley.html.

23 Bianca Bosker, "Why Beheadings Belong on Facebook," *HuffPost*, December 6, 2017, https://www.huffpost.com/entry/facebook-beheading-videos_n_4144886.

24 Issie Lapowsky, "Twitter Steps Up, Suspends Accounts That Share Horrific Beheading Video," *Wired*, August 20, 2014, https://www.wired.com/2014/08/costolo-video; "YouTube to Remove Video of Alleged James Foley Killing," *Irish Times*, August 20, 2014, https://www.irishtimes.com/news/world/middle-east/youtube-to-remove-video-of-alleged-james-foley-killing-1.1902815.

25 Tom Risen, "Twitter, Facebook, YouTube Grapple with Islamic State Censorship," *US News & World Report*, September 5, 2014, https://www.usnews.com/news/articles/2014/09/05/twitter-facebook-youtube-navigate-islamic-state-censorship.

26 Walter Reich, "Show the James Foley Beheading Video," *Washington Post*, August 29, 2014, https://www.washingtonpost.com/posteverything/wp/2014/08/29/why-facebook-and-youtube-should-show-the-james-foley-beheading-video/.

27 Jeff Jacoby, "James Foley Video Is Grim, but We Owe It to Him to Bear Witness," *Boston Globe*, August 22, 2014, https://www.bostonglobe.com/opinion/2014/08/22/james-foley-video-grim-but-owe-him-bear-witness/wWG9Jkprv49QJbA28BG8wM/story.html.

28 Armin Rosen, "Erasing History: YouTube's Deletion of Syria War Videos Concerns Human Rights Groups," *Fast Company*, March 7, 2018, https://www.fastcompany.com/40540411/erasing-history-youtubes-deletion-of-syria-war-videos-concerns-human-rights-groups.

29 Joel Kabot, "ISIS Is Winning the Cyber War. Here's How to Stop It.," *Hill*, March 21, 2017, https://thehill.com/blogs/pundits-blog/defense/325082-isis-is-winning-the-cyber-war-heres-how-to-stop-it.

30 Sheera Frenkel, "Facebook Will Use Artificial Intelligence to Find Extremist Posts," *New York Times*, June 15, 2017, https://www.nytimes.

com/2017/06/15/technology/facebook-artificial-intelligence-extremists-terrorism.html.

31 Abdul Rahman Al Jaloud et al., "Caught in the Net: The Impact of 'Extremist' Speech Regulations on Human Rights Content," Electronic Frontier Foundation, May 30, 2019, https://www.eff.org/wp/caught-net-impact-extremist-speech-regulations-human-rights-content.

32 Avi Asher-Schapiro, "YouTube and Facebook Are Removing Evidence of Atrocities, Jeopardizing Cases Against War Criminals," *The Intercept*, November 2, 2017, https://theintercept.com/2017/11/02/war-crimes-youtube-facebook-syria-rohingya.

33 Megha Rajagopalan, "The Histories of Today's Wars Are Being Written on Facebook and YouTube. But What Happens When They Get Taken Down?," BuzzFeed News, December 22, 2018, https://www.buzzfeed news.com/article/meghara/facebook-youtube-icc-war-crimes.

34 "Warrant of Arrest," International Criminal Court, August 15, 2017, https://www.icc-cpi.int/Pages/record.aspx?docNo=ICC-01/11-01/17-2.

35 Asher-Schapiro, "YouTube and Facebook Are Removing Evidence."

36 "GifCT," Global Internet Forum to Counter Terrorism, http://www.gifct.org.

37 "Civil Society Letter to the European Parliament on the GIFCT hash database," February 4, 2019, https://cdt.org/wp-content/uploads/2019/02/Civil-Society-Letter-to-European-Parliament-on-Terrorism-Database.pdf.

38 Facebook, "Next Steps for the Global Internet Forum to Counter Terrorism," September 29, 2019, https://about.fb.com/news/2019/09/next-steps-for-gifct/.

39 Emma Llansó, "Human Rights NGOs in Coalition Letter to GIFCT," Center for Democracy and Technology, July 30, 2020, https://cdt.org/insights/human-rights-ngos-in-coalition-letter-to-gifct/.

40 Emma Llansó, "Human Rights NGOs in Coalition Letter to GIFCT."

41 Emma Llansó, "Human Rights NGOs in Coalition Letter to GIFCT."

42 "Terrorism and Violent Extremism Policy," Twitter Help Center, March 2019, https://help.twitter.com/en/rules-and-policies/violent-groups.

43 JTA and Haaretz, "Twitter Blocks Hamas, Hezbollah Accounts Following Israeli Pressure," *Haaretz*, March 3, 2018, https://www.haaretz.com/twitter-blocks-hamas-hezbollah-accounts-in-israel-under-pressure-1.6240629.

44 Sarah E. Needleman and Bowdeya Tweh, "Twitter Suspends Accounts Linked to Hamas, Hezbollah," *Wall Street Journal*, November 4, 2019, https://www.wsj.com/articles/twitter-suspends-accounts-linked-to-hamas-hezbollah-11572888026.

45 Risen, "Twitter, Facebook, YouTube Grapple."

46 "The Crime of Speech: How Arab Governments Use the Law to Silence Expression Online," Electronic Frontier Foundation, April 25, 2016,

https://www.eff.org/pages/crime-speech-how-arab-governments-use-law-silence-expression-online.

Chapter 6: Twenty-First-Century Victorians

1   A. Victor Coonin, *From Marble to Flesh: The Biography of Michelangelo's David* (Florentine Press, 2014), 92.
2   Online Museum Victoria and Albert Museum, "David's Fig Leaf," June 24, 2011, http://www.vam.ac.uk/content/articles/d/davids-fig-leaf/.
3   CjCB, "Facebook, Curator of Culture," *New York Academy of Art* (blog), January 31, 2011, https://newyorkacademyofart.blogspot.com/2011/01/facebook-curator-of-culture.html.
4   CjCB, "New York Academy of Art."
5   Rebecca Greenfield, "Facebook Explains That Nipplegate Was a Mistake," *Atlantic*, September 11, 2012, https://www.theatlantic.com/technology/archive/2012/09/facebook-explains-nipplegate-was-mistake/323750.
6   Robert Mankoff, "Nipplegate," September 10, 2012, *New Yorker*, https://www.newyorker.com/cartoons/bob-mankoff/nipplegate.
7   Adrian Chen, "Inside Facebook's Outsourced Anti-Porn and Gore Brigade, Where 'Camel Toes' Are More Offensive Than 'Crushed Heads,'" *Gawker*, February 16, 2012, http://gawker.com/5885714/inside-facebooks-outsourced-anti-porn-and-gore-brigade-where-camel-toes-are-more-offensive-than-crushed-heads.
8   Marion Cocquet, "L'origine Du Scandale," *Le Point*, February 17, 2011, https://www.lepoint.fr/culture/l-origine-du-scandale-17-02-2011-1296611_3.php.
9   Phiilppe Sotto, "French Court Issues Mixed Ruling in Facebook Nudity Case," *Seattle Times*, March 15, 2018, https://www.seattletimes.com/business/french-court-issues-mixed-ruling-in-facebook-nudity-case.
10 Jillian Steinhauer, "Leaked Document Lays Out Facebook's Policy on Sex and Nudity in Art," *Hyperallergic*, May 22, 2017, https://hyperallergic.com/380911/leaked-document-lays-out-facebooks-policy-on-sex-and-nudity-in-art.
11 Hakim Bishara, "Facebook Settles 8-Year Case with Teacher Who Posted Courbet's 'Origin of the World,'" *Hyperallergic*, August 6, 2019, https://hyperallergic.com/512428/facebook-settles-8-year-case-with-teacher-who-posted-courbets-origin-of-the-world.
12 Maggie Fick and Paresh Dave, "Facebook's flood of languages leave it struggling to monitor content," April 23, 2019, https://www.reuters.com/article/us-facebook-languages-insight/facebooks-flood-of-languages-leave-it-struggling-to-monitor-content-idUSKCN1RZ0DW.
13 Xeni Jardin, "Richard Metzger: How I, a Married, Middle-Aged Man, Became an Accidental Spokesperson for Gay Rights Overnight," *Boing Boing*, April 19, 2011, https://boingboing.net/2011/04/19/richard-metzger-how.html.

14 Ibid.

15 "Facebook Opens Governance of Service and Policy Process to Users," Facebook Newsroom, February 26, 2009, https://newsroom.fb.com/news/2009/02/facebook-opens-governance-of-service-and-policy-process-to-users.

16 Jardin, "Richard Metzger."

17 "Gay Kissing Pic Banned from Facebook, So Why Are All the Hetero Pics Still There?," *AMERICAblog*, April 18, 2011, http://gay.americablog.com/2011/04/gay-kissing-pic-banned-from-facebook-so-why-are-all-the-hetero-pics-still-there.html.

18 Radhika Sanghani, "Instagram Deletes Woman's Period Photos - but Her Response Is Amazing," *Telegraph*, March 30, 2015, https://www.telegraph.co.uk/women/life/instagram-deletes-womans-period-photos-but-her-response-is-amazing.

19 Sarah Myers West, "Raging Against the Machine: Network Gatekeeping and Collective Action on Social Media Platforms," *Media and Communication* 5, no. 3 (2017): 28, https://doi.org/10.17645/mac.v5i3.989.

20 Myers West, "Raging Against the Machine," 28.

21 Myers West, "Raging Against the Machine," 28.

22 Kate Klonick, "What I Learned in Twitter Purgatory," The *Atlantic*, September 8, 2020, https://www.theatlantic.com/ideas/archive/2020/09/what-i-learned-twitter-purgatory/616144.

23 Kate Klonick, "The New Governors: The People, Rules, and Processes Governing Online Speech," *Harvard Law Review* 131 (2017): 73.

24 Klonick, "The New Governors," 73.

25 Courtney Demone, "I Am a Trans Woman. Will Facebook Censor My Breasts?," *Mashable*, September 30, 2015, https://mashable.com/2015/09/30/do-i-have-boobs-now.

26 Jenna Wortham, "Facebook Won't Budge on Breastfeeding Photos," *Bits Blog* (blog), January 2, 2009, https://bits.blogs.nytimes.com/2009/01/02/breastfeeding-facebook-photos.

27 Tarleton Gillespie, *Custodians of the Internet: Platforms, Content Moderation, and the Hidden Decisions That Shape Social Media* (Yale University Press, 2018).

28 Tom Pollard, *Sex and Violence: The Hollywood Censorship Wars* (Routledge, 2015).

29 "Barnes v. Glen Theatre, Inc.," LII / Legal Information Institute, https://www.law.cornell.edu/supremecourt/text/501/560.

30 Judith Lynne Hanna, *Naked Truth: Strip Clubs, Democracy, and a Christian Right* (University of Texas Press, 2012).

31 "Update to Our Nudity and Attire Policy," Twitch, April 7, 2020, https://blog.twitch.tv/en/2020/04/07/update-to-our-nudity-and-attire-policy.

32 Tristan Greene, "Tumblr's 'female-presenting nipples' language isn't semantic — it's oppression," December 14, 2018, https://thenextweb.

com/opinion/2018/12/14/tumblrs-female-presenting-nipples-language-isnt-semantics-its-oppression/.

33 Jillian York, "Facebook Celebrates Pride, Except Where Homosexuality Is Illegal," *Vice*, June 20, 2017, https://www.vice.com/en_us/article/pay4m7/facebook-celebrates-pride-except-where-homosexuality-is-illegal.

34 Kristina Cooke, Dan Levine, and Dustin Volz, "INSIGHT – Facebook Executives Feel the Heat of Content Controversies," Reuters, October 28, 2016, https://www.reuters.com/article/facebook-content-idCNL1N1CY01A.

35 Jamie Ballard, "Almost Seven in 10 Americans Are Comfortable with Women Breastfeeding Next to Them in Public," YouGov, September 27, 2019, https://today.yougov.com/topics/education/articles-reports/2019/09/27/breastfeeding-public-formula-feeding-poll-survey.

36 Ben Wagner, *Governing Internet Expression: The International and Transnational Politics of Freedom of Expression* (Phd Diss, 2013, European University Institute). In his dissertation, Wagner posits that the United Kingdom, the United States, Germany, AOL, Google, and Facebook are the key actors that have defined acceptability online

37 Wagner, *Governing Internet Expression.*

Chapter 7: The War on Sex

1 J Michel Metz and Rod Carveth, "Misunderstanding Cyberculture: Martin Rimm and the 'Cyberporn' Study," Popular Culture Association National Conference, Las Vegas, 1996.

2 David Kushner, "A Brief History of Porn on the Internet," *Wired*," April 9, 2019, https://www.wired.com/story/brief-history-porn-internet.

3 Matt Richtel, "For Pornographers, Internet's Virtues Turn to Vices," *New York Times*, June 2, 2007, https://www.nytimes.com/2007/06/02/technology/02porn.html.

4 Jacqui Cheng, "Porn 2.0 Is Stiff Competition for Pro Pornographers," Ars Technica, June 6, 2007, https://arstechnica.com/uncategorized/2007/06/porn-2-0-is-stiff-competition-for-pro-pronographers.

5 danah boyd, "White Flight in Networked Publics? How Race and Class Shaped American Teen Engagement with MySpace and Facebook," in *Race after the Internet*, eds. Lisa Nakamura and Peter Chow-White (Routledge, 2011).

6 Nick Summers, "Facebook's 'Porn Cops' Are Key to Its Growth," *Newsweek*, April 30, 2009, https://www.newsweek.com/facebooks-porn-cops-are-key-its-growth-77055.

7 Brad Stone, "Policing the Web's Lurid Precincts," *New York Times*, July 18, 2010, https://www.nytimes.com/2010/07/19/technology/19screen.html.

8 Jacqui Cheng, "Porn Pranksters Have a Field Day with YouTube Injection Flaw," Ars Technica, July 5, 2010, https://arstechnica.com/tech-policy/

news/2010/07/pranksters-have-a-field-day-with-youtube-injection-flaw.
ars.

9 Steven Musil, "Hackers Add Porn to Sesame Street YouTube Channel,"
   CNET, October 16, 2011, https://www.cnet.com/news/hackers-add-
   porn-to-sesame-street-youtube-channel.

10 "How Did The Pornography Make It On To Facebook?," *Allfacebook* (blog), November 17, 2011, available at https://web.archive.org/
   web/20111117004056/http://www.allfacebook.com/facebook-quietly-
   pulls-pornographic-posts-from-site-2011-11.

11 Adam Clark Estes, "Of Course Flickr Has a Porn Problem," *Atlantic*, July
   29, 2011, https://www.theatlantic.com/technology/archive/2011/07/
   course-flickr-has-porn-problem/353465; Larry Sanger, "What Should We
   Do about Wikipedia's Porn Problem?," *Larry Sanger Blog*, May 29, 2012,
   http://larrysanger.org/2012/05/what-should-we-do-about-wikipedias-
   porn-problem; Ben Parr, "Should Twitter Crack Down on Pornography?,"
   Mashable, July 3, 2009, https://mashable.com/2009/07/03/twitter-
   pornography.

12 Bardot Smith, "Silicon Valley's Cult of Male Ego," *Model View Culture*
   (blog), September 8, 2014, https://modelviewculture.com/pieces/silicon-
   valley-s-cult-of-male-ego.

13 CEO Jeff D'Onofrio, "A better, more positive Tumblr," *Tumblr Blog*,
   December 3, 2018, https://staff.tumblr.com/post/180758987165/a-better-
   more-positive-tumblr.

14 "Liaraslist," liaraslist, https://liaraslist.org.

15 Vijaya Gadde and Kayvon Beykpour, "Setting the Record Straight on
   Shadow Banning," Twitter (blog), July 26, 2018, https://blog.twitter.com/
   en_us/topics/company/2018/Setting-the-record-straight-on-shadow-
   banning.html.

16 "Hackinghustling.Com," http://hackinghustling.com.

17 John Constine, "Instagram Now Demotes Vaguely 'Inappropriate'
   Content," *TechCrunch* (blog), April 10, 2019, http://social.techcrunch.com/
   2019/04/10/instagram-borderline.

18 Russell Brandom, "Facebook's Report Abuse Button Has Become a Tool
   of Global Oppression," *Verge*, September 2, 2014, https://www.theverge.
   com/2014/9/2/6083647/facebook-s-report-abuse-button-has-become-a-
   tool-of-global-oppression.

19 "(1) Cindy Gallop - I've Been Silent on Facebook for the Past Few Days
   ...," Facebook, March 29, 2018, https://www.facebook.com/cindy.
   gallop/posts/10156464487798313.

20 Erika Lust, "Mom Are the People in Your Films Always Naked?," in
   Coming Out Like a Porn Star: Essays on Pornography, Protection, and Privacy,
   ed. Jiz Lee (Stone Bridge Press, 2015).

21 Emily Dixon, "Twitter and Facebook under Fire for Removing the Word
   'Vagina' from Ads for Gynecology Book," CNN, September 2, 2019,

https://www.cnn.com/2019/08/30/tech/us-twitter-vagina-bible-scli-intl/index.html.

22 Eric Johnson, "In Her New Book, 'The Uterus Is a Feature, Not a Bug,' Sarah Lacy Says Women Should Fight Back, Not 'Lean In,'" Vox, November 16, 2017, https://www.vox.com/2017/11/16/16658534/sarah-lacy-uterus-feature-not-bug-book-feminism-sheryl-sandberg-lean-in-recode-media-peter-kafka.

23 Lora Grady, "Women Are Calling Out Instagram for Censoring Photos of Fat Bodies," *Flare*, October 28, 2018, https://www.flare.com/news/instagram-censorship-fat-plus-size/.

24 Amber Madison, "When Social-Media Companies Censor Sex Education," *Atlantic*, March 4, 2015, https://www.theatlantic.com/health/archive/2015/03/when-social-media-censors-sex-education/385576.

25 Megan Farokhmanesh, "YouTube Is Still Restricting and Demonetizing LGBT Videos—and Adding Anti-LGBT Ads to Some," *Verge*, June 4, 2018, https://www.theverge.com/2018/6/4/17424472/youtube-lgbt-demonetization-ads-algorithm.

26 Lorelei Lee (missloreleilee), "WE NEED YOU TO CALL YOUR SENATORS," Instagram, March 5, 2018, https://www.instagram.com/p/Bf9NOCzBZDJ.

27 "Amicus Brief of Center for Democracy & Technology in Support of Plaintiffs-Appellants," Electronic Frontier Foundation, February 28, 2019, https://www.eff.org/document/orrected-brief-amicus-curiae-center-democracy-technology-support-plaintiffs-appellants.

Chapter 8: From Humans to Machines

1 "Fun People Archive – 15 Apr – AOL.COM Took the *WHAT* out of 'Country?,'" April 15, 1996, http://www.langston.com/Fun_People/1996/1996ASK.html.

2 Ernie Smith, "Scunthorpe Problem: What Made Scunthorpe Famous," *Tedium*, July 26, 2016, https://tedium.co/2016/07/26/scunthorpe-problem-profanity-filter-history.

3 "F-Word Town Censors Itself," NEWS.com.au, August 1, 2008, https://web.archive.org/web/20080818120216/http://www.news.com.au/story/0,23599,24112394-23109,00.html.

4 Paul Festa, "Food Domain Found 'Obscene,'" CNET, April 27, 1998, https://www.cnet.com/news/food-domain-found-obscene.

5 Jude Sheerin, "How Spam Filters Dictated Canadian Magazine's Fate," BBC News, March 29, 2010, http://news.bbc.co.uk/2/hi/technology/8528672.stm.

6 Lester Haines, "Porn Filters Have a Field Day on Horniman Museum," *Register*, October 8, 2004, https://www.theregister.co.uk/2004/10/08/horniman_museum_filtered.

7   Kris Maher, "Don't Let Spam Filters Snatch Your Resume," *CollegeJournal*, October 23, 2006, https://web.archive.org/web/20061023111709/http://www.collegejournal.com/jobhunting/resumeadvice/20040426-maher.html; Daniel Oberhaus, "Life on the Internet Is Hard When Your Last Name Is 'Butts,'" *Vice*, August 29, 2018, https://www.vice.com/en_us/article/9kmp9v/life-on-the-internet-is-hard-when-your-last-name-is-butts.

8   "Perspective," accessed January 25, 2020, https://www.perspectiveapi.com/#/home.

9   caroline sinders, "Toxicity and Tone Are Not the Same Thing: Analyzing the New Google API on Toxicity, PerspectiveAPI.," Medium, February 24, 2017, https://medium.com/@carolinesinders/toxicity-and-tone-are-not-the-same-thing-analyzing-the-new-google-api-on-toxicity-perspectiveapi-14abe4e728b3.

10   One widely shared list of "bad words" demonstrates the bluntness of keyword filtering: https://www.cs.cmu.edu/~biglou/resources/bad-words.txt.

11   Jillian York, "Google's Anti-Bullying AI Mistakes Civility for Decency," *Vice*, August 18, 2017, https://www.vice.com/en_us/article/qvvv3p/googles-anti-bullying-ai-mistakes-civility-for-decency.

12   "Drag Queens and Artificial Intelligence: Should Computers Decide What Is 'Toxic' on the Internet?," *InternetLab* (blog), June 28, 2019, http://www.internetlab.org.br/en/freedom-of-expression/drag-queens-and-artificial-intelligence-should-computers-decide-what-is-toxic-on-the-internet.

13   Rolfe Winkler, "The Imperial Powers of the Tech Universe," *Wall Street Journal*, December 27, 2019, https://www.wsj.com/articles/the-imperial-powers-of-the-tech-universe-11576630805.

14   Shoshanna Zuboff, "A Digital Declaration," *Frankfurter Allgemeine*, September 15, 2014, https://www.faz.net/aktuell/feuilleton/debatten/the-digital-debate/shoshan-zuboff-on-big-data-as-surveillance-capitalism-13152525.html.

15   Spandana Singh, "Everything in Moderation," New America, July 22, 2019, http://newamerica.org/oti/reports/everything-moderation-analysis-how-internet-platforms-are-using-artificial-intelligence-moderate-user-generated-content.

16   "There's an Algorithm to Fight Online Extremism," *Science Friday* (blog), January 27, 2017, https://www.sciencefriday.com/segments/theres-an-algorithm-to-fight-online-extremism.

17   "There's an Algorithm to Fight Online Extremism."

18   Evelyn Douek (@evelyndouek), Twitter, September 11, 2019, https://twitter.com/evelyndouek/status/1171823591870124038.

19   "AI Advances to Better Detect Hate Speech," Facebook AI, May 12, 2020, https://ai.facebook.com/blog/ai-advances-to-better-detect-hate-speech.

20   Singh, "Everything in Moderation."

21 Amanda Holpuch, "Facebook Still Suspending Native Americans over 'Real Name' Policy," *Guardian*, February 16, 2015, https://www. theguardian.com/technology/2015/feb/16/facebook-real-name-policy-suspends-native-americans; Matthew Moore, "Woman Called Yoda Blocked from Facebook," *Telegraph*, August 27, 2008, https://www.telegraph. co.uk/news/newstopics/howaboutthat/2632170/Woman-called-Yoda-blocked-from-Facebook.html.

22 Maggie Zhang, "Google Photos Tags Two African-Americans as Gorillas through Facial Recognition Software," *Forbes*, July 1, 2015, https://www. forbes.com/sites/mzhang/2015/07/01/google-photos-tags-two-african-americans-as-gorillas-through-facial-recognition-software.

23 Dave Gershgorn, "The Reason Why Most of the Images That Show Up When You Search for 'Doctor' Are White Men," Quartz, April 14, 2017, https://qz.com/958666/the-reason-why-most-of-the-images-are-men-when-you-search-for-doctor.

24 Maggie Frick and Paresh Dave, "Facebook's Flood of Languages Leave It Struggling to Monitor Content," Reuters, April 13, 2019, https://www. reuters.com/article/us-facebook-languages-insight/facebooks-flood-of-languages-leave-it-struggling-to-monitor-content-idUSKCN1RZ0DW.

25 "U Khin Maung Saw, "(Mis)Interpretations of Burmese Words: Part I," Scribd, https://www.scribd.com/document/24696342/Misinterpretations-of-Burmese-Words-1.

26 Thant Sin, "Facebook Bans Racist Word 'Kalar' in Myanmar, Triggers Collateral Censorship," *Global Voices Advocacy* (blog), June 2, 2017, https://advox.globalvoices.org/2017/06/02/facebook-bans-racist-word-kalar-in-myanmar-triggers-collateral-censorship.

27 Richard Allan, "Hard Questions: Who Should Decide What Is Hate Speech in an Online Global Community?," *About Facebook* (blog), June 27, 2017, https://about.fb.com/news/2017/06/hard-questions-hate-speech.

28 Sin, "Facebook Bans Racist Word 'Kalar' in Myanmar."

29 Allan, "Hard Questions."

30 Kate O'Flaherty, "YouTube Keeps Deleting Evidence of Syrian Chemical Weapon Attacks," *Wired UK*, June 26, 2018, https://www.wired.co.uk/article/chemical-weapons-in-syria-youtube-algorithm-delete-video.

31 Sheera Frenkel, "Facebook Will Use Artificial Intelligence to Find Extremist Posts," *New York Times*, June 15, 2017, https://www.nytimes. com/2017/06/15/technology/facebook-artificial-intelligence-extremists-terrorism.html.

32 Janes F. Peltz, "Twitter Says It Suspended 1.2 Million Accounts for Terrorism-Promotion Violations," *Los Angeles Times*, April 5, 2018, https://www.latimes.com/business/la-fi-twitter-terrorism-accounts-20180405-story.html.

33 Singh, "Everything in Moderation."

34 Singh, "Everything in Moderation."

35 Tarleton Gillespie, *Custodians of the Internet: Platforms, Content Moderation, and the Hidden Decisions That Shape Social Media* (Yale University Press, 2018).

36 Taylor R. Moore, "Trade Secrets and Algorithms as Barriers to Social Justice," Center for Democracy & Technology, August 2017, p. 13; AI Now Institute, "Reports," AI Now Institute, https://ainowinstitute. org/reports.html; "IEEE Standard for Algorithm Bias Considerations (P7003)," *UnBias* (blog), April 12, 2017, https://unbias.wp.horizon. ac.uk/work-packages/wp4-stakeholder-engagement/ieee-standard-for-algorithm-bias-considerations-p7003.

Chapter 9: The Virality of Hate

1 Brian Cuban, "Open Letter to Facebook CEO Mark Zuckerberg," May 10, 2009, https://web.archive.org/web/20131204021241/http://www. briancuban.com/open-letter-to-facebook-ceo-mark-zuckerberg.

2 Ki Mae Heussner, "Facebook Under Fire for Allowing Holocaust Deniers," ABC News, May 12, 2009, https://abcnews.go.com/Technology/Ahead oftheCurve/story?id=7566812&page=1.

3 International Convention on the Elimination of All Forms of Racial Discrimination, UN Human Rights Office of the High Commissioner, https:// www.ohchr.org/en/professionalinterest/pages/cerd.aspx.

4 Clarence Brandenburg, Appellant, v. State of Ohio, Cornell Law School, Legal Information Institute, https://www.law.cornell.edu/supremecourt/ text/395/444.

5 "Brandenburg v. Ohio," Columbia University, Global Freedom of Expression, https://globalfreedomofexpression.columbia.edu/cases/ brandenburg-v-ohio.

6 Anthony Shadid and Kevin Sullivan, "Anatomy of the Cartoon Protest Movement, *Washington Post*, February 16, 2006, https://www.washington post.com/wp-dyn/content/article/2006/02/15/AR2006021502865.html.

7 Danish Prime Minister Anders Fogh Rasmussen's New Year Address 2006, https://www.stm.dk/_p_11198.html.

8 Ehsan Ahrari, "Cartoon and the Clash of 'Freedoms,'" *Global Beat Syndicate*, February 15, 2006, https://www.bu.edu/globalbeat/syndicate/ ahrari021506.html.

9 UN Commission on Human Rights, *Racism, Racial Discrimination, Xenophobia And All Forms Of Discrimination, Report submitted by Mr. Doudou Diène, Special Rapporteur on contemporary forms of racism, racial discrimination, xenophobia and related intolerance* , 18 January 2006, E/ CN.4/2006/16, available at: https://www.refworld.org/docid/441182080. html.

10 Michelle Malkin, "Banned on YouTube," *UNZ Review*, October 4, 2006, https://www.unz.com/mmalkin/banned-on-youtube-3.

11 Michelle Malkin, "When YouTube Banned Me, but Not the Hate Imams," *Unz Review*, June 7, 2017, https://www.unz.com/mmalkin/when-youtube-banned-me-but-not-the-hate-imams.

12 Deepa Seetharaman, "Facebook Employees Pushed to Remove Trump's Posts as Hate Speech," *Wall Street Journal*, October 21, 2016, https://www.wsj.com/articles/facebook-employees-pushed-to-remove-trump-posts-as-hate-speech-1477075392?mod=e2tw.

13 Deepa Seetharaman, "Facebook Employees Try to Censor Trump," Fox Business, October 21, 2016, https://www.foxbusiness.com/politics/facebook-employees-try-to-censor-trump.

14 Anas Qtiesh, "Spam Bots Flooding Twitter to Drown Info About #Syria Protests," *Global Voices Advocacy*, April 18, 2011, https://advox.globalvoices.org/2011/04/18/spam-bots-flooding-twitter-to-drown-info-about-syria-protests/.

15 Gabriella Coleman, "Everything you know about Anonymous is wrong," *Al Jazeera*, May 8, 2012, https://www.aljazeera.com/indepth/opinion/2012/05/201255152158991826.html.

16 Ashe Schow, "#EndFathersDay, the latest ridiculous hashtag from the feminist outrage machine," *Washington Examiner*, June 13, 2014, https://www.washingtonexaminer.com/endfathersday-the-latest-ridiculous-hashtag-from-the-feminist-outrage-machine.

17 "Rachelle Hampton, "The Black Feminists Who Saw the Alt-Right Threat Coming," *Slate*, April 23, 2019, https://slate.com/technology/2019/04/black-feminists-alt-right-twitter-gamergate.html.

18 Ibid.

19 Ibid.

20 John Biggs, "The rise of 4chan politics," *TechCrunch*, December 21, 2016, https://techcrunch.com/2016/12/21/the-rise-of-4chan-politics/.

21 Mary Anne Franks, *The Cult of the Constitution* (Stanford University Press, 2019): 228.

22 Vegas Tenold, "Little Führers Everywhere," *Longreads*, February 21, 2018, https://longreads.com/2018/02/21/little-fuhrers-everywhere/.

23 NPR, "Big Tech Companies Are Struggling With How To Best Police Their Platforms," July 11, 2019, https://www.npr.org/2019/07/11/740871352/big-tech-companies-are-struggling-with-how-to-best-police-their-platforms.

24 Francie Diep, "How Social Media Helped Organize and Radicalize America's White Supremacists," *Pacific Standard*, August 15, 2017, https://psmag.com/social-justice/how-social-media-helped-organize-and-radicalize-americas-newest-white-supremacists; "Social Media Used to Identify Charlottesville Protesters," VOA, August 17, 2017, https://learningenglish.voanews.com/a/social-media-used-to-identify-charlotesville-protesters/3989596.html.

25 "Tech Companies Have the Tools to Confront White Supremacy," *Wired*,

August 14, 2017, https://www.wired.com/story/charlottesville-social-media-hate-speech-online.

26 Bryan Menegus and Tom McKay, "Airbnb Won't Put a Roof Over the Heads of Nazis [Updated]," Gizmodo, August 7, 2017, https://gizmodo.com/airbnb-won-t-put-a-roof-over-the-heads-of-nazis-1797585928.

27 Keith Collins, "A Running List of Websites and Apps That Have Banned, Blocked, and Dropped Neo-Nazis," Quartz, August 16, 2017, https://qz.com/1055141/what-websites-and-apps-have-banned-neo-nazis-and-white-supremacists.

28 Adi Robertson, "YouTube Bans Neo-Nazi Channel after Criticism over Hate Speech Rules," *Verge*, February 28, 2018, https://www.theverge.com/2018/2/28/17062002/youtube-ban-atomwaffen-neo-nazi-channel-hate-speech-rules.

29 Dottie Lux, "Facebook's Hate Speech Policies Censor Marginalized Users," *Wired*, August 14, 2017, https://www.wired.com/story/facebooks-hate-speech-policies-censor-marginalized-users.

30 Maya Kosoff, "Oculus Founder Does Damage Control After Outing Himself as Pro–Trump Donor," *Vanity Fair*, September 26, 2016, https://www.vanityfair.com/news/2016/09/oculus-founder-damage-control-outing-himself-pro-trump-donor; Tina Casey, "In Wake of Gawker Case, Peter Thiel Drags Facebook into White Nationalist Territory," June 14, 2016, https://www.triplepundit.com/story/2016/wake-gawker-case-peter-thiel-drags-facebook-white-nationalist-territory/25131.

31 Fathimath Afiya and John-Khalid Bridgen, "Maldives," Global Information Society Watch, https://www.giswatch.org/en/country-report/economic-social-and-cultural-rights-escrs/maldives.

32 "Pulling the Plug: A Technical Review of the Internet Shutdown in Burma," OpenNet Initiative, 2007, https://opennet.net/research/bulletins/013.

33 Nart Villeneuve and Masashi Crete-Nishihata, "Control and Resistance: Attacks on Burmese Opposition Media," in *Access Contested: Security, Identity, and Resistance in Asian Cyberspace* (MIT Press, 2011).

34 "Crisis in Arakan State and New Threats to Freedom of News and Information," RSF, June 28, 2012, https://rsf.org/en/reports/crisis-arakan-state-and-new-threats-freedom-news-and-information.

35 "Why Is There Communal Violence in Myanmar?," BBC News, July 3, 2014, https://www.bbc.com/news/world-asia-18395788.

36 "Internet Freedom: Cyberspying, Censorship and Other Challenges," East-West Center Media Conference: Yangon 2014, March 11, 2014, https://www.ewcmedia.org/yangon2014/2014/03/11/cyber-challenges.

37 Ethan Zuckerman, "Myanmar, No Longer Closed, Still Complicated," *My Heart's in Accra* (blog), March 12, 2014, http://www.ethanzuckerman.com/blog/2014/03/12/myanmar-no-longer-closed-still-complicated.

38 Zuckerman, "Myanmar, No Longer Closed."

39 Ray Sharma, "Telenor Brings Zero-Rated Wikipedia and Facebook Access

via Opera Mini to Myanmar," Fast Mode, November 2, 2014, https://www.
thefastmode.com/technology-solutions/2923-telenor-brings-zero-rated-
wikipedia-and-facebook-access-via-opera-mini-to-myanmar.

40 "In Myanmar, Facebook Is the Internet and the Internet Is Facebook," Yale
University, Modern Southeast Asia, October 2, 2018, https://seasia.yale.
edu/myanmar-facebook-internet-and-internet-facebook.

41 Denelle Dixon, "Mozilla Releases Research Results: Zero Rating Is Not
Serving as an On-Ramp to the Internet," *Mozilla Blog*, July 31, 2017,
https://blog.mozilla.org/blog/2017/07/31/mozilla-releases-research-
results-zero-rating-not-serving-ramp-internet.

42 Olivia Solon, "'It's Digital Colonialism': How Facebook's Free Internet Service Has Failed Its Users," *Guardian*, July 27, 2017, https://
www.theguardian.com/technology/2017/jul/27/facebook-free-basics-
developing-markets.

43 Timothy McLaughlin, "How Facebook's Rise Fueled Chaos and Confusion
in Myanmar," *Wired*, July 6, 2018, https://www.wired.com/story/how-
facebooks-rise-fueled-chaos-and-confusion-in-myanmar.

44 Steve Stecklow, "Why Facebook Is Losing the War on Hate Speech
in Myanmar," Reuters, August 15, 2018, https://www.reuters.com/
investigates/special-report/myanmar-facebook-hate.

45 Alan Davis, "How Social Media Spurred Myanmar's Latest Violence," Institute for War and Peace Reporting, September 12, 2017, https://iwpr.net/
global-voices/how-social-media-spurred-myanmars-latest.

46 McLaughlin, "How Facebook's Rise Fueled Chaos and Confusion."

47 "Zuckerberg Responses to Commerce Committee QFRs1," Scribd,
https://www.scribd.com/document/381569055/Zuckerberg-Responses-
to-Commerce-Committee-QFRs1.

48 Stephanie Nebehay and Simon Lewis, "U.N. Brands Myanmar Violence a 'Textbook' Example of Ethnic Cleansing," Reuters, September
11, 2017, https://www.reuters.com/article/us-myanmar-rohingya/u--
n-brands-myanmar-violence-a-textbook-example-of-ethnic-cleansing-
idUSKCN1BM0QF.

49 Tom Miles, "U.N. Investigators Cite Facebook Role in Myanmar
Crisis," Reuters, March 12, 2018, https://www.reuters.com/article/
us-myanmar-rohingya-facebook/u-n-investigators-cite-facebook-role-in-
myanmar-crisis-idUSKCN1GO2PN.

50 "UN: Facebook Has Turned into a Beast," BBC News, March 13, 2018,
https://www.bbc.com/news/technology-43385677.

51 Andy Sullivan, "Facebook's Zuckerberg vows to work harder to block
hate speech in Myanmar," Reuters, April 11, 2018, https://www.reuters.
com/article/facebook-privacy-myanmar/facebooks-zuckerberg-vows-to-
work-harder-to-block-hate-speech-in-myanmar-idUSL1N1RN290.

52 Ezra Klein, "Mark Zuckerberg on Facebook's Hardest Year, and What Comes
Next," Vox, April 2, 2018, https://www.vox.com/2018/4/2/17185052/

mark-zuckerberg-facebook-interview-fake-news-bots-cambridge.

53   "Myanmar – Open Letter to Mark Zuckerberg," Google Docs, April 5, 2018, https://drive.google.com/file/d/1Rs02G96Y9w5dpX0Vf1LjW p6B9mp32VY-/view?usp=sharing&usp=embed_facebook.

54   Stecklow, "Why Facebook Is Losing."

55   Stecklow, "Why Facebook Is Losing."

56   "Update on Myanmar," *About Facebook* (blog), August 15, 2018, https://about.fb.com/news/2018/08/update-on-myanmar.

57   Olivia Solon, "Facebook's Failure in Myanmar Is the Work of a Blundering Toddler," *Guardian*, August 16, 2018, https://www.theguardian.com/technology/2018/aug/16/facebook-myanmar-failure-blundering-toddler.

58   "Removing Myanmar Military Officials from Facebook," *About Facebook* (blog), August 28, 2018, https://about.fb.com/news/2018/08/removing-myanmar-officials.

59   "After Facebook Ban, Myanmar Military Accounts Are Moving to Russian Social Media Site VKontakte," *Global Voices Advocacy* (blog), September 7, 2018, https://advox.globalvoices.org/2018/09/07/after-facebook-ban-myanmar-military-accounts-are-moving-to-russian-social-media-site-vkontakte.

60   Oliver Spencer and Yin Yadanar Thein, "Has Facebook Censored Myanmar's Commander-in-Chief?," *Frontier Myanmar*, August 29, 2018, https://frontiermyanmar.net/en/has-facebook-censored-myanmars-commander-in-chief.

61   Russell Brandom, "Activists from Myanmar, Syria, and beyond Call for Facebook to Fix Moderation," *Verge*, May 18, 2018, https://www.theverge.com/2018/5/18/17369570/facebook-coalition-myanmar-syria-sri-lanka-moderation-transparency-audit.

Chapter 10: The Future Is Ours to Write

1   "Keeping People Safe and Informed about the Coronavirus," *About Facebook* (blog), June 3, 2020, https://about.fb.com/news/2020/06/coronavirus/.

2   Kate Klonick, "What I Learned in Twitter Purgatory," *The Atlantic*, September 8, 2020, https://www.theatlantic.com/ideas/archive/2020/09/what-i-learned-twitter-purgatory/616144/.

3   Zeynep Tufekci, *Twitter and Tear Gas: The Power and Fragility of Networked Protest* (Yale University Press, 2017).

4   Shoshanna Zuboff, *Frankfurter Allgemeine*, "Dark Google," April 30, 2014, https://www.faz.net/aktuell/feuilleton/debatten/the-digital-debate/shoshanna-zuboff-dark-google-12916679.html.

5   Renata Avila Pinto, "Digital Sovereignty or Digital Colonialism?," *Sur: International Journal on Human Rights* 15, no. 27 (2018), https://sur.conectas.org/en/digital-sovereignty-or-digital-colonialism.

6 "The Santa Clara Principles on Transparency and Accountability in Content Moderation," Santa Clara Principles, https://santaclaraprinciples. org ; Alex Hern, "Facebook Relaxes 'Real Name' Policy in Face of Protest," *Guardian*, November 2, 2015, https://www.theguardian.com/technology/2015/nov/02/facebook-real-name-policy-protest.

7 {Updating}

8 Juan Ortiz Freuler, "The case for a digital non-aligned movement," *OpenDemocracy*, June 27, 2020, https://www.opendemocracy.net/en/oureconomy/case-digital-non-aligned-movement/.

9 Ibid.

10 The Santa Clara Principles on Transparency and Accountability in Content Moderation, https://santaclaraprinciples.org/.

11 Jillian York, "Speaking Freely: An Interview with Ada Palmer," 2019, https://www.eff.org/pages/speaking-freely-ada-palmer.

12 Ibid.

Index